D0438898

NEW THEORIES OF THE
MULTINATIONAL ENTERPRISE

New Theories of the Multinational Enterprise

Edited by Alan M. Rugman

ST. MARTIN'S PRESS NEW YORK

St. Martin's Press, Inc., 175 Fifth Avenue, New York, N.Y. 10010
Printed in Great Britain
First published in the United States of America in 1982

Library of Congress Cataloging in Publication Data
Main entry under title:

New theories of the multinational enterprise.
     "Proceedings of a conference held in October 1981
at Dalhousie University, Canada . . . sponsored by the
Centre for International Business Studies . . ." -— Pref.
     1. International business enterprises — Congresses.
I. Rugman, Alan M. II. Dalhousie University. Centre
for International Business Studies.

HD2755.5.N485   1982   338.8'8'01   82-6003
ISBN 0-312-57058-9   AACR2

CONTENTS

PREFACE

These essays on the theory of the multinational enterprise are the proceedings of a conference held in October 1981 at Dalhousie University, Canada. This conference was sponsored by the Centre for International Business Studies, which is affiliated with the School of Business Administration of Dalhousie University. The financial support of the Centre is gratefully acknowledged. The organization of the conference itself was greatly facilitated by the excellent help of Pat Zwicker, Administrative Secretary of the Centre.

The participants who met in Halifax for the conference came from a variety of backgrounds in economics, finance, business policy and management but all shared a common interest in the multinational enterprise (MNE). Several of the participants had been active in developing the theory of the MNE while others were attempting to integrate their related work into a relevant framework for analysis of the MNE. All were invited to prepare papers at the frontiers of their respective fields, so that the new theories of the MNE could be discussed at the conference.

The essays in this volume reflect the wide background and knowledge of these leading experts on the MNE as they seek to develop a common analysis of this dominating worldwide organization. While no clear consensus emerges about what is a general theory of the MNE, many of the authors accept internalization (or one of its variants, the eclectic approach) as the paradigm for which we have been searching.

The readers of this volume will have to determine for themselves the extent to which the new theories of the MNE, discussed herein, become a single theory. If this issue is not fully resolved here, then at least these essays should provoke further analysis of the theoretical determinants of the MNE.

Alan M. Rugman
Columbia University
New York

To the memory of Harry G. Johnson and Stephen Hymer

Two Canadians whose seminal ideas on multinational enterprises are in the great tradition of independent scholarly enquiry.

1 INTERNALIZATION AND NON-EQUITY FORMS OF INTERNATIONAL INVOLVEMENT

Alan M. Rugman

Introduction

In this introductory chapter I review and explain the modern theory of the multinational enterprise. This is the theory of internalization. I then offer a summary and synthesis of recent theoretical work in this area, including the chapters published in this volume.

The objective of this book is to review carefully all new theoretical explanations of the multinational enterprise. Papers were commissioned so that alternative theories of the multinational enterprise can be analysed and synthesized. The major focus of these papers is to examine possible advances to the theory of internalization; in particular, exceptions to the use of internal markets are explored. Empirical work at industry and firm level is also reported as it reflects on the theory of the multinational enterprise.

The authors of these chapters address themselves to one or another of three key issues:

(a)   To what extent is internalization a general theory of foreign direct investment?
(b)   What exceptions, if any, are there to the process of internalization? Are there any sectors or nations where the theory is not readily applicable?
(c)   What empirical support, if any, is there for the theory of internalization?

While these questions are not answered in a definitive manner, the chapters in this volume provide valuable insights into these current areas of professional inquiry on the multinational enterprise.

The Theoretical Issues

The focus of the chapters in this book is the theory of the multinational enterprise (MNE). They extend the theory of internalization, with its emphasis upon the organization of an internal market, and incorporate recent developments which have considered non-equity forms of international involvement. These contractual arrangements are of increasing importance in international production and marketing. Contractual arrangements are mainly in the forms of licensing and joint ventures but also include types of intermediate involvement where some degree of post-contractual control is retained.

It is demonstrated in the chapters on internalization that the nego-tiation of a contractual agreement for a non-standardized product is a very difficult task. There is a danger that the firm's specific advantage (in knowledge, technology, organization, managerial or marketing skills) may be dissipated by the use of non-equity forms of inter-national involvement. It is argued that incorrect prices for proprietary information are likely to be negotiated in contractual agreements which lack the discipline of market constraints.

It is found in several papers that the internal market of the MNE is a superior device to non-equity forms of international involvement, since the costs of internalization are less than the costs of contracting. The costs of internalization depend on, first, the organization of an effective communications network within the MNE and, second, the additional costs of social distance and political risk associated with entry to an unfamiliar foreign environment. These costs are high enough to have eliminated any excess profits from the earnings of the largest US and non-US MNEs. For example during the 1970–9 period only 6 of the fifty largest US MNEs had a return on equity of 18 per cent or more (i.e. 50 per cent above the all-industry mean return of 12 per cent). These MNEs with excess profits were offset by a simi-larly sized group of MNEs earning 50 per cent below the mean (see Rugman, 1981a).

The costs of non-equity forms of involvement include the risk of dissipation of the firm-specific advantage by the premature or in-appropriately priced sale of knowledge and the danger of loss of control over the use of the firm's knowledge advantage by a poorly conceived contractual arrangement. The visible costs of contracting include the costs of policing the licence (or other non-equity forms of involvement) plus the costs of insurance which have to be paid by either or both parties to the contractual agreement.

It is still concluded, however, that non-equity forms of international involvement are increasing due to:

(a)   the growth of standardized products;
(b)   the increasing segmentation of world goods and factor markets

which make resale to third parties a more difficult task; and
(c)   the increased amount of government regulation of foreign direct investment and the MNE, which acts to increase the incentive for contractual arrangements with local participation.

Internalization Theory

All of the chapters in this book start from the premise that internalization is the modern theory of the multinational enterprise (MNE). The theory of internalization has been explained in detail in Rugman (1981a).

Briefly, internalization theory demonstrates that the MNE is an organization which uses its internal market to produce and distribute products in an efficient manner in situations where a regular market fails to operate. In particular, the MNE allocates intermediate products such as knowledge to desirable world markets. The internal market of the MNE is a device which permits the organization to assign property rights in knowledge to itself, such institutional control over this intermediate product being required since there is no regular (external) market for the pricing of knowledge, a public good. Yet the generation of knowledge involves the firm in private costs, in the form of expenditures on research and development. Therefore in most circumstances (in fact with the exception of public subsidies for research and development) it is necessary for the firm to overcome this appropriability problem by the creation of a monopolistic internal market where the knowledge advantage can be developed and explored in an optimal manner on a worldwide basis.

There are many kinds of natural market failure associated with the pricing of knowledge, or similar firm-specific intangible advantages. These occur in the areas of technology, managerial skills, corporate organizational structures and other aspects of the internal market of the firm. The firm, in short, is an alternative to a market. It develops its own managerial hierarchy to solve the allocation and distributional decisions that a regular market makes automatically but it does so inside the firm and therefore at a greater cost. The visible hand of the firm costs more to administer than does the invisible hand of a regular market. There is no such thing as a free lunch, or in this case, a free administered market. The costs of running the internal market need to be weighed against the advantages of internalization in order to find the point at which the growth and profitability of the firm is limited.

All of these arguments carry over into an international dimension as the world markets provide the MNE with the opportunity for greater sales and revenues than within the home nation alone. It is important that the MNE retain the firm-specific advantage it has generated in its home market; so foriegn subsidiaries tend to be branch plants (miniature replicas) of the parent firm. Control over its foreign subsidiaries and their integration into its worldwide internal market permits the MNE to avoid any dissipation of the firm-specific advantage.

The Literature on Internalization Theory

Developed mainly in North America and England, the theory of internalization has been shown by a growing number of scholars to be a valuable explanation of the MNE. The theory integrates elements from industrial organization and international economics.

From industrial economics internalization recognizes the existence of transactions costs and market failure. Under certain conditions, as first demonstrated by Coase (1937), it is more efficient for a firm to create and use an internal market, rather than incur the prohibitive transactions costs of an outside market. Indeed, in some cases of market failure such a regular market may not exist, for example, in the pricing of proprietary information generated within a firm but taking on the attributes of a public good. The assignment of property rights to a firm, and the firm's use of an internal market to monitor and control the use of such a firm-specific advantage in knowledge is the essence of internalization.

The natural market imperfection cited above (in the failure of a market to price a public good) is one of many such imperfections. In addition, there exist frequently many restrictions on the use of a market. Such restrictions are often imposed by governments and take the forms of regulations, taxes, controls and so on. These serve to distort market prices and again act as an incentive for the firm to create an internal market. When either natural or unnatural market imperfections exist across nations, for example, in the case of restrictions on such trade as tariffs, then there is an incentive for the MNE to create an internal market, in the same manner as a domestic firm responds to market failure and regulation. Indeed, as there are many more regulations between nations than within them, there is an even greater incentive for the MNE to have an internal market. These points are developed in Rugman (1981a).

The first application of the market imperfections approach in an international context was by Hymer in his 1960 dissertation, subsequently published in Hymer (1976). He identifies imperfections in factors and good markets, such as monopoly control of raw materials or managerial and research skills, any one of which has led to the development of a firm-specific advantage for the MNE. This work was extended by Caves (1971) and several others at that time. The notion of internalization itself was coined by Buckley and Casson (1976) and it has become a central tenet of the theory of the MNE developed by economists associated with the University of Reading in England. A recent exposition of internalization appears in more detail in Casson (1979).

On a parallel track John Dunning (1977, 1979, 1981b) has sought to explain the MNE in terms of an eclectic theory of international production. This approach seeks to integrate internalization theory, with its focus upon a firm's ownership-specific advantage, with other elements of international economics such as the location-specific variables which also determine foreign direct investment. In my work (Rugman, 1981a), I treat the latter country-specific factors as exogenous parameters, since they are basically the elements in an aggregate production function. They explain trade patterns between nations rather than intra-firm trade. For the latter to occur, firm-specific advantages must exist.

There is essentially no substantial difference between the eclectic theory developed by Dunning and internalization theory once the assumption is made that market imperfections are exogenous. The potential differences in the theories arise only if the MNE is assumed to have the power to generate its own firm-specific advantages over time, that is, to endogenize them. In essence, this is not a substantive difference, merely a choice of the suitable method to model the MNE.

As stated earlier there are costs of running an internal market. These serve both to limit the power of the MNE in exploiting its advantage and to reduce its ability to earn excess profits in the long run. The costs of co-ordination and control within a firm have been analysed by Williamson (1975) in a domestic context. His identification of the hierarchical structure and resulting factors which limit the growth of the firm's internal market can be extended to an international dimension to explain the limits to the power of an MNE. While each MNE has essentially a monopoly in its firm-specific knowledge advantage, the opportunities available to the firm for the successful exploitation of this advantage are limited over time by the costs and difficulties in expanding its internal organization.

Along similar lines Edith Penrose (1959) has identified the difficulty of expanding the management team as a key constraint on the growth of a (domestic) firm. Buckley and Casson (1976) explore these problems of the limits of expansion of a firm's organization structure on an international scale. Chandler (1962), Wrigley (1970) and others also discuss the complexities which result in the administration of the internal market of a large organization. The literature on strategy and structure stemming from Chandler's seminal work is applicable, with suitable modification, to the MNE and can help explain both its dramatic post-war growth and the more recent limits to its development. The extent to which large US firms (including some MNEs) are multi-divisional (M form) firms in Williamson's terminology has been explored recently be Teece (1981).

It can be concluded that the benefits of internalization act as an incentive for constant drives towards the discovery and use of new technology by the MNE. The need to develop new knowledge advantages, specific to the MNE, is a dynamic requirement. Yet the performance of the MNE is constrained by the costs of running a successful internal market. Such costs limit the ability of the MNE to exploit its firm-specific advantage in a sub-optimal manner over time.

Non-Equity Forms of Foreign Investment

Licensing and joint ventures are alternatives to subsidiary production by the MNE. In some nations, such as Japan, they are more important than FDI, but in most nations licensing accounts for only about 10 per cent of foreign activity whereas FDI is over 40 per cent (with exporting being the other half). These data are discussed in Buckley and Davies (1979).

In general, I argue that contractual arrangements arise only when the risk of dissipation of the firm-specific advantage of the MNE is low. This occurs when the MNE is producing a standardized product or when resale is difficult, for example when foreign markets are highly segmented. These conditions are hard to satisfy except for a few limited products and cases, so the number of contractual arrangements is unlikely to increase dramatically. To a large extent licensing occurs when the requirements for internalization are weakest. Once we have a theory of the MNE we also have a theory of licensing; that which need not be internalized can be licensed (or exported, if the conditions for free trade were to hold). To repeat, in terms of internalization theory the key characteristic of the MNE is its control over the firm-specific advantage; the licensing modality is only a valid option when the risk of dissipation is minimized.

The key characteristic of the MNE is that it has a firm-specific advantage in knowledge. Therefore, by definition, the MNE is a monopolist. Naturally there are potential competitors and seekers of the knowledge of the MNE, but as long as the MNE retains control over its firm-specific advantage it retains its monopoly. To keep control over the use of its monopolistic advantage the MNE is compelled to favour use of an internal market. Contractual arrangements, such as licensing and joint ventures, are fraught with danger for the MNE. An inappropriate form of non-equity involvement has the potential to destroy the firm-specific advantage of the MNE, without which it ceases to be a monopolist and runs the risk of fading away into nothing.

With this outline of the theory of internalization and its converse, the licensing modality, I now turn to a review of recent academic work on internalization and its alternatives.

Recent Applications of Internalization Theory

Boddewyn (1981) has adapted the eclectic model of Dunning (1979) to examine the reasons for divestment. In fact he suggests that the reasons for FDI given by Dunning can be reversed when divestment is to be explained. Dunning's three conditions for FDI are that there be a firm-specific advantage, that this be internalized within the MNE, and that foreign production take place rather than exporting or licensing. Boddewyn hypothesizes that divestment takes place when a firm loses its firm-specific advantage or the reasons for internalization cease or when alternative modes of servicing a foreign market replace FDI. In practice all these three reasons for FDI (or its failure) are inter-related, so it is not possible to separate them out as individual explanatory reasons for divestment. Also, as Boddewyn recognizes, there are other managerial variables of relevance in the divestment decision, and these have not yet been successfully incorporated into the model.

Contractor (1981) elaborates upon the robust nature of the licensing modality. He observes that licensing occurs at a simultaneous stage as FDI, and not necessarily at a later time when the risk of dissipation of the firm-specific advantage has been minimized by the product becoming standardized. Contractor lists a dozen circumstances under which licensing is a superior strategy to internalization. Then he presents evidence that licensing and other contractual arrangements amount to a very large number (five billion dollars of licensing income to US firms). The question not answered is how important this number is relative to FDI; the answer instead is to be found in the Buckley and Davies (1979) study, where licensing is only about 10 per cent of all foreign activity, as reported above.

A useful attempt has been made by Robock (1980) to build a geo-business model of international business. The strength of this model is its emphasis upon the spatial (geographical) dimension of the firm. It makes a stronger case for inclusion of location-specific factors than does work on the eclectic theory by Dunning (1977) or internalization theory by Rugman (1981a). Its weakness is that it is too broad a model: 'It covers all strategy alternatives available to the enterprise and is not limited to either trade or direct investment.' As a result many non-economic variables have to be included as well as economic ones and not enough variables are made exogenous. I believe that the theory of the MNE must be distinguished from the wider theory of international business. The MNE is the principal institution of international business and it exists due to market imperfections which have prevented alternative forms of international business transactions such as exporting or contractual arrangements. Therefore, once the reasons for MNEs are explained then the alternatives of exporting and licensing are themselves explained (as redundant cases). No separate theory is required.

Moxon (1980) has extended the Hirsch (1976) model to explain the conditions required for export platform production instead of foreign subcontracting or domestic production. Moxon finds that export platforms are chosen by the MNE when the firm-specific advantage of the MNE in marketing and technology is greater than the costs of control of its subsidiary. His use of special costs for exporting and foreign direct investment is similar to that in Chapter 3 of Rugman (1981a) who also explores the export platform case, although in less detail than Moxon.

A Review and Synthesis of the Chapters in this Volume

Casson demonstrates that a leading transaction cost is buyer uncertainty in the purchase of products (especially consumer goods and services). There is a lack of information about the quality of such products and this tends to lead to the development of brand name products. Such brand names are provided by the seller in an effort to reduce the buyer's uncertainty and thereby encourage regular transactions from which there may well result a mutual gain from exchange.

Casson's hypothesis is that consumer product type MNEs occur in industries where the incidence of quality control is most severe. The MNEs frequently engage in backward integration to ensure quality control of their goods and services. They then sell to the upper end of the market, where the provision of good quality products is demanded and where a premium for this knowledge advantage can be realized. Examples occur, first in the international hotel industry where buyer uncertainty is reduced by the provision of a good quality service through a worldwide reservation system, mainly for businessmen. Second, in the banana industry, where multinational food processors integrate backwards to control supply sources and then distribute a product of standard quality at the optimal time for appropriate consumption. In both cases the MNE can meter the use of its good or service to ensure quality and thereby reduce buyer uncertainty, to the extent that potential consumers identify the brand name of the MNE as synonymous with a risk-free choice.

Casson's work illustrates the extension of the theory of the MNE to include transactions costs as a sufficient condition for the development of the MNEs even in the consumer goods industries. Previously advocates of internalization theory, such as Dunning (1981b) and Rugman (1981a) have argued that MNEs occur in response to a market failure, for example in the pricing of knowledge, or where some other type of firm-specific advantage occurs. Casson accepts that MNEs exist to exploit a knowledge advantage and predominate in R and D-intensive industries. They also exist where backward integration permits control over a raw material resource. Yet now Casson suggests that MNEs also occur in the more general case where information asymmetries arise between buyer and seller, such that buyer uncertainty can be reduced by the MNE using its internal market to ensure quality control in the provision of its brand name product. In this case the 'advantage' of the MNE lies in its ability to generate sufficient know-how to guarantee a good quality product to consumers.

Calvet observes that much FDI is often in the form of mergers; this suggests that the theory of industrial organization needs to be utilized, as it explains merger activity. At the very least, Calvet argues, industrial organization theory needs to be integrated with the general theory of

FDI in order to explain mergers and other types of foreign takeovers. Yet it is difficult to reconcile industrial organization theory with FDI theory for at least two reasons.

First, mergers take place in a domestic (US) context in a cyclical pattern. There have been several waves of mergers in the US economy in the 1962–77 period, and these have spilled over into foreign takeovers in Canada. This indicates that to understand FDI (mergers) activity in Canada it is necessary to observe current merger activity in the United States. The US mergers appear to take place due to different expectations held by US entrepreneurs about the current and future value of the corporations involved. These expectations, in time, are influenced by new information, especially technological knowledge, which arrives in a random (unpredictable) manner and thereby generates a valuation gap in the expected earnings of corporations. The valuation gap leads to opportunities for trading in the shares of corporations perceived by some to be undervalued at current stock market prices. There is apparently some type of synergistic advantage in a merger which takes place under such conditions of imperfect information and different expectations about valuation.

Second, as is discussed throughout this book, the theory of FDI is a theory of the MNE, namely the theory of internalization. This is, however, more of a theory of the real goods market rather than a financial market theory such as the one that explains merger activity. The essence of the MNE is that it is engaged in international production. The MNE operates an internal market and is an efficient organization structure in a world of market failure.

It would seem that the weakness of Calvet's theory is that, while it explains mergers, it does not explain fully the aspect of FDI other than foreign takeovers. Yet much of the activity of MNEs is in the form of international production by new foreign subsidiaries. These are formed to avoid tariffs, to enter markets protected by non-tariff barriers, to avoid other market imperfections or to retain control over a firm-specific advantage in knowledge or some other asset. In the MNE there is no risk of dissipation of the firm-specific advantage if control is exercised; yet with a takeover such control may be difficult unless similar products are produced.

Calvet offers a reconciliation of the industrial organization and internalization theories. The link is the valuation gap. This exists due to information asymmetries between buyers and sellers. While the seller knows the value of the technology or good being sold, no market price can be set because the buyer does not. He (or she) has insufficient information to make a purchase and this leads to different expectations about the value of an asset, or a corporation in this case. This is an example of the type of market failure that, in other contexts leads to the development of internal markets by MNEs. Here it leads to merger activity, either in a domestic, or an international context. It is apparent that this reconciliation is much in the spirit of Williamson (1975) and closely parallels Casson's chapter in this volume. The special focus of Calvet on mergers alone is instructive, since it reveals the relevance of buyer uncertainty (and hierarchical behaviour as a response) in this particular area of FDI activity.

Calvet shows that the common aspect of industrial organization theory and FDI theory is the ways in which decisions are made to internalize existing or potential market transactions with a firm (or hierarchy). Once the motivation for hierarchical decision-making is established we have an explanation of merger activity in particular and FDI activity in general. The motive for such internalization is simple — it lies in market failure in the pricing of information and knowledge. I conclude that Calvet's explanation of merger activity is a special case of internalization theory.

The wide-ranging chapter by Giddy and Young attempts to find exceptions to the market imperfections (internalization) explanation of the MNE. They argue that this new theory, already 'conventional', also applies to small-scale MNEs, MNEs from developing nations, or Japanese MNEs. They also argue that these 'deviate' or 'unconventional' MNEs are, in fact, pretty common, and that internalization is a rich enough theory to explain them.

I am convinced by the Giddy-Young chapter that internalization theory has sufficient explanatory power to accommodate the unconventional MNEs that they identify. All of them have some sort of firm-specific advantage that is consistent with the essential element of internalization theory. Many of the criticisms made by Giddy and Young of the Kojima model are, by extension, criticisms of the product cycle model rather than of the modern version of internalization theory.

Dunning and McQueen apply the eclectic theory of the MNE to the international hotel industry. This work complements related papers by Dunning and Norman (1979 and 1981) on the application of the eclectic model to the determination of multinational office location. Both studies examine the conditions under which the theory is relevant in the service sector; they are consequently valuable additions to a literature which has as its first focus the role of MNEs in manufacturing industry.

In this volume Robert Grosse examines the location of regional offices of multinational firms but before proceeding to his chapter it is useful to summarize the work of Dunning and Norman. They take the three eclectic theory conditions (ownership advantages, internalization advantages, and location advantages) and use them to study the location of international offices. One of their interesting findings is that quality control is more difficult and costly for office services than for international hotel chains and that the fixed costs of FDI in offices are lower than in hotels. Therefore the barriers to FDI are lower for office services than for international chain hotels.

The key factor influencing the location of multinational branch offices is the ownership advantage developed in the home nation and exploited abroad to satisfy local markets. This is a similar activity to the classic branch plant operations of multinational manufacturing subsidiaries in host nations such as Canada. In office location the specific location factors of relevance are market size, resource availability and a good communications network. Regional offices fill the dual role of garnering local information in new markets and products while at the same time acting as a conduit for the dissemination of the firm-specific advantage of the parent multinational into the host nation's market. These advantages of internalization outweigh those of licensing; the latter modality involving excessive costs of control.

The chapter by Robert Grosse is mainly empirical and its results conform to the implications of internalization theory. He finds that regional offices of MNEs specialize in the marketing function and act as information intermediaries. Thus regional office behaviour is a fundamental aspect in the development of the internalization theory.

Dunning and McQueen test the eclectic theory for another part of the service sector in a case study of the international hotel industry. They identify three conditions as being necessary for multinational activity; ownership, location and internalization advantages. They find that the eclectic theory broadly explains the patterns of FDI in this industry with the exception of location advantages (which are irrelevant). Ownership advantages operate as a brand name 'experience good' in the hotel chains, which also internalize knowledge or other types of firm-specific advantages.

Peter Cory's chapter is an ambitious attempt to extend the premises of internalization theory to explain various non-equity types of foreign investment. In particular, he focuses upon joint ventures, industrial co-operation and other types of contractual arrangements necessary in Eastern European nations. His empirical work is based upon an extensive study of the transfer of technology to Yugoslavia.

One interpretation of his empirical findings is that there exist many forms of intermediate-level foreign involvement in planned socialist economies. Under such contractual arrangements transaction costs and buyer uncertainty are reduced by a process of mutual business relationships. These non-equity alternatives to internalization are found to be often very close substitutes for foreign direct investment. Such quasi-internalized contractual arrangements reveal that MNEs can adapt quite well to the regulated environment of Eastern Europe.

Adrian Tschoegl applies the concepts of internalization to test reasons for foreign bank entry into Japan and California. He finds that the Hymer-Kindleberger variant of internalization, which works well to explain the MNE, also broadly explains multinational banking. Banks tend to enter foreign markets at a relatively low stage of organization and advance later to higher forms of organization. They exploit a knowledge advantage, reflected in their experience in multinational operations, this bank-specific advantage being similar to the firm-specific advantage of the MNE. Tschoegl's chapter is only a first step in the vital task of adding empirical substance to the theoretical work on multinational banking by Grubel (1977) and others. However, it is a useful piece of evidence in support of the application of internalization theory to explain multinational banking activity.

Rutenberg's chapter is an interesting attempt to explore the applicability of internalization theory to the food processing industry, using the fishing industry to sharpen the analysis. It asks relevant questions about the limitations of the internal market concept in an industry where the product is perishable and the erratic availability of fish is not mitigated by integration of the MNE.

The fishing industry is characterized by large numbers of independent fishermen, often in protected and subsidized regions. Institutional constraints and socio-historical cultural values have so far been unsuccessful in modernizing this situation. The MNE is therefore in the position of a fish buyer, subject to variable supply and quality due to the seasonal nature and unpredictable availability of the various species of fish. However, the MNE is in a better position than the individual buyer of fish in that it enjoys scale economies in the production and distribution of fish, so it is able to absorb quality variations more efficiently than smaller firms.

Rutenberg models the fish processing companies as brand managers. They attempt to provide the final consumer with a well-known product, fresh fish, packaged in an easily identifiable name and available in frozen or canned form. The seasonal variations in fish species can be overcome by offering a strategic 'portfolio' of fresh fish products, i.e. the MNE sells fish rather than particular varieties of fish. This brand name or core skill of the MNE food processor is similar to the intangible knowledge advantage of R and D-intensive MNEs. It is an advantage, internalized by the MNE, so that its use can be monitored, metered and controlled in the same way that other MNEs perform.

The perishable nature of the product in Rutenberg's fish model is similar to the perishable banana example of Casson, However, whereas banana MNEs have been successful in integrating backwards to control source quality, the fish MNEs have not yet been able to master quality control. The compelling advantages of control of supply to the fish MNE is now so obvious that some MNEs are devising arrangements or close relationships with governments to secure property rights at the fishing end of the business. A species can then be fished simultaneously in many oceans. Furthermore, fish farms are growing so that the quality of the fish can be controlled and the variance of availability of supply reduced to an optimal level. As Japanese- and Swedish-based MNEs succeed in controlling the variance of their fish supply it can be predicted that there will be increasing pressure to manage quality. Eventually this will lead to brand management by fish MNEs.

Peter Gray defines a macroeconomic theory of foreign direct investment as one focused upon country-specific factors. These can be usefully contrasted with the microeconomic theories which dominate this book; namely those focused upon firm-specific, ownership or internalization advantages. The micro explanations stem from the industrial economics, market imperfections approach whereas the macro theories are related more to trade and the field of international economies. Thus one of the three macro theories examined by Gray is that of Kojima, with its emphasis on comparative advantage as a determinant of the appropriate type of foreign direct investment. Other macro theories examined are Aliber's country-specific capitalization rate hypothesis and the very recent work of Dunning on the level-of-development.

Peter Gray raises many intriguing questions about each of these theories and is particularly critical of the narrow framework of the Kojima analysis, the current irrelevance of Aliber's model and the empirical treasure hunt in Dunning's speculative paper. These criticisms should be kept in perspective, however, since it is apparent that none of these theories is strictly macroeconomic. Each one has strong elements of micro-level considerations, as sometimes noted by Gray himself. It is also clear that a generalized theory of foreign direct investment must integrate both macro and micro variables, as is achieved explicitly in Dunning's eclectic theory and implicitly in internalization theory.

The macroeconomic variables are only implicit in internalization theory since such country-specific factors are usually modelled as exogenous environmental parameters. Internalization theory then sets firm-specific factors as the determinants of multinational activity. Yet changes in the macroeconomic environment will affect the foreign investment decision. Such macro effects include changes in tariffs and taxes, political risk, variations in wages and interest rates due to differential inflation rates or other factors, and so on. Even national factor endowments may change over time. In internalization theory these macro variables are set as parameters for simplicity in modelling but a richer theory will explore the effect of changes in key representative variables. The danger of relaxing too many parameters at once is that the theory ceases to be predictive, and we end up with good descriptive lists of relevant variables but no model. For this reason I believe that internalization theory is a more useful explanation of the multinational enterprise than more eclectic approaches.

The masterly survey of the recent work on the transfer of technology by Richard Caves is the final chapter in this volume. Professor Caves is one of the progenitors of the industrial organization, market imperfections approach which led to the development of internalization theory. In his chapter Caves uses internalization as a key concept to explain the efficiency of technology flows within the MNE. Amongst other issues of internalization he examines the extent to which R and D is centralized and the risk of dissipation of the firm-specific advantage of the MNE by inappropriate licensing of technology. His chapter is a fitting epilogue to this volume on the theory of the MNE.

2 TRANSACTION COSTS AND THE THEORY OF THE MULTINATIONAL ENTERPRISE

Mark C. Casson

Introduction

The theory of internalization is now widely accepted as a key element in the theory of the multinational enterprise (MNE) (McManus, 1972; Buckley and Casson, 1976; Dunning, 1979; Rugman, 1981a). Internalization is in fact a general theory of why firms exist, and without additional assumptions it is almost tautological. To make the theory operational it is necessary to specify assumptions about transaction costs for particular products and for trade between particular locations. It is typically asserted that:

(1) It is very costly to license unpatentable know-how, so that the market for know-how must be internalized. This leads to the vertical integration of production and R and D, and, because of the public good characteristics of know-how, to the consequent horizontal integration of production in different locations.

(2) It is difficult to specify and enforce long-term futures contracts, so that the market for raw materials used by capital-intensive production processes must be internalized by backward integration.

(3) *Ad valorem* tariffs, international tax differentials, and foreign exchange controls create incentives for transfer-pricing, which are most easily exploited through internalization.

With these additional assumptions about the relative costs of internal and external markets, the theory predicts that MNEs will predominate in R and D-intensive industries — particularly those where patents are difficult to register or enforce — in resource-based industries, and in situations where the international division of labour is inhibited by fiscal intervention which can be avoided by transfer-pricing.

It is apparent, however, that not all industries where MNEs operate fulfil these conditions. MNEs occur in many low-technology manufacturing industries, and are also quite important in the service sector. It is true that US-based MNEs are predominantly R and D-oriented, but this does not apply to the same extent to European MNEs, and certainly not to Japanese MNEs.

The object of this chapter is to extend conventional theory in order to explain the rationale of non-R and D-intensive MNEs. It has been suggested by Giddy and Young (see Chapter 4, below) that this can be done simply by broadening the concept of know-how to include a wide range of marketing skills. This chapter suggests that instead the non-R and D-intensive MNE is best explained by extending the scope of internalization theory to take account of additional sources of market imperfection.

The chapter falls naturally into three parts. The first part reformulates internalization theory in the context of a more general theory of transaction costs. The second part focuses upon a particular component of transaction cost, arising from the need to monitor for product quality, and shows how this may be reduced through internalization. Using case studies, it is argued that this motive for internalization explains the presence of MNEs in some non-R and D-intensive industries. The final part considers how far orthodox theory can be regarded as a special case of this more general theory of transaction cost and internalization.

The Nature of Transaction Costs

Orthodox internalization theory starts from the neoclassical norm of perfectly competitive markets in general equilibrium, and then introduces imperfections which appear as deviations from this norm. These imperfections are obstacles to trade, and are usually assumed to be exogenous to transactors. The imperfections are sometimes identified with transaction costs, but this is not strictly correct. The opportunity cost of obstacles to trade is measured by the gains from trade foregone. Transaction costs are incurred in attempting to overcome these obstacles. Table 2.1 identifies these obstacles and indicates the 'market-making' activities required to overcome them.

The table may be interpreted in two ways. The conventional interpretation is that of an inventory of possible deviations from perfect competition. On this view it is appropriate to analyse each obstacle to trade, and its corresponding market-making activity, as though it were the only deviation present. The objections to this view are twofold. First, it is unrealistic, for in practice many markets exhibit several simultaneous obstacles to trade. Second, and much more fundamental, is that the effectiveness of a market-making activity designed to overcome one obstacle may be strongly influenced by the presence of other obstacles. For example, if contact-making is difficult then markets will be fragmented, transactors will tend to be bilateral monopolists, and so

Table 2.1: Classification of Market-making Activities

Obstacle to trade	Market-making activity	Major resource input
No contact between buyer and seller	Contact-making *via* search or advertisement	Administrative labour
No knowledge of reciprocal wants	Specification of the trade and communication of details to each party	Administrative labour
No agreement over price	Negotiation	Administrative labour
No confidence that goods correspond to specification	Monitoring: i.e. screening of quality, metering of quantity, timing of instalments, observation of 'contingent' events	Administrative labour
Need to exchange custody of goods	Transport	Energy, applied *via* manual labour or utilization of transport equipment
Tariffs, taxes on gains from trade, price regulations, quotas	Payment of taxes and tariffs. Avoidance or evasion of taxes, tariffs, regulations or quotas	Administrative labour
No confidence that restitution will be made for default	Enforcement	Administrative labour

price negotiation may be more difficult too. Again, the accuracy with which the product has to be screened for quality will depend upon the detail with which the product is specified, and this will in turn depend upon the ease with which product specifications can be communicated.

An alternative interpretation is that the table exhibits the logical sequence of steps necessary to take transactors from mutual isolation, through anarchy (or a Hobbesian state of nature, perhaps), by way of strategic haggling towards successful completion of a trade. Logically the first step in a trade is for transactors to make contact, and then to communicate reciprocal wants which are embodied in the contractual specification. It is assumed that they exchange two types of good, one of which may be designated 'the product' and the other 'the payment'. The contractual specification may allow for product supply and/or payment to take place in various instalments at different dates, for the arrangements to be contingent upon particular events on or before these dates, and for various penalties or compensations to be paid in the event of default. After negotiating a price the two parties exchange custody of the goods and pay any taxes or tariffs due on the transaction. Each party monitors the exchange: he screens the quality and meters the quantity of the good he offers, and checks the other party's screening and metering of the good which he has received (though in certain cases it may be possible to eliminate this duplication of screening and metering — see below). Failure of the quantity or quality to comply with the specification constitutes default. In the final stage the penalties and compensations due in respect of default are enforced.

Specialization in Market-making

All market-making activities incur costs, and have (at least to some extent) an uncertain outcome. There is always a risk that the transaction may break down, so that the costs of market-making will have been incurred without anything to show for them.

Suppose to begin with that all transactors are risk-neutral and there is no fiscal intervention (which implies, amongst other things, that taxes and tariffs are zero). In this case economic efficiency requires that expected transaction cost should be minimized for any given set of transactions. Transactions should be effected up to the margin where the increment in transaction cost is equal to the value of the incremental gain from trade.

The minimization of transaction costs normally calls for the specialization of market-making activities. There are two main reasons for specialization. The first is to exploit economies of scale arising from increased utilization of purpose-designed indivisible assets. The classic example of this is the use of a brokerage facility (e.g. a purpose-built communication network) to reduce contact-making costs. Secondly, specialization permits each resource to be concentrated on the market-making activity in which it has a comparative advantage. For most market-making activities the major resource is administrative labour. Thus for example specialization allows people with a comparative advantage in monitoring to specialize in activities such as quality control, while people with a comparative advantage in contact-making can specialize in brokerage.

Specialization in Risk-bearing

Suppose now that some individuals — possibly all — are risk-averse. The risks associated with each market-making activity are described in Table 2.2. Typically the risks associated with any given transaction are related to the nature of the product and to the personal characteristics of the buyer and seller, as well as to other more general factors. The influence of product characteristics and transactor characteristics on market-making risks is exhibited in Table 2.3.

In the first instance, the risks associated with each transaction, or attempted transaction, will be shared between the buyer and the seller. Prior to contract, the allocation of risk between the two parties will depend upon who takes the initiative in making contact, communicating specifications and opening negotiations. The allocation of the remaining risks will be determined by the provisions of the contract and by the arrangements made for its enforcement.

In principle most risks are to some extent insurable. This means that ultimately the risks associated with any transaction do not have to be borne solely by the buyer and the seller — they can be shared with other people. It is apparent that in any transaction the buyer's risk and the seller's risk are to some extent inversely correlated. Provided that the contractual form is efficient, in the sense of avoiding unnecessary risk, then the greater is the risk borne by the buyer the less is the risk borne by the seller, and vice versa. Furthermore the risks associated with different transactions will normally be less than perfectly correlated with each other. Both these factors provide individual transactors

Table 2.2: Risks Associated with Market-making Activities Listed in Table 2.1

Risk	Loss
Failure to make contact	Sunk costs of search and advertising
Misunderstanding of specification	Sunk costs of setting up the transaction which led to receiving the misspecified commodity, *plus* the capital loss incurred on resale of the unwanted good, *plus* the transaction costs incurred in the resale
Failure to agree over price	Sunk costs of negotiation
Default on specification caused by dishonesty or incompetence of other party	Costs of remedying the problem *plus* indirect costs of damage or disruption to other activities
Default in transport	Ditto
Failure to enforce	Compensation that would have been due *plus* sunk costs of attempted enforcement

Table 2.3: Product Characteristics and Transactor Characteristics Influencing Market-making Risks

Risks	Product characteristics						Transactor characteristics						Other
	Fewness of potential buyers and/or sellers	Novelty of the product	Complexity of the product's function	Difficulty of inspecting for quality before use	Lag in evaluating performance after use	Difficulty of metering	Market-awareness	Knowledge-ability of products	Screening ability	Metering ability	Dishonesty	Legal experience	
Failure to make contact	X						X						
Misunderstanding of specification		X	X					X					
Failure to agree over price							X						
Default on specification				X	X	X			X	X	X		
Default in transport													X
Failure to enforce												X	X

with an opportunity to reduce their exposure to risk through mutual assurance. Instead of each individual bearing either all the buyer's risk or all the seller's risk in each transaction in which he is involved, each individual can hold a small share of the buyer's and seller's risk associated with all the transactions taking place. By diversifying his portfolio of risk, the 'unsystematic' element of market-making risk is eliminated from his portfolio. If all individuals diversify, then the risk associated with any given level of transaction cost, and any corresponding level of expected gains from trade, is minimized. As a result, economic efficiency is increased (see e.g. Fama, 1976).

When individuals differ in their degree of risk-aversion, economic efficiency also requires that the least risk-averse individuals should specialize in risk-bearing, i.e., the least risk-averse should insure the 'systematic' risks of the most risk-averse.

Finally, it is necessary to consider the economic implications of the fact that many market-making risks are subjective. They are subjective in the sense that different individuals will form different estimates of the risks associated with the same transaction. *Ex ante*, economic efficiency requires that if two individuals have a similar degree of risk-aversion and one takes a more optimistic view of some risk than does the other, then it should be the most optimistic individual who insures the risk. Thus *ceteris paribus* the insurance of each risk is specialized with the person who takes the most optimistic view of it.

The Optimal Degree of Specialization

It has been shown that economic efficiency calls for the specialization of the resources used in market-making activities, and also for the specialization of the bearing of market-making risks. However, specialization is effected using markets, and the greater is the degree of specialization the more markets are required. It must then be recognized that transaction costs will be incurred not only in the markets where the original obstacles to trade were encountered, but also in the markets for market-making services, and the markets for the allocation of market-making risk. These markets too will face obstacles to trade, and require their own market-making activities whose costs will offset some of the gains stemming from specialization. In the context of the economy as a whole, therefore, economic efficiency requires that the specialization of market-making activities and of the bearing of market-making risks should be extended only up to the point at which the additional transaction costs incurred as a result of greater specialization are equal to the savings in transaction costs achieved elsewhere as a result of it.

The Rationale of the Firm

This section summarizes the arrangements for the specialization of market-making, and of its associated risks, that most commonly prevail in the private sector of developed capitalist economies.

(1) The supply of market-making services is generated from plants, most of which take the form of offices, showrooms, trading posts, or some combination of these (e.g. a retail shop). These plants combine complementary resources to 'produce' market-making services. The typical plant is constituted as a legal entity, i.e. as a firm (or a part of one). The firm hires the market-making resources and owns the market-making services that are produced. The residual income stream from the sale of these services is profit which accrues to the owners of the market-making firm.

(2) Market-making plants sell their services to households and to other plants. To avoid transactors having to make two separate transactions, one for the purchase of market-making services and the other for the purchase or sale of the product itself, the market-making activity is usually integrated with the purchase or sale of the product. So far as households are concerned, for consumer products they buy their market-making services from the firm that sells them the product, and for factor services they buy their market-making services from the firm that buys their factor services (e.g., the employer that buys their labour). This means for example that if two households were to trade with each other they would purchase their market-making services from an intermediary. This intermediary would buy the product from the seller and resell the product to the buyer. Ostensibly this doubles the number of transactions, but in fact it actually minimises the number of transactions required to sell to the households the market-making services supplied by the intermediary which are required to accomplish the transaction.

(3) Market-making services are usually sold using a pricing system through which the seller of the services insures the buyer against the risk of failure, by charging for the service only if the transaction is successful. This is most apparent in the relation between firms and households. In consumer product markets, firms take the initiative

in contacting households by advertising and/or by renting retail premises on sites convenient to households. Households are only charged for making contact if the contact leads to a trade, in which case a contribution to the overheads of contact-making is included in the price paid by the household. This arrangement insures the household against contact-making risks (a) by reducing the household's direct expenditure on seeking out the product supplier and (b) pricing the supplier's contact-making service so that if the contact is unsuccessful no charge is made. Firms also reduce the risks borne by households in respect of negotiation. They reduce the time the household needs to spend on negotiation by adopting a convention of always quoting their best price first, i.e. they quote an initial price on which they subsequently refuse to concede. Once the household recognizes this, there is no point in wasting time on negotiation (an exception may be made in the case of very valuable commodities, or where households have a very low opportunity cost of time, in which case haggling may occur). These price quotations are normally freely available, and can still be taken up after the household has solicited other quotations for comparison. This protects the household against the risk that protracted negotiations may result in breakdown; the household only pays for the firm's price quotation service if the negotiation is successful, in which case the negotiated price includes a contribution to the firm's overheads.

Similar principles apply when firms purchase factor services from households. Although the firm and the household reverse their role of buyer and seller, it is still by and large the firm that takes the initiative in seeking out the household (e.g. by advertising job vacancies) and in quoting prices (e.g. in quoting non-negotiable wage rates for the job).

(4) Many firms are constituted as joint-stock companies. This means that no one individual is obliged to bear all the risks incurred by the firm in its market-making activities. Each household can hold equity shares in different firms involved in different transactions, and so avoid unsystematic risk through equity diversification. Households who are not risk-averse can avoid holding equity altogether, and so obtain complete insurance against market-making risk.

(5) Each firm specializes in making a particular market, or group of markets. This enables those individuals who take an optimistic view of the risks associated with a particular market to back their judgement by acquiring equity in the relevant firm. Taken together (4) and (5) indicate how the equity market functions to achieve an efficient allocation of market-making risk.

Quality Control and Backward Integration

The preceding discussion sets the scene for our main hypothesis, which is concerned with the role of firms in providing quality control. Quality control is a special case of monitoring activity. As Table 2.1 indicates, monitoring activity also encompasses the control of quantity and the timing of supply, but in the present context these may be regarded as of secondary interest.

A household purchasing a product demands insurance against the risk that the product will be substandard. At very least the household needs to have confidence that its contractual or legal right to replacement of a faulty item can be enforced. Since prevention is better than cure, it is preferable that the quality can be assured before the product is used. In certain cases the buyer may be able to establish the quality by inspecting the good before use. However such inspection by the buyer may well replicate inspection by the seller prior to the sale. Such replication is wasteful and is only done because of the buyer's lack of confidence in the seller.

If the seller assumes that the buyer will screen for product quality anyway then he may be inclined to abandon screening himself. This will resolve the problem of duplication of screening. However, there are two objections to this strategy. First, the buyer may not be able to establish the quality of the good by inspection, and may not even be able to screen for quality by trial use. If the potential damage caused by utilization of a substandard good is very great, then it is essential that quality is checked before the buyer takes delivery. This is a special case of our second, and more general, proposition, that the seller of a product has a natural advantage over the buyer in screening for product quality because he is one step closer to the producer, and may indeed be the producer himself. Information about product quality is generated naturally as a joint product of the production process and accrues in the first instance to the person supervising production. The costs of quality control may be reduced significantly by drawing upon this information instead of replicating its discovery at a subsequent stage.

Economic efficiency in quality control therefore normally requires that the producer should assume reponsibility for quality control, and that people buying from the producer should have confidence in the producer's quality control (assuming that this confidence is well founded). If the product is an intermediate product, which is going to be transformed or resold again before final use, then it is important that there be a chain of confidence whereby the final buyer has confidence in the seller's quality claims, and the seller has confidence in his own claims because he has confidence in the claims of the intermediate product producer as well as confidence in his own work that has added value to the intermediate product.

There are three main strategies available for giving buyers confidence in the seller's quality control. The first is simply to build up this confidence through successful experience of repeated trade between the same buyer and seller. If the same seller trades with several buyers then he may be able to build up a reputation among them. This reputation may be disseminated more widely by word-of-mouth recommendations, or may be actively promoted by the seller through advertising. This is really the only feasible method for sellers of final products who wish to build up household confidence in the quality of a consumer good.

The second strategy is for the seller to agree to the buyer supervising the production of his own good. The disadvantage of this is that while it gives the buyer confidence, it may require him to interrupt his other work. In the case of a firm which subcontracts a great deal of work to another firm in which it has relatively little confidence this strategy may be quite reasonable, however, as the volume of trade may justify placing a full-time agent of the buyer (e.g. one of his employees) on the seller's premises.

The third strategy is for the buyer to integrate backwards into production, i.e., to internalize the product market in order to achieve better quality control. Once internalization has been achieved the buyer has free access to all the information about quality generated in the course of production, as well as full discretion to take remedial measures without having to negotiate with another party (the seller) first. Equally, a seller who feels it will be a slow or difficult business to build up confidence among buyers may decide to integrate forward into the use of his product.

Internalization is applicable to the household in only a very limited sense (e.g. 'do-it-yourself' is a simple form of internalization of the market for manual labour services). Internalization is however likely to be an important strategy for which the market-making firm can guarantee the quality of the product it offers to consumers. A speculative intermediator who wishes to establish a reputation for the quality of the product in which he deals may wish to integrate backwards into production, so that he can have confidence in the validity of the claims he makes for his product in his advertising. If the product he sells is in turn an assembly of different components then he may be involved in backward integration into a number of different production processes. It is this case which is of most direct relevance to the theory of the MNE.

Applications to the MNE

For the purpose of this chapter it is useful to work with a very simple definition of the MNE, namely that an MNE is any firm which owns outputs of goods or services originating in more than one country. This definition supposes only a minimal threshold level of multinationality. In particular it includes firms which merely operate foreign sales subsidiaries, since these subsidiaries produce market-making services and so qualify as foreign locations of production, within the terms of the definition. Note also that the MNE does not need to be a foreign direct investor, since all resources (except possibly inventories) in the foreign location can be hired rather than owned outright. This reflects the fact that the definition employs an income, or value added, concept of production, rather than a capital or asset concept, as do some other definitions.

The simplicity of the definition above emphasizes the fact that the MNE is simply a multiplant firm whose operations span national boundaries. The advantages of backward integration from consumer market-making into production mean that any firm which services a host market with imports of a new or sophisticated product is liable to become an MNE. The most elementary example is of a two-country MNE with production located in one country and sales located in the other. There is no need for the firm to have any internationally transferable advantage in market-making. All that is required is that the firm utilizes host-country resources which have a comparative advantage in marketmaking, that international comparative advantage encourages production elsewhere, and that there are economies of integrating production and market-making.

There are four main reasons why a market-making MNE may operate in many different countries at once. First, there may be major economies of scale in production which make it efficient to service several entire national markets from the same plant. If the market-makers in each host country were independently to attempt to integrate backward, they would find themselves all trying to share ownership of the same production facility (or alternatively, being obliged to produce in independent plants of below the efficient scale). The solution is for the market-making activities in each of the host countries to be integrated within a single firm which owns the production facility as well.

A second reason is that buyers of the product may be internationally mobile, i.e. they may travel frequently between countries. It reduces the buyer's transaction costs if there is a single market-making firm offering its services within easy reach of any location for the buyer then avoids having to identify separate market-makers in each location. The international mobility of the clientele encourages market-making firms to replicate their activities in many different countries. It should be emphasized that in this case each market-making branch plant can impose severe external costs on the others by failing to provide satisfactory service. Poor service offered by one plant will reduce the consumer's goodwill not only towards that plant but towards all other plants carrying the same name. As a result, the maintenance of strict accountability of branch plants is crucial to the success of the firm as a whole.

The third reason is related to the second, but is logically distinct from it. It is that buyers of the product may wish to place orders in one location for supply at another location. In this case part of the market-making service (contact-making, specification and negotiation) is effected in one country, and another part (exchange and monitoring) in the other country. In principle, of course, the buyer could communicate direct with the market-making facility nearest to where he wishes to take delivery of the product. However, the cost of international communication may be relatively great to the buyer, particularly if he does it only occasionally and therefore lacks expertise. It may be cheaper, and certainly less risky to the buyer, if international communication is internal to the firm. The buyer will therefore prefer to trade with a firm which offers a facility for placing an order through one branch office to be executed by another. It is obvious that the success of this arrangement depends upon close liaison between the two branch plants involved. The extent to which the operations of the branch plants are integrated is even greater than in the second case, and the need for accountability to avoid potential externalities is correspondingly intensified.

The final reason is that the firm has an internationally transferable absolute advantage in market-making. This brings the analysis to an interface with the orthodox theory of the MNE. The interface is more obvious if the absolute advantage is described as propriety know-how regarding the differentiation of products (Caves, 1971). The exploitation of an absolute advantage would tend to create a set of market-making activities in each country operated on broadly similar lines, but without necessarily any of the special features identified in the first three cases. The only link between the market-making branch plants in the different countries might be a common dependence on the firm-specific market-making skills. In this case the potential externalities between the branch plants would be limited to aggressive action such as a tendency to compete against each other in territories not specifically identified as a particular branch plant's market area. At the same time, the firm as a whole would exhibit the familiar characteristics of firms possessing unpatentable proprietary know-how, such as extreme secrecy regarding their operating methods, a tendency to 'lock in' key employees who have partial access to the know-how, and so on.

In the context of this final case the present analysis has little to add to orthodox theory, except to provide more rigorous foundations for the general concept of market-making skills such as product differentiation. These analytical foundations suggest, however, that the efficiency implications of product differentiation are far more complex than a naive application of partial equilibrium monopolistic competition theory used by other writers might suggest.

Towards a More General Theory of the MNE

The analysis above suggests that in the light of the theory of transaction costs, the MNE may be a far more common species of firm than the orthodox theory would suggest. In particular, it highlights a new kind of MNE which specializes in making markets in consumer products. The firm improves the quality of service to the consumer by integrating backward from market-making into production.

Almost all consumer products are likely to have at least some buyers who value quality of service. Perhaps the only exceptions are inferior goods which are consumed only in very low-income countries where consumers are too near subsistence to afford to purchase quality. Consequently there are very few markets where the presence of market-making MNEs can *prima facie* be ruled out. The theory predicts, however, that in whatever markets MNEs occur they will be most strongly represented in those segments of the market where quality is at a premium. Thus in markets where backward-integrated MNEs operate alongside non-integrated indigenous firms the MNEs will be positioned at the high quality-high price end of the market, and the indigenous firms at the low quality-low price end of the market.

Another major implication of the theory is that the presence of MNEs in low-techology consumer product markets does not need to be interpreted as a manifestation of an absolute advantage in product differentiation. It may be due to this, but it is not necessarily so. It can in fact be argued that recent research on MNEs in non-R and D-intensive industries supports the view that an absolute advantage in product differentiation is not always the crucial factor.

Dunning and McQueen (Chapter 5, below) have examined the involvement of MNEs in the hotel industry (see also McManus, 1972). Although Dunning and McQueen interpret their findings in terms of Dunning's eclectic theory, their data can just as easily be interpreted without this theory. The authors confirm that MNEs are concentrated at the high quality-high price end of the hotel market, and not suprisingly cater principally for international travellers and in particular for the businessman. The hotels use an internationally standardized brand name, as one would expect when catering for an internationally mobile clientele. This suggests that the hotel firms represent the MNE of the second kind distinguished in the previous section. Many of the hotel firms offer an international reservation system, which in the past has proved important in attracting first-time visitors to foriegn locations, though the authors argue that its importance is diminishing now that repeat-visit business has become relatively larger. Subject to this qualification, it appears that the MNE of the third kind is also significant among hotel firms.

The hotel industry is unskilled labour-intensive, and one of the crucial elements in maintaining product quality is the efficient management of unskilled labour. Many hotel groups train their own managers, and the authors interpret this, quite reasonably, as a method of imparting firm-specific management skills to their senior employees. It is however possible to regard this backward integration into vocational training simply as a method of achieving quality control. Given the key role of the manager, and the potential diseconomies that an isolated failure of management may create, the internalization of training does not need to be justified by the imparting of monopolized skills; it may be justified simply in terms of a lack of confidence in managers who have been college-trained or who have just quit jobs with competing firms. Intuitively, it may be suggested that if each MNE in the hotel industry has a monopolistic advantage in some aspect of hotel management then there would be far greater diversity in the hotel services offered by the different groups. The MNEs in the hotel industry do not on the whole appear to be characterized by major product differentiation, but by the supply of a fairly standardized service with rigorous quality control.

Our second, and final, example is based upon Read's work on MNEs in tropical agricultural export industries (Read, 1981). Read provides an interesting case study of the banana industry in which, despite the apparent homogeneity of the product, MNE involvement in the export trade is relatively strong. Here again MNEs specialize in the high quality-high price trade in a branded product, offering year-round supplies of carefully ripened bananas distributed through selected retail outlets (typically large supermarket chains). The arm's-length export trade which is carried on alongside is predominantly a seasonal trade in unbranded bananas which are sold through small independent retailers. The MNEs invest heavily in quality control using custom-designed reefer ships for transport, and they tag all bananas so that the packing station on the plantation can be readily identified should defects be observed at the point of final sale. The ability of the MNE to control the growing and packing on the plantation gives it the confidence to make the claims for product quality which, through advertising, it hopes that consumers will identify with its brand name.

Because of the economies of scale and agglomeration in plantations (arising from indivisibilities in the infrastructures — e.g. road and rail links) several national markets can often be supplied from a single group of neighbouring plantations. In this respect MNEs in the banana industry exemplify the MNE of the first kind distinguished above: production is concentrated in just one or two countries, with numerous sales subsidiaries servicing the various export markets supplied from these locations. It is quite possible that the MNEs also possess certain monopolistic advantages, such as proprietary know-how regarding disease-resistant strains. It is equally apparent, however, that because of the very limited set of locations in which it is feasible to grow bananas, this factor alone cannot explain the multinationality of the operations of banana producers. The key to multinationality lies rather in the integration of market-making and production in order to improve quality of service, and in particular to maintain effective quality control.

Relation to the Theory of Buyer Uncertainty

The previous discussion has emphasized some important differences between the general theory of internalization based upon transaction costs and those applications of the theory which focus exclusively upon the internalization of firm-specific advantage. It is worth noting, however, that there is a close analogy between the concept of quality control used above and the concept of buyer uncertainty which occurs in discussions of the licensing decision. Essentially the buyer uncertainty which complicates the licensing decision is an extreme case of the buyer uncertainty which complicates the sale of any product. In each case buyer uncertainty arises, not because no one knows the quality of the product, but because those who do cannot communicate the information to those who do not. The seller knows the quality, but cannot communicate it to the buyer. There is an initial asymmetry of information which remains impacted (Arrow, 1975; Williamson, 1975).

In the case of licensing, the information remains impacted for an important strategic reason. Where know-how is concerned, information about the product quality is difficult to separate from the information which constitutes the product itself. The proprietary value of the information can only be protected by enforcing a right of exclusion, and in the absence of patent protection a right of exclusion can be encorced only by secrecy. Maintaining secrecy about the product itself implies that only very limited information about product quality can be divulged. Consequently the seller of know-how cannot allow the buyer to become too well informed about its quality.

As noted earlier, buyer uncertainty is overcome most efficiently by giving the buyer confidence in the seller's competence and integrity. The buyer's knowledge of the seller's personal characteristics acts as a surrogate for knowledge of product quality. Typically this confidence is built up by the successful repetition of trades. However in the case of know-how, although there is a high value of trade there is a relatively small number of separate transactions, and hence a relatively infrequent repetition of trades between the same two parties. This makes it extremely difficult for confidence to be built up and hence for buyer uncertainty to be overcome.

It appears therefore that the concept of quality control used in our extension of internalization theory is not entirely new to the internalization literature. However, while it has been implicit in earlier discussions of the licensing decision, its wider implications have not been fully appreciated.

Alternatives to the MNE

At present there is considerable analytical and policy interest in the issue of contractual alternatives to the MNE. The analysis above has an important bearing on this issue, for its focuses attention on the question of alternatives to internalization as a method of overcoming buyer uncertainty regarding quality.

An alternative to internalization mentioned above (see p. 35) is that the seller allows the buyer to monitor his production process. When buyer and seller have a long-term contract for supply then this may be an attractive proposition. Indeed it is a method which is quite widely used by sellers of branded products who subcontract production (e.g., retail chains selling own-brand products, and manufacturers assembling electronic products from components).

A potential difficulty for the seller is that it may be difficult to separate the functions of monitoring and control. Conflict may arise when the buyer's agent appears to interfere excessively in the management of production. One way of resolving this conflict is for the seller to allow the buyer full discretion in the day-to-day management of production — i.e. to enter into a management contract with the buyer at the same time as the contract for supply is made. In this case the parties negotiate a composite long-term contract in which the buyer supplies the management and the seller supplies the production facilities. Contracts of this kind are fairly common in East-West trade and are a special case of industrial co-operation agreements.

The introduction of a buyer's agent or management team into the seller's premises is a reasonable solution so long as the seller does not have any proprietary know-how to protect. However if the seller possesses such know-how (e.g. an advanced technology) then the introduction of a buyer's agent is likely to result in a premature dissipation of his property rights. For this reason theory predicts that the buyer's direct involvement in production will only occur in firms or industries in which the seller has little proprietary know-how (e.g. in industries where there is a fairly standard production technology).

When sellers have proprietary know-how to protect it is extremely difficult to overcome buyer uncertainty except through the creation of mutual confidence. But to build up mutual confidence it is necessary at the very least to get some trade between the two parties initiated, out of which this confidence can grow. It is therefore desirable to have some form of intervention or intermediation in order to 'prime' the trading process. One solution is to introduce an 'honest broker'. The honest broker is usually someone who is legally prohibited from entering into competition with either the buyer or seller — i.e. he is barred from production or use of the product. As a result the seller may be willing to accord privileges to the honest broker which he would not be willing to accord to the buyer. Similarly the buyer may be willing to employ the honest broker as an agent, because the broker is unlikely to use the information he acquires from the seller to undermine the buyer's trading position with the seller. The buyer will accept assurances about product quality from the broker because the broker, unlike the seller, has no incentive to mislead.

However there are very few economic agents who have the reputation necessary to operate as honest brokers. This function is normally institutionalized in major banks, politically stable governments and international agencies. It would appear that in many instances the creation of a viable alternative to the MNE will depend upon such reputable institutions being able to extend their role of honest broker into the underwriting of product quality in a wide range of industries. Whether these institutions — or any other kind of institution that could be devised — can develop the necessary skills in monitoring product quality must remain an open question.

3 MERGERS AND THE THEORY OF FOREIGN DIRECT INVESTMENT

A. Louis Calvet

Introduction

The coexistence of business enterprises and markets is an important feature of the industrial structure of a modern economy. On the international scene, the same feature is very much present: the international transfer of resources is mediated by both markets and business firms. Furthermore, it is a fact that (1) a large number of these business firms — the multinational enterprises (MNEs) — operate in various domestic economies, and (2) domestic markets are not completely segmented. This creates a network of interrelationships among economies which renders dubious any analysis that neglects either the influences that domestic and international forces have over each other, or the reasons why markets substitute for firms or vice versa in the organization of economic activity, be it domestic or international. Surprisingly, these basic interrelationships have been neglected for many years. Economists have studied thoroughly the function of markets, leaving to the administrative sciences the investigation of the inner working of business organizations. And, within economic science, international trade theory and industrial organization have evolved along separate lines, thus failing to provide a comprehensive view of the institutional organization of the international transfer of resources.

There are, fortunately, strong indications that the decade of the 1980s will see an integration of the various strands of research in ways which will enhance our understanding of economic phenomena. From the standpoint of this chapter, this integration is taking place at two different levels. First, the new institutional economics is bringing the sciences of administration and economics closer than ever before.[1] Central to the new approach is the idea that the organization of economic transactions (production and distribution) can be accomplished through firms, markets or federations.[2] Firms, which are basically managerial hierarchies, appear to have superior co-ordinating properties in certain circumstances, thus making them more efficient at times than the other two institutional arrangements. The progress made in understanding the reasons for the rise of business enterprises has implications for the analysis of the international transfer of resources via markets or MNEs. (Multinationals are indeed business hierarchies which internalize international transactions within their administrative machineries.) The second area of integration concerns the fields of international trade and industrial organization.[3] Recognition is being given to the fact that international forces impact on domestic market structures and that the latter influence the competitive position of domestic economies. Here again the MNE plays a central role since it represents a crucial link between the various national markets and brings its influence to bear on domestic as well as foreign market structures.[4]

The previous comments suggest that it is not proper to isolate domestic from international business behaviours. They also hint at a similarity between the basic motives underlying the rise of domestic business hierarchies and international hierarchies. Following upon these ideas, the present paper explores a phenomenon situated at the crossroad of the markets v. hierarchies approach, the theory of industrial organization and the theory of foreign direct investment (FDI): domestic and international mergers.[5] The phenomenon of merger activity relates to the question of markets v. hierarchies because mergers are examples of internalization within a single administrative machinery of existing or potential market-mediated transactions. Mergers also fall within the realm of industrial organization and of theories which explore the determinants of international production. As would be expected from the previous comments, these last approaches to merger activity have remained relatively apart. Foreign direct investment theories have dealt at length with the determinants of international production but have somehow neglected the study of the specific means by which firms engage in international investment, in particular through the takeover of an existing local firm. On the other hand, industrial organization and specifically merger theories have approached acquisition activity in the domestic context but have failed to provide an explanation for a widespread international phenomenon, i.e. the takeover of host country firms.

The argument presented here is that, when viewed in a markets and hierarchies perspective, there are theoretical reasons for a unified approach to FDI and merger behaviour. This implies that, in general, movements in domestic acquisition activity must be in harmony with international mergers of domestic firms, over time and across industrial sectors. Empirical support for this hypothesis is shown in the case of domestic acquisition activity in the US, and that of foreign — mainly US — acquisition activity in Canada. This chapter does not offer, however, a validation of the markets v. hierarchies approach or, for that matter, of FDI theories; nor does it pretend to give a definite answer to the still puzzling merger phenomenon. But it establishes an interesting link between two phenomena which had not been looked at jointly before.

The first part discusses merger behaviour and its relation to FDI in a markets and hierarchies framework. The second part presents the data base, the statistical model and the results. To conclude, implications are drawn and areas for further research identified.

Merger Behaviour and Foreign Direct Investment

The pattern of foreign ownership in any country's industries is the result of: (1) the takeover of domestically-owned firms; (2) the creation of *de novo* subsidiaries; and (3) the further growth of foreign-controlled firms. Baumann (1975), who first suggested this taxonomy, associated merger theories with foreign direct investment, although these two fields have evolved relatively apart.[6]

The economic literature has looked at mergers from essentially two viewpoints: when they occur — the particular timing of their occurrence; and why they take place — the motives underlying acquisition behaviour. On the question of timing, there exists a general phenomenon of fluctuations in merger rates with periods of frenzied activity, such as in the late 1960s, followed by relatively calm years. It is the tendency to observe merger waves or cycles which presents researchers with difficulties in finding a general theory of mergers. If mergers are indeed prompted by economic motives, at least some motives must be present when there is intense merger activity and must disappear afterwards. In particular, motives such as the quest for economies of scale, for economies of vertical integration, for creating more efficient firms or simply for increasing market power would therefore be subject to strange cycles corresponding to the ones observed for mergers.

The problems in identifying clear-cut motives for mergers have led to a search of the conditions under which they would be expected to occur. Nelson (1959) proposed a 'valuation gap' approach to merger waves, where divergent expectations among entrepreneurs encourage those with favourable expectations to expand and acquire the firms of those with low expectations. Gort (1969) synthesized most of the research conducted in this area when he proposed an economic disturbance theory of mergers. He contended that economic disturbances increase the variance in valuations of income-producing assets mainly because the past contributes less and less to the predictions about the future. Among the various economic shocks that can alter the structure of expectations, he mentioned rapid changes in technology in either new products or processes of production.

There seems to be overall agreement among researchers that mergers can be explained only by assuming that there are differences in the valuation of future earning streams, or of risks associated with these flows, between the acquiring and the would-be acquired firm.[7] If this is true for domestic takeovers, the same should hold true for foreign acquisitions. Discrepancies in expectations must exist between the foreign firm and the host country firm, irrespective of what causes these discrepancies to occur.[8] However, because foreign acquisitions are a major vehicle for foreign investing they must not only conform to this general framework but they must also be compatible with foreign direct investment explanations.

The FDI literature upholds the idea that foreign investors must possess a countervailing advantage over local firms as compensation for the costs of operating in an unfamiliar environment. This advantage is generally in the form of superior knowledge, be it in products, processes or managerial skills, and, as such, motivates firms to seek foreign involvement in the pursuit of profits and/or growth (Hymer, 1976; Kindleberger, 1969). The involvement in foreign markets is not necessarily one of controlled, equity-based ownership. The desire to internalize the transactions with the foreign market within an administrative structure must in turn be based upon additional justifications. The traditional industrial organization argument had been that higher rents could be gained by establishing foreign subsidiaries. Recent work on the theory of the MNE suggests that such a reason is clearly not satisfactory. Teece (1976), in a comparative study of international technology transfer, points to the high costs of using market mechanisms to license know-how, as compared to using the internal machinery of the firm. Magee (1977) relates the alleged preference for majority control of MNEs to appropriability considerations; that is, the desire of these large firms to ensure the private appropriation of the returns of knowledge — a public good *par excellence*. Other authors claim that markets for intermediate products and factors are very imperfect and internalizing transactions is an efficient way to handle international production (Buckley and Casson, 1976).[9]

In the context of FDI explanations, however, foreign takeovers are no different from establishing a new subsidiary firm. But, in light of our earlier discussion of the merger theory, foreign takeovers must meet the necessary condition for a merger to take place: that is, the existence of a valuation gap. The obvious way to reconcile the two approaches is to view the foreign acquiring firm and the domestic, would-be acquired firm, as being engaged in an exchange characterized by information asymmetries. On the one hand, the foreign firm possesses some sort of valuable knowledge unknown to the domestic firm. On the other hand, the domestic firm experiences difficulties in pricing that superior knowledge, because it cannot assess the impact it will have on its operations. To make matters worse other factors militate against a market transaction: the fear of the foreign firm to have its knowledge dissipated; the difficulties in specifying and later monitoring a long-term contract; and the inherent costs to license un-patentable know-how. In contrast, because of its familiarity with the knowledge, the acquiring firm has a better idea of the latter's final impact on the future cash flows of the target firm. Furthermore, if that knowledge is likely to alter substantially the future growth opportunities of the domestic firm, the foreign firm can price the local enterprise above its current value. Hence, albeit no market price can be struck for the particular knowledge, a valuation differential is likely to arise in that the two owners will diverge in their expectations as to the present value of the domestic firm. The impossibility of exchanging that knowledge via the market gives rise to a valuation gap (in terms of assets) and to a foreign takeover.

To appreciate better the way in which the valuation gap arises, one must think of the stock price of the would-be acquired firm as the capitalized value of earnings under a no-growth policy, plus the present value of growth opportunities (PVGO), that is:

$$P_0 = \frac{EPS_1}{r} + PVGO \tag{1}$$

where P_0 is the current stock price, EPS_1 are the earnings per share expected at the end of year 1, and r the discount factor applied to those earnings.[10] The ratio EPS_1/r represents the present value of the earnings to be generated by the assets already in place, while PVGO is a factor capturing that part of the stock price to be attributed to future growth opportunities of the firm. Both the foreign and the domestic firms are likely to have a similar estimation for the ratio EPS_1/r because it is relatively straightforward to evaluate the capitalized value of assets already in place. Where the firms are more likely to diverge is the valuation of PVGO in equation (1). What is being suggested here is that the foreign firm attaches a higher value to PVGO as a result of its inside knowledge of the technology it possesses and the latter's forecasted impact on the would-be acquired firm. This higher value of PVGO can, in turn, result from either one or both of the following reasons: (1) the expected cash flows (from the technology) by the foreign firm are higher than those forecasted by the domestic firm; (2) the discount rate applied to those risky cash flows is lower for the acquiring firm. In general, one would expect that both reasons would be present.[11]

The argument presented above is in line with FDI and merger theories. Conceptually, some sort of cyclicality would be expected in mergers, for divergences concerning the PVGO factor are likely to be more frequent whenever innovation and technological advances are on the upswing. Magee (1977) suggested that mergers tend to be most frequent in young industries where there is a rapid pace of product and market development. Moreover, empirically, the evidence shows that FDI is mostly of a 'horizontal' type, although by no means only so, and tends to be sector-specific, i.e. predominant in certain industries characterized by high degrees of R and D and of innovation in products and processes. The selectivity shown by foreign investors and by acquiring firms is to be expected, for information asymmetries and different perceptions of risk are most likely to occur in particular industries, rather than to be uniformly spread across all the economy. Incidentally, the scant historical evidence available to support the markets and hierarchies approach also points to the rise of modern business enterprises, primarily in the so-called new-product industries (Chandler and Daems, 1980).

The common basis for both FDI and merger theories, coupled with the underlying support provided by the markets and hierarchies approach, would guarantee that movements in foreign acquisition activity across industries and over time did not deviate substantially from those occurring domestically. This is certainly not an exact relationship for there are obviously other forces at work on the international scene. However, the behaviour of domestic firms, as a group, expanding abroad via acquisitions is not independent of changes in the industrial market structure at home, and vice versa. The two conditions that would seem necessary for such a pattern to hold true are: (1) the market for mergers and the ability to engage in FDI should not be strictly regulated by governments; and (2) information asymmetries must be traced to a common source, say, technology, and not to other factors such as cross-border changes which would not affect the domestic industrial structure. To the extent that these two restrictions are met, a comparison of domestic merger activity and foreign direct investment is warranted.

The Data Base, Model and Results

The data base consists of information regarding: (1) foreign acquisition activity in Canada, and (2) large domestic acquisitions in the US, during the period 1962–77.[12] Foreign acquisitions are taken as a proxy for US acquisitions in Canada since no disaggregated data by country are available over the period considered here. This is not an unreasonable assumption because the bulk of foreign acquisitions is of US origin. The data base indicates the industrial classification of the acquiring and acquired firms, at the two-digit SIC level for Canada and the US. In all, 1,002 foreign acquisitions were recorded in Canada over the 16 years considered for the 19 manufacturing industries of the two-digit SIC classification, while there were 941 large domestic mergers in the US over the same period and in the same industries. The grand total was therefore 1,943 observations.

These observations were next used to construct cross-classified tables of inter-industry distributions of acquisitions in the two countries on a yearly basis. Hence each cell represents the number of acquisitions by companies from industry i into industry j in a specified year and for a particular country. Subsequently, the data were collapsed into two vectors by summing over (1) the columns and (2) the rows, in order to compare, in turn, the behaviour of acquiring and acquired industries between the two countries involved.[13]

The hypothesis to be tested is that movements over time in US domestic acquisition activity were similar to those of foreign (mainly US) acquisition activity in Canada, both in acquiring and acquired industries – similar in that there exists a parallelism in the frequencies with which acquisitions took place in a particular industry over the years for the two countries.

The tests were made using loglinear analysis, which is a multivariate technique applicable to the structure of large contingency tables.[14] It allows for the necessary interactions between the three variables used, i.e. (1) industrial classification, (2) year, and (3) country, in that a series of 'unsaturated' models is proposed and compared to the 'saturated' model which includes all the variables, as well as their interactions, and fits the data perfectly. All unsaturated models are hierarchical, that is, a higher order interaction cannot be present unless all lower order interactions are also included in the model. In this case the complete model can be written as:

$$\ln F_{ijk} = \theta + \lambda_i^I + \lambda_j^Y + \lambda_k^C + \lambda_{ij}^{IY} + \lambda_{ik}^{IC} + \lambda_{jk}^{YC} + \lambda_{ijk}^{IYC} \qquad (2)$$

where I stands for industrial classification, Y for year, C for country, and $F_{ijk} = E(f_{ijk})$ is the expected value of the observed frequencies; ln stands for natural logarithm; θ is the overall mean of the $\ln F_{ijk}$; and, the λs are called effects, with the superscripts indicating the variables to which the effects refer. The λs with a single superscript are first order effects corresponding to the dimensions of the contingency table. The λs with a double superscript are interaction terms for dimensions taken two at a time. The λ with a triple superscript is an interaction term of the three categories being analysed.

The basic strategy of loglinear analysis is to formulate a model which explains variations in cell frequencies. When applied to the hypothesis tested here, it implies that the frequencies of takeovers across industries within one country are proportional to the frequencies of takeovers within the other country. Specifically, the 'no difference' in acquisition patterns between the countries corresponds to having $\lambda^{IYC} = 0$, i.e. the interaction industry-year is independent of the country chosen.[15]

The statistical assessment of the fit of a particular model is obtained using procedures comparable to the chi-square hypothesis testing. Theoretical estimates of the frequencies to be expected are derived and compared against the observed frequencies by means of the chi-square (χ^2) and the likelihood ratio (G^2) statistics. Both are asymptotically distributed as chi-square, with n-p degrees of freedom (df) where n is the number of cells and p is the number of estimated independent parameters.

The results of the inter-country behaviour of acquiring and acquired industries are reported in Tables 3.1 and 3.2, respectively.

By examination of the chi-square statistics and the associated p-value, it appears that the null hypothesis of the no third order interaction term is accepted. That is to say, a model which includes first order effects and second order interactions fits the data well, while a third order interaction term, i.e. λ^{IYC}, is not necessary.[16]

The results of Table 3.2 are similar. The null hypothesis of the no third order interaction effect is accepted. Thus, to summarize, the model incorporating all main effects and pair-wise interaction terms

Table 3.1

Model tested	df	x^2	p-value	G^2	p-value	decision
1. No first order effects	607	1961.42	0.00	2453.49	0.00	reject
2. No second order interactions	573	787.65	0.00	829.22	0.00	reject
3. No third order interactions	270	279.39	0.33	262.64	0.61	accept

Table 3.2

Model tested	df	x^2	p-value	G^2	p-value	decision
1. No first order effects	607	1883.71	0.00	2354.45	0.00	reject
2. No second order interactions	573	811.16	0.00	937.44	0.00	reject
3. No third order interactions	270	287.38	0.22	273.95	0.42	accept

appears to fit the data best. It can be written as:

$$\log F_{ijk} = \theta + \lambda^I + \lambda^Y + \lambda^C + \lambda^{IY} + \lambda^{IC} + \lambda^{YC}. \tag{3}$$

One concludes that the trend of differences in merger behaviour among industries is the same for both countries when viewed from the standpoint of acquiring and acquired industries. This is tantamount to saying that the time pattern of inter-industry acquisition activity is similar for US domestic firms in the US and for US firms in Canada. The hypothesis that the interaction year-industry is independent of the country factor is thus confirmed.

Conclusion

This paper has shown that there are important insights to be gained by combining two or more economic theories which have developed separately but have, each on its own, dealt with the same phenomenon in different contexts. In the case of merger waves, the findings of this work would suggest that they also manifest themselves via foreign acquisitions and within the same industrial sectors. Not only are FDI theories brought closer to merger theories, but also two major implications can be drawn from this study. First, since mergers in the US follow a cyclical pattern and FDI into Canada via acquisitions conforms to the same cycles, one would expect that FDI into Canada will fluctuate accordingly.[17] Periods of intense merger activity in the US would probably be followed by international expansion in Canada and abroad by US firms in the same industrial sectors. Hence, inferences could be made about the magnitude and composition of FDI into Canada on the basis of takeover activity in the US. Second, from the standpoint of designing policies aimed at controlling foreign acquisitions, it would be advisable not to attribute to foreign investors a behaviour which is solely determined by their foreign expansion, when in fact it is the behaviour of a whole industry, be it at home or abroad, and which one should be concerned. The relevant question would therefore be: what are the factors in an industry that may trigger a domestic wave of takeovers and at the same time drive firms to internalize their international transactions? Future work on this phenomenon of mergers between the US and Canada should also be to verify whether acquisitions by Canadian-controlled firms follow the same industrial pattern over time as was found for foreign mergers in Canada.

Notes

1. See, for instance, the symposium on the Economics of Internal Organization, *Bell Journal of Economics*, Spring and Autumn 1975, as well as the main contribution of Williamson (1975).

2. For a definition and comparison of these three modes of mediating transactions, see Chandler and Daems (1980).

3. See, for instance, the symposium on International Trade and Industrial Organization, in the *Journal of Industrial Economics*, December 1980, which tries to correct the lack of communication that previously existed between scholars working in each field, and particularly the introduction by Caves (1980).

4. Several authors had established the relations between domestic market structure and the MNE (Hymer, 1976; Kindleberger, 1969; Caves, 1971) but none went as far as to question the validity of basic concepts, such as that of a national market, with the exception of Dunning (1975).

5. The terms merger, acquisition and takeover will be used interchangeably hereafter.

6. Clearly takeovers of host country firms are only one means of engaging in FDI. Merger theory could only be a partial explanation for FDI.

7. The financial economics literature is unanimous on these points (Myers, 1976) although the fact that these valuation gaps are more frequent in bull markets is still something to be explained.

8. The currency factor has been suggested as a possible cause (Aliber, 1970).

9. For a review of the theories of the MNE see Calvet (1981b) and Dunning (1979). Also Rugman (1981a) provides a good explanation of the internalization theory.

10. It is a well-known property of financial valuation that prices are a function of the earnings generating power of currently held assets *and* of opportunities for future growth.

11. The lower discount rate applied by the foreign investor may result from the lower riskiness of the cash flows, for instance. Note that the gains from mergers will accrue to either the domestic or the foreign shareholders depending on whether the market for acquisitions is perfectly competitive or not, respectively. It is well known that in the US market, the stockholders of the acquired firms earn abnormal gains from mergers. See Mandelker (1974).

12. The Canadian data were obtained from the Merger Register of the Federal Department of Consumer and Corporate Affairs. The US data were collected from the Federal Trade Commission publications, which only record 'large' mergers, i.e. those in which the acquired firm's assets are over 10 million dollars. The Canadian data were reclassified to conform to the US Standard Industrial Classification. The US data, in turn, although available at a more disaggregated level, were considered at the two-digit level to render compatible both sets of data.

13. The large number of zero entries in the matrices made it necessary to examine separately the behaviour of acquiring and acquired industries.

14. See, Fienberg (1977) for a simple presentation of these models and their applications, and, more recently, DeSarbo and Hildebrand (1980).

15. Note that the hypothesis of 'no difference' in the time pattern of inter-industry acquisitions is equivalent to testing the null hypothesis of no third order interactions which is, in turn, equivalent to testing the good fit of the two-way interaction effect model.

16. The statistical interpretation of the table is as follows: if the null hypothesis H_0 were true, the probability of obtaining a calculated χ^2 of 279.39 or more would be 0.33 (Type I error). Alternatively, the calculated χ^2 is less than the theoretical χ^2 at a 0.05 significance level. This in turn implies that the null hypothesis is to be accepted. The theoretical value of χ^2 at the 0.05 level with 270 degrees of freedom can be computed by recalling that $\chi^2 - \nu/\sqrt{2\nu}$ follows a standardized normal distribution, where ν and $\sqrt{2\nu}$ are the mean and the standard error of the χ^2 distribution with ν degrees of freedom. In this case the calculated $\chi^2 = 279.39$ is less than the theoretical $\chi^2_{0.95}(270) = 308.23$. All the tests were run on BMDP3F, 1979 version.

17. Actually the inflow of FDI into Canada took a drop after 1973 coinciding with the slowdown in merger activity in the US. See Edwards (1977).

4 CONVENTIONAL THEORY AND UNCONVENTIONAL MULTINATIONALS: DO NEW FORMS OF MULTINATIONAL ENTERPRISE REQUIRE NEW THEORIES?

Ian H. Giddy and Stephen Young

Introduction

Picture a multinational enterprise. What do you see? Few will not visualize what Raymond Vernon describes as

> the giants of modern industry, commerce and banking: the big oil companies such as Mobil, Shell and Gulf; the leading chemical companies such as BASF and DuPont; the major electrical-machinery producers such as AEG and General Electric; the largest drug companies such as Pfizer and Hoffman-LaRoche; and so on through the upper ranks of Fortune's various lists of the world's leading firms.[1]

These are the firms that dominate the world of international business, and it is their characteristics that have been of primary interest to students of the modern multinational enterprise. A decade's research confirmed that most multinationals were large, mainly American or European-based corporations, operating with oligopolistic industries at home and abroad. These firms were, moreover, clustered within technologically advanced industrial sectors, the developed countries were the main recipients of their direct investment activity and the wholly-owned subsidiary was the most favoured form of involvement.[2]

The theories of multinational enterprise currently evolving in the literature have inevitably focused heavily on these features of multinationality. Product differentiation, brand names, marketing or more general managerial skills, unique technology and various financial factors associated with capital market imperfections have all been suggested as sources of advantage to the multinational firm. A number of these characteristics are associated with large firm size and oligopolistic behaviour; and the industrial organization model formally linked monopolistic and oligopolistic market structure and behaviour to multinationality. Of the unique assets possessed by such companies, most emphasis had been placed upon in-house technology, derived from research and development (R and D) activity. High-income countries

55

provide an environment suited to the development of large, R and D-intensive firms, and to specialization in technologies and products that will later be sought in countries that have achieved a similar income level. This seems to explain why most of foreign direct investment flows from the Western industrialized countries, and why much of it goes to other countries of comparable income levels.

Yet many forms of the multinational enterprise seem not to fit the conventional paradigm. During the past few years several writers have drawn attention to what may be termed unconventional multinationals.

The growth of direct foreign investment from Japan in the 1970s and the emergence of multinationals from low-income countries are two developments that seem to demand explanation. There is also evidence of many small multinational enterprises and of mulitnationals in low-technology industries.[3] Focus on the most visible aspects of international business was justifiable while there remained major areas of ignorance concerning conventional MNEs. Now, however, the field has reached the point of needing to bridge some of the more glaring gaps. What the present chapter seeks to consider is whether or not 'conventional' theories are adequate to explain the overseas expansion of these 'non-conventional' MNEs, or whether new paradigms are warranted.

Interpreting Existing Theory

What, specifically, is conventional theory? While the theory of the multinational enterprise has its roots in the 1960 work of Hymer,[4] it has only received sustained attention from economists within the last few years. Although attempts have been made recently to synthesize the various models and produce a comprehensive theory of international production,[5] there is still not total agreement as to the constituents of a theory. Nevertheless there are a number of key elements which explain the growth of the multinational enterprise.

Ownership-specific Advantages of Firms

Within an imperfectly competitive environment, firms are able to develop new products or processes; skills in marketing, organization or finance; expertise in differentiating products, and so forth. These unique assets developed by the firm represent monopolistic advantages which are required to enable the company to compete successfully in unfamiliar foreign environments. In comparison with a local competitor abroad, the MNE has additional costs. These arise from cultural, legal, institutional and linguistic differences, lack of knowledge of local market conditions and the increased expense (in terms of communications and misunderstandings) of operating at a distance. It has been suggested that these costs will prove a particular barrier to foreign direct investment by small firms.[6] So for foreign direct investment to prove profitable, the firm entering an overseas market must have some advantages not shared by its local competitors.

The question then arises as to the type of company which is able to create barriers to direct competition, which are effective in many national markets and not simply in the domestic market. It is on this issue that the industrial organization explanation for multinationality becomes particularly pertinent. Large, oligopolistic firms are most obviously identified with multinationalism for a variety of reasons. Product differentiation derived from large-scale advertising represents a major barrier to entry in some markets, and this is frequently associated with oligopolistic industry structures. Second, large firm size is an important attribute in financing research and development. Moreover, size may be a source of the market power necessary to defend activities such as organization, finance and distribution. Finally, oligopolists are in a strong position to delay the inevitable erosion of barriers to entry, through controls over suppliers and markets, cartels and other collusive forms of behaviour.

Internalization[7]

The above comments do not *per se* explain why a domestic firm should choose to exploit its monopolistic advantage by foreign production rather than by producing at home and exporting, or by licensing a manufacturer abroad. The resolution of this dilemma lies in the concept of internalization. Simply stated, the firm will undertake co-ordinating activities itself (that is, undertake foreign production) where it is more efficient to do this than to use the market, or where missing external markets make it essential.

Problems in the efficiency of markets arise most obviously in the case of technology.[8] The creation of this technological know-how requires long-term R and D, but at any stage before project completion, the value of the knowledge obtained may be difficult to establish, if the firm were contemplating selling. Once the knowledge has been created, furthermore, the firm is faced with the problem of obtaining an adequate return from the R and D investment, given the public good characteristics of knowledge.[9] The use of an internal market permits the corporation to retain control over the know-how (whereas with licensing the knowledge will be dissipated); and, by the application of techniques such as price discrimination and transfer pricing, appropriate the returns from its investment in information creation.

Most emphasis in the literature relating to internalization has been placed upon proprietary know-how. Some mention has been made of other types of firms which may find internalization across national boundaries an attractive proposition. These include companies whose monopolistic advantage lies in sophisticated management or market techniques (and the creation of brand images). In such cases the expertise may be inseparable from the firm or may face uncertain returns on the external market. Again, in general, large oligopolistic companies are assumed to be involved.

Over time, monopolistically-held specific advantages will be eroded and barrers to entry will therefore fall. Through research and investment, however, it may be possible to generate and retain ownership-specific advantages in a dynamic manner. Once again focus has been placed on technology, and on the continuous up-grading of technology as the revenues earned in domestic and foreign markets provide the funds for new R and D projects.

Location-specific Factors

The monopolistic advantages possessed by potential multinational firms and the internalization process provide a necessary but not always a sufficient condition for foreign direct investment. With the possession of these firm-specific advantages, the company could simply export to overseas markets. To explain the choice of foreign direct investment, it is necessary therefore to take into consideration location-specific factors in either home or host countries. These include variables such as trade barriers and other government policies, market characteristics, costs and productivity. Where such factors favour a foreign rather than a domestic location, then the foreign direct investment route will be chosen in place of exports.

Concluding this review of received theory, these three sets of conditions must be fulfilled for a firm to engage in foreign direct investment. First, the firm must possess net ownership advantages over firms of other nationalities. These advantages must be sufficient to offset the additional costs of operating in a foreign environment. Second, it must be more profitable for the company possessing these unique assets to utilise them itself through foreign direct investment, rather than to sell the rights to their use to other parties, through licensing agreements, management contracts, etc. That is, it must be more beneficial to use an internal market (taking account of both the costs and returns from internalization) than to externalize the property rights. Third, assuming the first two conditions are satisfied, it must be advantageous for the firm to exploit its unique assets through production outside its home country rather than through exports. This condition will be met when there are either positive (e.g. lower labour costs) or negative factors (e.g. trade barriers) deterring production at home or encouraging production abroad.

So much for the theory. Now for some ostensibly counter-theoretical facts.

Non-conventional Multinationals: the Evidence

What characterizes the deviate multinational? Three sets of evidence — on the source, size, and technological level of some international firms — suggest that a theory that fails to encompass these firms misses a lot.

First, there is evidence that the *sources* of foreign direct investment are becoming more diffuse and encompass a number of *small and lower-income countries*. India provides a striking example of a newly-emerged source country. A survey of Indian joint ventures abroad at the start of 1976 found that of 65 projects abroad, nearly half were less than two years old, and 63 more such investments were in process at the time.[10] In the Central American Common Market, according to another survey, 7.5 per cent of 572 identified foriegn-owned ventures came from other Latin American countries.[11] A recent study by Eduardo White[12] documents substantial intra-Latin American direct investment (see Table 4.1), especially by firms from Brazil, Mexico, Argentina, Venezuela and Uruguay. Table 4.1 demonstrates the preponderance of investment between neighbouring countries — Brazilian firms in Argentina, Colombian firms in Ecuador and Venezuelan firms in Colombia, for example. Table 4.2, taken from a United Nations study, indicates substantial investment in Asia stemming from Korea, Singapore, the Philippines and, particularly, Hong Kong.[13]

Developing country-based MNEs as well as those from Japan seem to posssess some characteristics that distinguish them from their Western counterparts. Commonly the firms are relatively small,[14] produce low-technology undifferentiated goods and direct their investment to poorer and smaller neighbouring states. Joint ventures are frequent, although effective control is probably retained by the investing firm in

Table 4.1: Intra Latin American Direct Investment

Countries of origin	Argentina 5/1979	Bolivia 1976	Brazil 6/1978	Colombia 12/1978	Chile 8/1978	Ecuador 12/1977	Mexico 12/1978	Peru 12/1977	Venezuela 12/1978	Total
					Host countries					
Argentina	*	441	20.031	1.061	662	10.846	986	1.771	2.058	37.856
Bolivia	n.a.	*	17	5	133	–	–	431	49	635
Brazil	35.962	1.301	*	2.404	13.969	4.752	734	949	338	60.409
Colombia	3.816	–	244	*	50	10.347	–	695	1.499	16.651
Chile	924	271	273	195	*	11.097	218	1.240	82	14.300
Ecuador	n.a.	–	148	17.620	100	*	–	825	21	18.714
Mexico	39.898	–	7.650	4.141	2.552	4.771	*	1.156	1.846	62.014
Paraguay	n.a.	–	1	–	–	–	–	–	77	78
Peru	–	594	14	1.720	47	1.186	133	*	193	3.886
Uruguay	120.482	–	16.475	1.110	300	–	–	2.256	3.812	144.435
Venezuela	n.a.	–	13.333	26.123	5.697	5.525	1.205	2.011	*	53.894
Other central America	n.a.	–	194	153	82	–	–	38	731	1.198
Total	201.082	2.607	58.380	54.532	23.592	48.524	3.276	11.372	10.706	414.071

Source: White (1979).

Table 4.2: Intra-regional Direct Investment Stock in Asia,[a] 1976 (millions of US dollars)

Home country	Thailand[b]	Host country Indonesia	Philippines	Hong Kong	Total
Malaysia	5.0	42.7	–	–	47.7
Hong Kong	10.9	728.3	14.2	–	753.4
India	2.4	19.4	–	–	21.8
Philippines	0.9	272.1	–	3.4	276.4
Singapore	2.2	115.6	–	13.4	131.2
Korea, Republic of	–	107.4	–	–	107.4
Thailand	–	–	–	29.7	29.7
Other Asian developing countries	22.1	102.9	3.1	7.3	135.4
Japan	74.5	1216.6	124.2	56.8	1,472.1

Notes: a. The data for Hong Kong, the Philippines and Thailand refer to assets; the data for Indonesia refer to approved project as of 1976.
b. 1975.
Source: United Nations Economic and Social Council, *Transnational Corporations in World Development*, Table III–41, p. 247.

the majority of cases.[15] The range of examples quoted in the literature is wide.[16] Over time, foreign direct investment from Hong Kong has progressed from the manufacture of basic household items and simple food processing, to the production of textiles and now more sophisticated goods in industries such as electronics. In Latin America, much private foreign direct investment within the region has taken place in light engineering industries, including machine tools and automobile parts, domestic appliances, other consumer durables and textiles. Filipino multinationals engage in activities ranging from management services to brewing; and Indian multinationals are involved in detergents, steel, machine tools, electronics and even hotels. It is not merely the case therefore that developing country MNEs are engaged solely in basic low-technology industries, although these sectors certainly account for the bulk of investment. Furthermore, even though the investments from low-income country MNEs mainly involve horizontal integration, there are also examples of both forward and backward vertical integration. The operation of Latin American oil refining companies in the Middle East provides an example of the latter. Conversely, Central American firms manufacture fertilizers in the United States, and Indian companies can shrimp in Ski Lanka.

The second characteristic of conventional multinationals is their size. Evidence from the traditional homes of direct investment, the USA and UK, suggests that it may be incorrect to associate multinationality exclusively with large, technologically advanced corporations. A recent project in the UK studied the overseas manufacturing experiences of a sample of firms, all of which had an annual turnover of less than $20 million. 'Clearly size is no great barrier to going international', commented the authors.[17] Even among large UK firms, Stopford has shown that there is a sharp distinction between two groups of multinationals.[18] In addition to a relatively small group of companies which are leaders in international oligopoly there is a much larger, less technologically advanced group of firms that have tended to concentrate on production in Commonwealth markets.

For the USA there is no denying that overseas direct investment has been dominated by large, research-intensive firms.[19] Within the United States, however, in 1976 over 90 per cent of plants had fewer than 250 workers and these firms provided more than one third of employment in manufacturing industry. Given this survival potential of the small firm it is hardly surprising that many of these companies have also become active in overseas ventures. A study by the Conference Board concluded that 'examination of the involvement in foreign manufacturing by company size (annual sales) suggests that product line and management attitudes are as important as size in determining whether a US firm's management assumes responsibility for overseas production'.[20] As Table 4.3 shows, even in the class of smallest firms ($21 million to $50 million in sales), at least 37 per cent had some foreign involvement and for 29 per cent this meant manufacturing abroad − in Canada or elsewhere. This in the country whose large domestic market has made its firms' insularity notorious.

Of the various non-conventional multinationals, the ones that have received most attention have been the Japanese. In recent years Japanese foreign investment has shifted from the typical trading company-manufacturing firm partnership towards fully-fledged direct investment abroad.[21] In several respects, however, Japanese multinationals resemble those from developing countries more than the Western giants. According to Ozawa, Japanese multinationals seem to be characterized as follows: [22]

(1) Japan's small and medium-sized manufacturers (with capital of yen 100 million or less, or 300 or fewer employees) have been very active in direct investment, particularly in the developing countries. Data to end 1975 indicate that 42 per cent of the number of manufacturing investments abroad were undertaken by these small and medium-sized firms.

(2) Much of Japanese manufacturing investment is in relatively

Table 4.3: Overseas Operations of US Manufacturing Companies With Total Sales Over $20 Million, 1975

Sales ranking[a] (millions of US dollars)	Number of companies	Per cent of companies				
		Manufacture in more than 1 country (excl. Canada)[b]	Manufacture in Canada only[b]	No manufacture but other foreign involvement[c]	No activity outside US	Unknown
21–50	294	21.4	7.5	8.2	46.6	16.3
51–100	328	32.0	9.1	13.7	34.5	10.7
101–500	592	45.3	10.1	12.0	25.3	7.3
501–1,000	122	76.2	2.5	9.0	11.5	0.8
Over 1,000	210	85.2	3.3	2.4	8.6	0.5
Total	1,546	45.8	7.9	10.0	27.9	8.4

Notes: a. 1973. b. Foreign plants 51% or more owned by US parent. c. Joint ventures, minority holdings, licences, sales offices, etc.
Source: Conference Board, *Announcements of Foreign Investment in US Manufacturing Industry, 1st Quarterly* (New York, 1977).

labour-intensive or technologically standardized goods, e.g. textiles, or involved unsophisticated products within the electrical appliance or chemical industries, e.g. batteries, fans, radios, plastics and paints.

(3) Japan's manufacturing investments are heavily concentrated in Asia and Latin America (particularly Brazil). In 1975, three-quarters of the stock was in developing countries in comparison with 17 per cent for the USA and 20 per cent for West Germany.

Apart from these differences, other distinctive features of the Japanese direct investment pattern include the importance of investment in extractive ventures and in services; the significance of minority-owned and joint-venture operations abroad; the prevalence of 'group' investment, where a number of companies participate in a particular venture abroad as co-investors; and, associated with this, the involvement of government agencies and government-affiliated financial institutions in foreign investment.

In sum, when the various pieces of evidence are assembled, it becomes clear that multinationality is far from being the exclusive domain of large, Western, research-intensive corporations. The question that requires an answer is whether or not existing theory is adequate to explain the overseas expansion of the smaller, non-Western, non-research-intensive firms. One alternative paradigm is the 'Japanese model'.

A Model of Japanese Multinational Operations

It is argued by some Japanese economists, led by Kojima of Hitotsubashi University, that received theory, largely derived from US experience, is inadequate to explain the pattern of Japanese outward direct investment.[23] Kojima makes the distinction between 'anti-trade oriented' American manufacturing investments and 'trade-oriented' Japanese investments. The US economy is claimed to have a dualistic structure consisting of oligopolistic, technologically-advanced industries alongside a traditional, stagnant, price-competitive sector (textiles, steel, agriculture). Foreign direct investment is seen as taking place only within the former sector as companies attempt to defend their markets and maintain their oligopolistic position. This overseas investment will take place at the top of the product cycle, although the motivation is seen as 'offensive' rather than 'defensive' as in the original Vernon model.[24] Direct investments of this kind are viewed as anti-trade oriented and working against the structure of comparative advantage. By the process of establishing foreign affiliates rather than exporting, increased imports are induced, jobs are lost at home and structural adjustment is hindered.

This alleged pattern of American multinationality is contrasted with the trade-oriented pattern of Japanese direct investment flows, where investment takes place in sectors in which the country has a comparative disadvantage. The theory argues that within the contracting sector of a home country, economic resources released can be used either internally — through intra-country sectoral transfers — or externally — through inter-country transfers. Marginally efficient companies within the declining sector are considered to find it easier to establish operations overseas, often assisted by the incentives offered by developing host countries. The firm applies its existing expertise within a more suitable factor-endowments framework abroad rather than facing the problems associated with entering a new industry at home. It is argued, therefore, that the marginal firms feel the greatest pressure to set up foreign manufacturing plants, utilizing cheap labour within the developing countries. Certain of the resources specific to the contracting sector, such as industry-unique technology and experience, could not, moreover, be transferred to the expanding sector domestically. Unless such released resources are transferred to other countries to develop the latter's comparatively advantaged industries, therefore, they would be wasted at home.

On the face of it, this explanation for Japanese foreign direct investment is quite different from conventional theory. In the first place, the 'advantage', which is usually assumed necessary to enable MNEs to compete successfully abroad, is not immediately obvious. Indeed, it is argued that the smaller the technological difference between the investing and host country industry, the easier it is to transfer operations. Moreover, what is being transferred is general technology, covering a wide range of production activities such as assembly techniques (e.g. cars, TVs, refrigerators); material selection, mixing and treatment techniques (e.g. dyes, inks and paints); machine operation and maintenance techniques (e.g. weaving and spinning); training of engineers and operatives; plant layout; installation of machinery and equipment; and quality, cost and inventory control techniques. Secondly, the type of firm involved in foreign manufacturing activity is the smaller, marginally efficient operation rather than the large, innovative corporation. Thirdly, oligopolistic or monopolistic market structures need not prevail in either home or host countries.

Some of these arguments were extended and elaborated by another Japanese writer, Ozawa,[25] who contrasted the microeconomic forces underlying the expansion of Western MNEs with the macroeconomic pressures behind Janapese multinationality. Ozawa sees Western MNEs as the outcome of an evolutionary process by which firms increase in size and organization sophistication. On the other hand, the motivations underlying the overseas growth of Japanese firms were basically macroeconomic in nature, via domestic factor shortages, insecurity of supply of industrial resources and environmental constraints. Multinationality by this view is a reflection of the collective way in which corporate objectives are set in Japan. Given their macroeconomic influences it is concluded that 'the more competitive the industry (that is, the less monopolistic or oligopolistic the industry, and the less technologically sophisticated the product), the greater the need so far for Japanese industry to resort to offshore production . . .'[26]

Although this model is applied solely to Japan, it does represent a challenge to any claims of universality in conventional theory. Is it valid?

Monopolistic Advantage and Within-industry Firm Characteristics

Part of the blame for neglect of small-firm characteristics must fall on empirical researchers. Most of past research on the sources of advantage to multinational firms has focused on (a) the features of source countries, (b) the industry-specific factors supporting direct investment, and (c) within-industry determinants. While empirical work on (a) and (b) is fairly substantial, the difficulty of obtaining systematic evidence has resulted in a neglect of *within-industry* differences between direct investors and stay-at-home firms. Much writing has relied on Horst's findings of size as the principal within-industry factor. Freeman's work, however, points to certain other characteristics or strategies that can influence multinationality, including investments in information that do not require large size to achieve any necessary economies of scale.[27] Freeman's typology of the strategies open to firms under technological change, while retaining the link with technology, shows that innovative competition does not require heavy research expenditures. Typical strategies are:

Offensive strategy. Companies pursuing this type of strategy are those aiming for technical and market leadership through innovation.

Such firms spend heavily on R and D, committing funds even for basic research work.

Defensive Strategy. These firms again invest in R and D, but their objective is to be fast followers rather than early leaders. The strength of such corporations may lie in adaptive research rather than in basic or fundamental work.

Imitative strategy. These companies introduce products well after their first appearance on the market. An imitative company may have particular advantages in production engineering, enabling it to manufacture at low cost; or it may have a labour cost advantage which has the same effect; or it may possess skills in adapting products to special market requirements. Or the company may be strong in marketing.

Dependent strategy. The firms operating dependent strategies are mainly subcontractors to finished goods manufacturers. Dependent firms will often be small, but may be highly profitable, capitalizing on the supply of perhaps an important component to a dominant company. The optimum scale of production may be too low for the dominant firm to consider it worth becoming involved. The expertise and familiarity built up over the years will be a valuable asset, and for the dominant firm the search costs associated with locating alternative suppliers with similar skills may be prohibitive.

Traditional strategy. The traditional corporations are those which find no reason to change their products. The market may prefer the traditional goods they product; product innovation may be a positive disadvantage to these firms. Alternatively, the companies concerned may survive on the basis of a local monopoly. They will tend to be small and will not engage in research and development work.

Opportunist strategy. The opportunist or niche-dependent company identifies an opportunity — a gap in the market — and survives by responding to it. It is doubtful if this represents a long-term advantage for a corporation since it relies heavily on a single, entrepreneurial decision (although it may provide a launching point for a longer-term plan).

Freeman's taxonomy enables us to identify the sorts of firms likely to engage in direct investment. We have tried to summarize each type of firm's special advantage in Table 4.4. Perhaps we should first draw attention to those firms that are *unlikely* to become direct investors despite their success in home markets.

First, *traditional* firms will often survive in the domestic market only because of the ability to charge a premium price based on some regional association (as in craft skills). This type of advantage is not readily transferable across national frontiers. Second, the on-off nature of the

Table 4.4: Principal Advantages of Successful Firms and their Applicability Abroad

Firm characteristic	Principal source of advantage[a]	Size of firm	R & D spending	Transferable abroad	Tied to firm?
Offensive	R & D capacity	Large	Heavy	Yes	Yes
Defensive	R & D capacity; applications and adaptation engineering; entrepreneurial skills	Large	Heavy	Yes	Usually
Imitative[b]	Production expertise – production engineering, quality control, applications and adaptations. Marketing expertise – product differentiation, brand names, marketing research, distribution	Large/small	Low	Yes	Sometimes
Dependent	Production engineering, applications and adaptation; production flexibility	Medium/small	Low/negligible	Yes	Yes
Traditional	Production craft skills; marketing association with traditionalism, regional image	Small	Negligible	No	Yes
Opportunist	Entrepreneurial skills	Small	Negligible	Not normally	Yes temporarily

Notes: a. Note the principal source of advantage may be backed up by other advantages. For instance, among firms in the offensive and defensive categories, large size will facilitate economies of scale in production and marketing and various advantages in the finance area.
b. Among large companies, skills may be either in production or marketing (supported by economies of scale, and advantages in finance, as above). Among small firms the advantages may accrue primarily from production.

opportunist strategy means that it is unsuitable for foreign direct investment; although entrepreneurs may occasionally identify one-shot opportunities abroad as well as at home; the occurency of such direct investment will be random and not amenable to systematic explanation; they will tend to be short term.

The conventional MNEs, upon which most attention has been focused, are those in the offensive and defensive categories: both groups spend heavily on R and D and exploit the knowledge advantage so gained through internalization across national boundaries.

As Table 4.4 shows, however, there is an in-between group of firms, not necessarily large or research-intensive, that has the potential for foreign direct investment. In many cases its domestic advantages are also those that drive direct investment: they are transferable abroad within the firm at little additional cost, and they are largely inseparable from the firm. These are the kinds of advantages whose exploitation tends to be internalized rather than sold in an open market.

Companies in the *dependent* category may be encouraged to establish production facilities by the dominant firm, or may see it in their interests to do so to prevent the latter developing other sybaritic relationships. The dominant company, for its part, may find it convenient to rely on the same suppliers in its foreign operations as it uses in the home market. Doing so removes some of the risks and costs associated with subcontracting to indigenous firms. The importation of components may be less satisfactory if, for instance, the country-specific advantages of the foreign location take the form of low labour costs. The establishment of UK operations by US-based oil industry subcontractors may represent a case in point.

The firm-specific assets which the satellite firm is selling in either of these may be rather different from the types of advantages normally identified, including: a general body of expertise relating to the manufacture and use of certain components; problem-solving skills in the application of these components within particular industries; flexibility of production; and possibly, though less essential, low-cost production.

Firms adopting *imitative* strategies may also develop internationally. This may in fact be that most important group, characterized as it is by low R and D intensity but without the close inter-firm links which exist within the dependent category. Both large and small companies may survive successfully with imitative strategies, but their unique assets will tend to be different. The large corporations may spend heavily on marketing to differentiate their products and ensure high penetration within distribution outlets. The marketing-oriented small firms, by comparison, lacking financial resources, will seek out market segments where they are insulated from the direct competition of the mass producers. A firm need not be big to have a strong reputation in a narrow community of specialist buyers.

For other imitative companies, production expertise may be important. Skills in physical production, adaptation to meet particular market (small?) or use (primitive?) conditions, or expertise in production engineering may create a reputation for quality and thereby provide a barrier to entry. For all of these types of firms, the advantages possessed may be transferable across national frontiers and in principle therefore permit foreign direct investment.

The Role of Location-specific Factors

In spite of the possibility of direct foreign investment among smaller and low-techology firms, the implication of the above discussion is that the monopolistic advantages possessed by these companies will be relatively small or temporary. The height of barriers to entry remains positively related to firm size and R and D intensity. It follows from this that the successful transplant of manufacture to a foreign environment will depend heavily on location-specific factors within the prospective host country: that is, the extent to which the foreign investor is at a disadvantage. The lower the monopolistic advantage, therefore, the greater the attention a firm must pay to minimizing the costs of foreignness. The following are some of the ways in which small or low-technology firms achieve this:

(a) Direct investment involving *joint ventures* with local partners. This can be a low-cost way of building up knowledge about the market and business methods and of minimizing capital requirements.

(b) Direct investment in countries where the main competitors are *home country firms*, meaning that the structure and form of competition is understood.

(c) Direct investment where *secure markets* are assured, as in the examples quoted earlier of subcontractors to end-user firms.

(d) Manufacture in host countries where *incentives*, such as tax holidays and subsidized interest rates, are offered to incoming foreign investors

(e) Direct investment in states which are *linguistically or culturally similar* to the home nation, or investment in neighbouring countries where distance costs may be reduced

(f) Direct investment in countries where the strength of indigenous competition is low, which will usually mean countries which are less developed economically than the home nation.

In summary, the possession of ownership advantages, taken together with favourable location-specific factors abroad may permit even small and low-technology firms to undertake direct investment. But if the above assertions are valid then the direct investment pattern will be completely different from that of conventional MNEs. This is so because of differences in products and industry sectors and the need to keep the additional costs associated with foreign manufacture to a minimum. In particular we would expect small-firm and small-country multinationals to have a much greater affinity for cultural, linguistic and geographical proximity than do conventional multinationals.

A Reinterpretation of the Japanese Model and Some Extensions

It has been argued above that notionally unconventional multinational business operations may be explained adequately within the broad framework of received theory. If this explanation holds good then it may be possible to reinterpret the Japanese foreign direct investment model as postulated by Kojima and Ozawa.

The basis of the latter model is that the pattern of Japanese investment cannot be explained within the monopolistic advantage model. The reasons for this are that Japanese producers 'rarely possess any decisive advantage to compensate for the intrinsic cost of being alien producers . . .' and that much of Japanese foreign direct investment takes place within 'market(s) devoid of such strongly monopolistic or oligopolistic characteristics as the monopolistic theory postulates'.[28] The arguments presented above, however, have shown that firms of different sizes and varying degrees of research intensity may co-exist. The non-traditional MNEs, without the advantages accruing from large firm size and heavy R and D intensity, may still be able to develop some advantage to enable them to survive both at home and abroad. The assets possessed by the smaller and medium-sized Japanese companies have already been indicated. These include general technology and production expertise, as possessed by firms pursuing imitative strategies, supported by a variety of other advantages. First, it has been shown that Japanese investment abroad is characterized by 'bunching'[29] within particular industries in developing countries. Rather than an oligopolistic form of behaviour in this instance, bunching may be considered both as a means of strengthening the market position of all firms and as a means of sharing the additional costs associated with manufacturing in a foreign environment. The latter are further minimized by the fact that investment takes place in neighbouring countries where socio-cultural conditions are not totally dissimilar. Second, the involvement of Japanese trading companies, banks and the explicit support of the Japanese government itself may provide investing firms with a variety of types of assistance to improve their competitive positions abroad. In a sense these factors may be considered as forms of company-specific assets and as ways of lowering operating costs overseas. Third, one should consider the extent to which intermediate output markets are internalized either within the firm itself or among associated Japanese companies (as, for example, where a small firm supplies most of its output to a larger company located within Japan or to the latter's affiliate in third-country markets).

So Japanese companies would seem to fit fairly readily into the model outlined earlier. The 'Japanese theory' makes a spurious distinction between trade and anti-trade oriented foreign investments and between the motivation for US and Japanese investment. It may be true that much of US direct investment abroad replaces US exports,[30] but there is no reason why this should work against the structure of comparative advantage. Provided US MNEs are able to appropriate the returns from their investment in R and D, this will permit further technological advance and a continuous upgrading of the United States' economy. Moreover, it is contended that the motives of US firms are to maintain an oligopolistic market position, while those of Japanese firms are to upgrade the industrial structures of both home and host economies. However if Japanese investment motives were so benign, then licensing would be a more satisfactory method of transferring technology from the host country viewpoint. Direct investment occurs to retain control and appropriate the returns from intangible factors.

Generalizing the monopolistic advantage concept from the case of Japan to that of other non-traditional foreign direct investors, studies have identified a number of firm-specific assets which may be possessed by such companies. These include:

(a) Production experience and know-how in manufacturing certain items which are not in sufficient demand in foreign countries to

support local production
(b) Skills in adapting machinery for low-volume production and in designing machinery to permit more flexible usage[31]
(c) Imperfections in the market for secondhand machinery, arising from lack of knowledge relating to the availability of such machinery, that is, communications failure[32]
(d) For the Third World multinationals most emphasis is placed on production rather than marketing expertise. Where marketing expertise is required, there is evidence of link-ups between developed and developing country firms, or indeed between developing-nation companies themselves[33]

In addition, operating a developing-country MNE in another developing country may capture rents from some imperfections in the market for high-skill labour. Expatriate managers and technical personnel will require much lower salaries and fringe benefits than equivalent specialists from developed countries. Building costs may be lower since developing-country MNEs are often accustomed to operating from unattractive premises. It has been suggested that the less formal organization structure of developing-nation MNEs may provide a further advantage, in making it easier for them to deal with off-book financial arrangements.

By and large, the advantages of LDC MNEs accrue from production experience, low costs and adaptability; they tend to be closest to imitative strategies.[34] Whatever their advantage, it is apparent that the alleged uniqueness of the Japanese model of multinational business operations is somewhat illusory. When the concept of monopolistic advantage and internalization is defined broadly, it becomes possible to provide an explanation for the emergence of a wide range of nonconventional multinational firms, including those from Japan.

Conclusions and Implications

The preceding discussion has suggested that firms of widely varying characteristics and from a broad range of countries may generate firm-specific advantages which are exploitable through foreign direct investment. Yet a number of issues remain unsettled. First, received theory predicts that there is a positive correlation between the incidence of multinationalism among companies and the height of barriers to entry. Barriers to entry will be highest where firms are large, oligopolistic and research-intensive. Conversely, among small corporations, relying heavily on cumulative production experience and entrepreneurial skills, barriers to entry and multinationalism will be commensurately lower. Where small-firm multinationalism does exist, one expects to find a relationship between these different types of multinationals and the location of their investments. The lower the entry barrier the greater the likelihood of investment in risk- and cost-minimizing locations. In general such locations will be fairly close in terms of distance, language and culture to the home country.

Another issue which poses certain problems when considering the multinationalism of non-conventional MNEs is that of the maintenance of entry barriers over time. It is true that the costs of foreignness will fall as MNEs become established in a host country, but this must be set against the erosion of their monopolistic advantages. The maintenance of monopolistic advantage on a dynamic basis would seem to be much more difficult for smaller and low-technology companies, particularly when these firms are operating in price-competitive industry sectors.[35]

A further issue concerns the lack of integration in the operations of developing-country MNEs.[36] This would again prove a disadvantage over time, although even among American MNEs it has been observed that integration is an evolutionary process. Thus in the early stages of multinationalism, affiliates tend to operate as fairly independent units. Integration has been shown to take place at a later stage, in some cases as a reaction to loss of initial technological advantage.

The above conclusions would, nevertheless, tend to indicate that there may be greater instability in the overseas manufacturing operations of MNEs possessing limited ownership-specific advantages.

A final interesting question relates to the predictions which may be derived from this broader interpretation of the theory of foreign direct investment. In particular it is possible to indicate the types of countries which may emerge as homes to MNEs in the future.[37] The emphasis in this paper has been on microeconomic issues, indicating the diversity of ways in which companies may acquire the types of advantages required for successful direct foreign investment. In the main, MNEs from low-income countries have emerged through the pursuit of imitative, adaptive and dependent strategies. There may be certain macroeconomic characteristics of home countries which seem likely to facilitate the development of such multinationals. These include:

(a) A high degree of communication with industrialized countries (e.g. Hong Kong)

(b) Government and social support for outward-looking development strategies (e.g. Japan)
(c) Scale and other economic similarities arising from market or production conditions (e.g. India)
(d) Regional economic co-operation

Complementing these factors in several newly industrializing countries is a climate that fosters entrepreneurship and human skills. Where firms are unable to compete through technical innovation and intensive research and development activity, then the company-specific assets must derive from human skills. It is here perhaps that government activity in Hong Kong provides some lessons, for the role of the state in this Crown Colony has been in providing maximum scope for entrepreneurs.[38] It would be relatively easy to associate entrepreneurship and human skills and firm advantages with the general level of economic development of a country and variables such as literacy levels. But in principle there is no reason why countries at fairly low levels of economic development should not produce entrepreneurs with the foresight and confidence to engage in manufacture with other countries with similar market and production conditions. Where political and cultural barriers are great, economies of scale and integrated operations dominate firms' own advantages and large, conventional multinationals alone can survive. Where barriers are few, small, adaptive unconventional multinationals can also thrive.

Notes

1. Raymond Vernon, *Storm Over the Multinationals* (Cambridge, Mass., University Press, 1977) p. 19.
2. For a comprehensive review of trends and patterns, see United Nations Economic and Social Council, *Transnational Corporations in World Development: A Re-examination*, Commission on Transnational Corporations 4th Session, E/C. 10/38 (New York, UN, 1978).
3. Other developments requiring explanation include the growth of state-owned multinationals, and even the emergence of substantial numbers of Soviet Union-based multinational companies. See Herbert E. Meyer, 'This Communist Internationale Has a Capitalistic Accent', *Fortune*, February 1977, pp. 134–48.
4. Hymer's thesis was completed in 1960, but the work was not published until 1976. See Stephen H. Hymer, *The International Operations of National Firms* (1976).
5. John H. Dunning, 'Trade Location of Economic Activity and the MNE: A Search for an Eclectic Approach', in Bertin Ohlin (ed.), *The International Allocation of Economic Activity* (London, Macmillan, 1977).
6. Richard E. Caves, 'International Organization', in John H. Dunning (ed.),

Economic Analysis and the Multinational Enterprise (London, Allen and Unwin, 1974). As Caves states on p. 130, 'because information costs associated with undertaking a foreign investment are both heavy and relatively fixed, small but rising firms that might someday find direct investment profitable may rationally postpone it until penetration of the home market is more advanced'. But there are ways in which these information costs may be substantially reduced. These include investment in neighbouring countries or in states which are culturally or linguistically similar to the home nation, or in countries where the structure and forms of competition are understood. The initial costs of establishing overseas operations may be low for other reasons too: a large body of experienced international personnel now exists, and there has been a rapid growth in multinational operations in the service sector to support direct investors.

7. The concept was first applied to the MNE in Peter J. Buckley and Mark C. Casson, *The Future of the Multinational Enterprise* (London, Macmillan, 1976). See also, Mark C. Casson, *Alternatives to the Mulitnational Enterprise* (London, Macmillan, 1979).

8. Alternatively termed 'knowledge' or 'information'.

9. This is the appropriability problem. See S.P. Magee, 'Information and the Multinational Corporation: An Appropriability Theory of Direct Foreign Investment', in J.N. Bhagwati (ed.), *The New International Economic Order* (Cambridge, Mass., MIT Press, 1977), pp. 317–40.

10. Cited in Raymond Vernon, *Storm Over the Multinationals*, p. 27.

11. Reported in Louis T. Wells, Jr, 'The Internationalization of Firms from the Developing Countries', in Tamir Agmon and Charles P. Kindleberger (eds), *Multinationals from Small Countries* (Cambridge, Mass., MIT Press, 1976).

12. Eduardo White, 'The International Projection of Firms from Latin American Countries', presented at the Conference on Third World Multinational Corporations, East-West Center, Honolulu, September 1979.

13. We should point out that there are doubts as to the reliability of the statistics quoted. Observers have suggested that some of the investment designated as developing country based, may actually be investment controlled by affiliates of Japanese or Western firms in these states. On the other hand, as a possible offsetting factor, it has been pointed out that in Hong Kong, at least, a large number of outward direct investments may not be reported at all.

14. 'LDC firms in Nigeria seemed to form an intermediate sector in size (defined in terms of employment) between the larger firms from the developed countries and the small indigenous ones,' according to C.N.S. Nambudiri. *et al.*, 'Third World Country Firms in Third World Developing Countries: The Nigerian Experience', presented at the Conference on Third World Multinational Corporations, East-West Center, Honolulu, September 1979, p. 3.

15. According to a study of Korean firms abroad, about two-thirds of foreign investments were wholly-owned subsidiaries, and about 23 per cent joint ventures with Korean majority ownership.

16. The examples are taken from a variety of sources apart from those already cited: Tamir Agmon and Charles P. Kindleberger, *Multinationals from Small Countries* (Cambridge, Mass., MIT Press, 1976); Louis J. Wells, Jr, 'Foreign Investment from the Third World: The Experience of Chinese Firms from Hong Kong', *Columbia Journal of World Business*, Spring 1978, pp. 39–49; R. Rowan, 'There's Also Some Good News About South Korea', *Fortune*, September 1977, pp. 171–6. The 1979 Conference on Third World Multinational Firms held at The East-West Center, Honolulu in September 1979 produced about a dozen studies on the subject.

17. G.D. Newbould, Peter J. Buckley and J.C. Thurwell, *Going International* (New York, John Wiley, 1978).

18. James M. Stopford, 'Changing Perspectives on Investment by British

Manufacturing Multinationals', *Journal of International Business Studies*, 7, 2, Winter 1976, pp. 15–27.

19. The classic study of Thomas Horst, 'Firm and Industry Determinants of the Decision to Invest Abroad: An Empirical Study', *Review of Economics and Statistics*, 54, 1972, pp. 258–66.

20. Conference Board, *Announcements of Foreign Investment in U.S. Manufacturing Industry 1st Quarter 1977*, New York, 1977.

21. See M.Y. Yoshino, *Japan's Multinational Enterprises* (Cambridge, Mass., Harvard University Press, 1976); and Y. Tsurumi, *The Japanese are Coming* (Cambridge, Mass., Ballinger, 1976).

22. T. Ozawa, 'International Investment and Industrial Structure: New Theoretical Implications from the Japanese Experience', *Oxford Economic Papers*, 31, 1, 1979, pp. 72–92.

23. K. Kojima, 'A Macroeconomic Approach to Foreign Direct Investment', *Hitotsubashi Journal of Economics*, 14, 1, 1973, pp. 1–21; K. Kojima, *Direct Foreign Investment: A Japanese Model of Multinational Business Operations* (London, Croom Helm, 1978).

24. Raymond Vernon, 'International Investment and International Trade in the Product Cycle', *Quarterly Journal of Economics*, 80, 1966, pp. 190–207.

25. T. Ozawa, 'International Investment and Industrial Structure: New Theoretical Implications from the Japanese Experience', *Oxford Economic Papers*, 31, 1, 1979, pp. 72–92.

26. T. Ozawa, 'International Investment and Industrial Structure: New Theoretical Implications from the Japanese Experience', *Oxford Economic Papers*, 31, 1, 1979, p. 89.

27. C. Freeman, *The Economics of Industrial Innovation* (Middlesex, England, Penguin, 1974).

28. The quotations are from T. Ozawa, *International Investment and Industrial Structure*, p. 78 and p. 73.

29. A form of behaviour first observed in F.T. Knickerbocker, *Oligopolistic Reaction and the Multinational Enterprise* (Boston, Mass., Harvard University Press, 1973).

30. Stobaugh has argued that most US investments serve to retain markets that would otherwise be lost, and hence do not replace exports. Robert B. Stobaugh *et al.*, *U.S. Multinational Enterprises and the U.S. Economy* (Boston, Mass., Harvard Business School, 1972).

31. David Lecraw, 'Direct Investment by Firms from Less Developed Countries', *Oxford Economic Papers*, 29, 3, pp. 442–57.

32. Dilmus D. James, *Used Machinery and Economic Development* (East Lansing, Michigan State University, 1974); Louis T. Wells, Jr, 'Economic Man and Engineering Man', *Public Policy*, Summer 1973, pp. 319–42.

33. For some details see David A. Heenan and W.J. Keegan, 'The Rise of Third World Multinationals', pp. 107–8; and Louis T. Wells, Jr, 'Foreign Investment from the Third World', p. 45.

34. It is worth noting that similar types of strategies have been observed in relation to MNEs from Australia. Helen Hughes describes the country as a 'technological intermediary', with Australian companies transmitting their scaled-down technology through investments in developing countries: H. Hughes, 'Technology Transfer: The Australian Experience', in Tamir Agmon and Charles P. Kindleberger, *Multinationals from Small Countries*, pp. 101–27.

35. One possibility is that company strategy changes over time. Among some Japanese firms a shift from imitative strategies to offensive strategies has been observed. Along with this there has been a change in the directional pattern of investment from South East Asia to Europe and North America. Similarly among

British MNEs there has been a reorientation of investment from the Common-wealth towards Europe and North America with, presumably, a greater stress on technological advance at the corporate level.

36. Louis T. Wells, Jr, 'Foreign Investment from the Third World'. On p. 42, Wells comments that he 'identified no Hong Kong firm that was, on its own, attempting to build a system of several affiliates that were integrated to gain economies of scale and lower costs'.

37. For another view of this issue, see John H. Dunning, 'Explaining Outward Direct Investment of Developing Countries: In Support of the Eclectic Model', presented at the Conference on Third World Multinational Companies, East-West Center, Honolulu, September 1979.

38. See J. Riedel, *The Industrialization of Hong Kong* (Tubingen, J.C.B. Mohr (Paul Siebeck), 1974).

5 THE ECLECTIC THEORY OF THE MULTINATIONAL ENTERPRISE AND THE INTERNATIONAL HOTEL INDUSTRY

John H. Dunning and Matthew McQueen

Introduction

The theory of the multinational enterprise has developed along three paths explaining *why* firms produce abroad (internalization advantages), *how* they are able successfully to compete with domestic firms (ownership advantages) and *where* MNEs of a particular nationality produce in particular host countries (locational advantages). These are, however, only partial explanations of international production. For example, the ability of MNEs to internalize markets may partly explain their ability to compete successfully in foreign locations but does not explain cases where the MNE has an absolute advantage over local producers derived from the knowledge, expertise and entrepreneurial flair of individuals within the enterprise. Ownership advantages must therefore be carefully distinguished from internalization advantages. Similarly, internalization theory cannot provide a complete explanation for the distribution of international production between countries. The eclectic theory integrates these three strands of economic theory to explain the ability of firms to service markets and the reasons why they choose to exploit this advantage rather than through exports or contractual resource flows, and to explain the direction of international production by the MNE. The principle hypothesis of the theory is that the propensity of a firm to engage in international production depends on three conditions being satisfied:

(i) the firm with headquarters in one country must possess net *ownership advantages* (which largely take the form of intangible assets) *vis à vis* firms of other nationalities in serving a particular foreign maket;

(ii) it must be profitable to the firm to combine these assets with factor endowments *located* in foreign countries (otherwise the foreign market would be served by exports);

(iii) it must be more beneficial to the enterprise possessing these advantages to use them itself rather than sell them, or the right to use them, to a foreign firm.

The existing theories of international production have been mostly applied to R and D-intensive industries; capital-intensive, resource-based activities where fiscal laws make it profitable to engage in transfer pricing; and some information intensive service sectors. This chapter reports on part of some research recently completed by the authors (Dunning and McQueen, 1981) which collected together a considerable amount of new data about the growing internalization of the hotel sector. The data provides an opportunity to test the applicability of the eclectic theory to a sector which operates with a very different and generally lower level of technology than that normally associated with MNE production. Second, the character of the foreign involvement in this industry suggests that some of the traditional ideas about the nature of international production may need to be re-modified. It is normally assumed that internalization advantages can only be achieved through the ownership of an equity capital stake sufficient to allow the enterprise *de jure* control over resource allocation. In the case of hotels, however, it appears that many of these benefits may be attained through some form of contract; we will call such control contract-based control to distinguish it from equity-based control. In this chapter we shall take international involvement to mean any form of transaction by an enterprise outside its national boundaries in which assets, rights or goods are transferred and there is some continuing *de facto* control over the use of these and/or complementary indigenous resources.

The chapter proceeds by looking into each of the three strands of the eclectic theory (ownership, locational and internalization advantages) and, for each, considers how far the theory explains the data, given the country- and firm-specific characteristics of these advantages. We do not test the theory by means of any statistical techniques (since the data to do so are not available) but rather by an examination of the characteristics of the product market; the organization of the firms and their forms of involvement; and the relationship between the geographical distribution and form of involvement of the MNEs and the characteristics of the host countries.

Ownership-specific Advantages

Our analysis of the transnational characteristics of the hotel business is limited to enterprises which had associations with two or more foreign hotels at the end of 1978. At that date, 81 international hotel chains from 22 countries were associated with 1,025 foreign hotels and

270,646 rooms. We believe that these account for at least 95 per cent of all the rooms in all foreign associated hotels and that no important MNE with hotel interests is omitted. They exclude the activities of referral chains, where these are solely reservation and marketing agencies. About one-half of foreign-based hotels, which had 56 per cent of the rooms, are associated with US enterprises, and, between them, French and United Kingdom MNEs account for another 30 per cent of foreign hotels and 25 per cent of the rooms.[1] Of the remaining important tourist generating countries, Japan accounts for 3.3 per cent, West Germany and Scandinavia 1.6 per cent each.

Industrial organization theory suggests that for enterprises of one nationality to be involved in an industry located in another country, they must possess or be able to generate or acquire income-generating assets not available to indigenous firms, sufficient to overcome the advantages which the latter firms have in that country. To evaluate the net advantages of foreign firms in the hotel industry, let us first examine the nature of the product supplied by the industry. Essentially it comprises three ingredients. The first, and most important, is a package of 'on premises' services which offer a particular life-style and ambience for the customer where he is a guest in the hotel. All hotels provide the basic services of lodgings and food and drink, but the kind and quality of accommodation and sustenance vary considerably as do those of other services offered.[2] The second ingredient is the provision, or arrangement, of *before*, *at the time*, or *after* 'off premises' services for their guests, e.g. transport from home or airport to hotel, reservations with restaurants and/or other hotels, local excursion and sightseeing tours, booking facilities for theatres, other entertainment, cultural, sporting events, etc. The third component of the product of hoteliers is the extent to which a customer may be assured that the services he is actually sold are those he expects to obtain. A 'trademark' of guarantee may be particularly important where customers are buying a product 'sight unseen' and have little real knowledge of what is being offered for sale; indeed it is characteristic of the international hotel industry that many guests are one-time visitors; and that knowledge of the product to satisfy wants can only be experienced after it is bought. In this important respect, hotel services can be regarded as 'experience goods' (i.e. those whose value to the consumer cannot be established by visual inspection) rather than 'search goods' (whose attributes can be examined and compared with the advertised claims of the supplier). An experience in one hotel in a chain which prides itself on providing identical or similar standards of accommodation throughout the world

Table 5.1: Share of Transnational-associated Hotel Rooms in Total Hotel Rooms in Selected Countries, 1978 (percentage)

Developed market economies	Share	Developing countries and territories	Share	Developing countries and territories	Share
North America		Middle East		Oceania	
Canada	7.3	Egypt	28.5	Cook Islands	15.2
United States	0.6	Iran	20.7a	Fiji Islands	27.7
		Israel	15.7	New Caledonia	44.6
		Jordan	33.0a	Tahiti (French Polynesia)	45.8
		Lebanon	30.7a		
		Syria	7.4		
		Turkey	9.2		
	1.5		16.0		28.7
Europe		Africa		Latin America	
Austria	1.5	United Republic of Cameroon	10.9a	Argentina	12.8
Denmark	7.9a	Cabon	53.8a	Brazil	1.8
France	1.8a	Ghana	...	Chile	4.5
Germany, Fed. Rep. of	1.7a	Ivory Coast	41.7a	Colombia	16.1
Greece	4.3	Kenya	13.1	Ecuador	2.8a
Ireland	4.1	Lesotho	28.0	Guatemala	13.8
Italy	1.0	Madagascar	46.1	Mexico	5.6a
Netherlands	10.1	Mauritius	4.9	Panama	25.5
Portugal	5.2	Morocco	16.6a	Peru	2.8a
Spain	3.1	Senegal	49.7	Venezuela	33.4
Sweden	4.3a	Seychelles	61.0a		
Switzerland	4.1	Tunisia	9.4		
United Kingdom	2.0	Zambia	39.2		
	2.2		17.7		4.6

Other areas		Asia		Caribbean, etc.	
Australia	3.4[a]	Afghanistan	11.1[a]	Antigua	32.2
Japan	9.6[a]	Bangladesh	6.2[a]	Bahamas	35.6[a]
New Zealand	11.0[a]	Hong Kong	34.0	Barbados	14.9
		India	10.2	Bermuda	46.7
		Indonesia	10.6[a]	Cayman Islands	...
		Malaysia	5.6	Dominican Republic	30.5[a]
		Pakistan	10.0	Jamaica	31.0[a]
		Philippines	43.9	Martinique	67.2[a]
		Korea, Republic of	27.5	Puerto Rico	43.4[a]
		Singapore	32.6	St Lucia	43.8[a]
		Sri Lanka	21.3	Trinidad and Tobago	42.6[a]
		Thailand	10.4		
	6.6		16.6		35.6
All developed market economies	2.1	All developing countries and territories	11.1	All countries	3.3

Note: a. 1976 or 1977 data.

Source: For all hotels (and similar establishments), information provided by tourist offices and WTO, *Regional Breakdown of World Tourism Statistics, 1973–1977* (1979 edition).

may powerfully influence its competitive position in an unfamiliar environment.

The knowledge of the kind of product consumers want, the ability to supply it, and the persuasion of potential customers to buy your product comprise the main competitive weapons of hotels. The question arises 'Why should hotels associated with foreign firms have an edge over indigenous firms in the provision of these services?'

It is worth emphasizing that outside North America, the affiliates of international hotel chains primarily serve the needs of foreign visitors, particularly businessmen, rather than domestic guests. Firms with a knowledge and appreciation of that particular market, either gained from experience in the tourist generating country or in providing similar services in other locations, will have, at least, an initial advantage over *de novo* indigenous firms. Proprietary knowledge of the market also enables MNE hotels to differentiate their product (Caves, 1971) from that of their competitors, while catering generally for the upper end of the market. The combination of the characteristic of hotel accommodation as an experience good with effective product differentiation, makes the marketing of the 'brand image' of the hotel a crucial element in the ownership advantage of international hotel chains. At the same time, the hotel sector is not characterized by specific pieces of knowledge which might be protected by a patent. The nearest to such an intangible asset is the hotel's trade mark and its reservation system. In developed industrialized economies, with a lively domestic market for luxury hotels, a well developed local tourist industry, and where indigenous hotels may have established a brand image in other parts of the world, one would not expect to find – and, in fact, does not find – such a strong presence of foreign associated hotels. In most developing countries, where these characteristics are less likely to be present, such hotels play a much more significant role. This is clearly illustrated in Table 5.1 which shows the share of MNE-associated hotel rooms in total hotel accommodation in 75 countries. The percentage share is for all hotel and similar accommodation and if it were possible to obtain comparable figures for luxury and first class accommodation then the MNE share would be higher, particularly for developing countries.

Given the information on *what* to produce, why should MNE hotels have an advantage over domestic firms on *how* to produce it? Our research indicates that it is the ability to innovate, produce and market a range of complementary products and services which determines market share. *Inter alia*, this would suggest that diversification and experience may play an important part and, to the extent that international hotel chains are larger, more diversified and experienced than their domestic rivals (or potential rivals), they are able to enter new markets more easily.

There may be various reasons for this; first, and most important, where the MNE is already involved in the hotel business, it has built up a set of intangible assets and logistical skills which it can make available to any newly associated hotel at a much smaller transaction cost than a *de novo* entry into the hotel business (Johnson, 1970). In general, the larger and more luxurious a new hotel, particularly if it is designed to serve business traffic, the greater the advantage of the kind of capacity possessed by MNEs. Second, and allied to the first, MNEs are able to draw upon the experience of operating hotels in their home country and/or other foreign hotels, and it would seem that there is a greater similarity between hotels in different countries under the same ownership than there is between hotels in the same country under different ownership, supplying similar groups of customers (reflecting product differentiation). Third, according to their degree of multi-nationality, their sourcing of management and professional staff, foodstuffs, beverages, furnishings and fitments, linen and china, etc., are likely to be wider (which add to the advantages of size, e.g. via quantity discounts, centralized purchasing procedures, etc.), can be supplied at lower marginal costs and may be of superior quality and design. Fourth, and related to the third, their managerial and organization expertise, their ability to invest substantial sums in training hotel staff, plus their detailed instruction manuals, often enable them to have superior expertise in the overall planning and design of hotel complexes and to employ technically superior methods of production in the day-to-day operation, control and maintenance of hotels, etc. and to recruit and retain better staff by offering good promotional prospects.

As research and development are often essential elements in the maintenance of the ownership advantages of MNEs in the manufacturing sector, so investment in training may be regarded as essential to MNE hotels. It is not possible to give a quantitative estimate of investment in training by international hotel chains but certainly for the larger chains, substantial sums are involved in direct staffing and resource costs (including the opportunity cost of staff receiving training), in maintaining training facilities at each hotel, regional centres and at the flagship hotel and in preparing training literature and manuals, organizing seminars, and in the constant dissemination of information on new designs, procedures, techniques, equipment, etc. Admittedly, part of the training costs arises from the size and geographical spread of the hotel chain and from its internalization of the markets for intermediate products (including skilled labour). Additional accounting and control information is required, compared to that needed by an individual hotel enterprise, while additional problems may arise from the need to ensure that the information collected is relevant, accurate and flows to all relevant parts of the organization, while at the same time remaining confidential to the MNE. However, the benefits outweigh the costs. Fundamentally, investment in training enables the MNE to maintain the quality of its distinctive brand image and hence its market share of this experience good. The competitive image of the MNE is also enhanced by internalizing training, because it can more accurately assess employees' abilities and prospects (Buckley and Casson, 1976), while maintaining a ready pool of skilled and mobile labour for expansion.

Casson (above Ch. 2) questions this interpretation and claims that international hotels produce an undifferentiated product of a high and reliable quality which appeals to an internationally mobile clientele because the guarantee of quality associated with the brand name reduces the buyer's transactions costs in identifying suitable accommodation. In addition, by using the international reservation system of the MNE, the buyer reduces the costs and risks associated with possibly unfamiliar international communication. According to Casson, MNEs in the international hotel industry can be explained simply in terms of their ability to internalize the training of management of unskilled labour and without relying on complexities of the eclectic theory.

It is our contention that this approach ignores important elements in the structure of the hotel industry and the nature of the 'product' which is produced. As we have previously stated, hotels do not just provide a standard room but a large number of ancillary services catering for the requirements of a particular clientele and this is closely reflected in their choice of location of the hotel, pricing and marketing strategy. For example, Holiday Inns, the world's largest international hotel chain, is generally aimed at the family group and lower-level management staff market, Inter-Continental Hotels and Hilton (respectively second and third largest) are geared more to meet the needs of the business traveller, while Sheraton (fourth largest) aims for the luxury end of the market. Hotels which are closely linked to international tour operators (wholesalers), such as Club Méditerranée, Thomson Hotels, Caledonian Hotel Management, Steigenberger Hotels and Neckerman und Reisen, cater for the middle-level three-star segment of the market. Trusthouse Forte (sixth largest) covers a large part of the range from luxury (e.g. George V, Paris) to small country hotels in England. The international hotel industry can therefore be viewed as producing differentiated products in the same way as, for example, the car or cosmetics industry.

Second, the internalization theory ignores the almost obsessive secrecy of the industry, where even the most co-operative of the MNEs refuse to divulge the contents of their manuals of operating instructions because these codify the essence of their proprietary knowledge. Furthermore, most MNEs, notably Hilton International, have a marked tendency to 'lock in' key employees and to follow a policy of promoting from within the organization.[3] This can only be interpreted as aimed at discouraging defection to a rival hotel group and thereby protecting the unpatentable proprietary knowledge of the enterprise (i.e. to produce a hotel 'product' different from those of its competitors). Casson also exaggerates the importance of buyer uncertainty and the costs of international transactions. In practice the hotel reservation system accounts for on average approximately one-quarter of total guest nights and most reservations are either direct from clients or made by local businesses. One would also predict from Casson's theory that MNE 'involvement', at least in developed countries, would be predominantly in hotel reservation and referral systems backed up by regular inspection to ensure standards of quality. It is certainly not obvious that the hotel sector in developed countries suffers from any significant market failure in the supply of trained personnel which would justify hotels engaging in the high costs associated with what are often quite elaborate training programmes. The central importance of product differentiation in what is essentially an oligopolistic market therefore provides a more convincing explanation for the existence, growth and behaviour of MNEs in the hotel sector.

Country-specific Characteristics of Ownership Advantages

The eclectic theory suggests that the ownership-specific advantages may be unevenly distributed according to the countries of origin and destination; and that it is possible to use traditional trade models to identify the determinants of these. In the case of the hotel industry, we have emphasized the importance of knowledge of the requirements and tastes, particularly of business visitors, from the tourist generating countries. We would therefore expect that the countries most likely to be involved in foreign hotel operations would also be those which tend to generate the most foreign direct investment. This is confirmed by the data. However, there do appear to be other factors. In particular, we have suggested that the size and structure of the hotel industry of the home country of the MNE may be important in generating management expertise, knowledge of markets and a pool of trained labour. The contrast between the USA (with 50 per cent of foreign associated hotels), France and the United Kingdom (with 15 per cent of foreign associated hotels), is instructive. Clearly the 2 per cent share does not reflect West Germany's importance in international trade and investment (and hence business travel). The explanation would appear to be that, unlike the other three countries, the West German domestic hotel industry is not characterized by chains of hotels and it is experience in the management of domestic hotel chains, i.e. multi-plant operations, which is a necessary condition for the establishment of international hotel chains.

Firm-specific Characteristics of Ownership Advantages

We have already mentioned size and investment in training as firm-specific variables determining ownership advantages, but within these categories variations occur. Some hotels emphasize their advantages in marketing and concentrate on referral systems (e.g. Best Western) and franchising (e.g. Holiday Inns). Others regard themselves as providing a package of professional, managerial and organizational services which cover every stage of hotel operations (e.g. Hilton International, which explicitly rejects involvement solely through franchise agreements).

Airline-associated MNE chains clearly have a marketing advantage in being able to arrange advertising and reservations in conjunction with that of the parent company airline. Economies of joint supply may also be attained through using the central purchasing facilities in furnishings, food, catering equipment, etc. of the airline. Similarly, hotels associated with tour operators (wholesalers) will also presumably be able to plan for and maintain higher occupancy rates because the parent company is in a central position in channelling tourists towards its own hotel.

Location-specific Advantages

Because the value of a hotel to a customer cannot be separated from its location, the choice of country from which the needs of hotel guests should be served is not one which normally has to be made. As in the case of some primary products, the location of hotels is country specific since they have to be situated where the tourists wants to be.

The only exceptions are the hotels sited near the border of one country from which tourists may pay day-time visits to another,[4] or those in countries *en route* to the ultimate destination of travellers.

This is not to say that the locational advantages of a country are irrelevant to an MNE considering a link with a foreign hotel. First, a choice has to be made on whether to be involved at all in the hotel business in a particular country and if so, *where* in that country, *what kind* and *how big* a hotel and *what form* should the participation take. Moreover, at a given moment of time, or over a period of time, there may be managerial or organizational constraints on the number of new hotels or expansions which can be effectively handled and to this extent, involvements in alternative locations may be mutually exclusive, even if each is profitable. The question comes down to *how* profitable — which is of the same order as the choice between exports and foreign production in a different setting.

Several factors will determine the attractions of a particular country for a hotel involvement — *given* the relative ownership advantage of the foreign and indigenous firms. These are broadly similar to those facing foreign firms in other sectors of economic activity, but there are some differences. First, and most obvious, are all the factors determining the size and rate of growth of tourism, particularly business tourism to a particular country. Second is the general infrastructure for tourism. Third, is the availability and quality of hotel inputs, including local hotel staff and essential services which cannot be imported. Fourth is the policy of government towards foreign direct investment in general. Fifth is the general political, social and economic stability of the country and attitude of the local population to foreign tourists. In view of this it is hardly surprising that the geographical pattern of foreign involvement in the hotel sector shown in Table 5.2 bears a close relationship to the geographical distribution of foreign direct investment. The factors which determine the profitability of MNE involvement in the hotel sector will also broadly determine the profitability of foreign direct investment, while the volume and direction of international trade and investment will determine the flows of international business tourists and thereby determine the location of MNE hotels, since they largely cater for this section of the market. Table 5.2 shows that the variation between home countries is nevertheless quite marked, for example French involvement in Africa, Japanese and US involvement in Asia, UK involvement in Europe. If the international hotel chains simply produced a 'quality' product which consumers were unable to distinguish between hotel chains then one might predict a

Table 5.2: Distribution by Country of Origin of Transnational Corporation-associated Hotels and Rooms in Main Host Regions, 1978 (percentages)

Host regions	United States		France		United Kingdom		Other Europe		Japan		Other developed market economies		Developing countries		All countries	
								Home countries								
	H	R	H	R	H	R	H	R	H	R	H	R	H	R	H	R
North America	19.1	14.7	0.6	1.7	4.7	7.4	26.1	29.0	26.1	28.3	3.1	6.6	2.7	3.8	13.4	13.0
Europe	26.6	26.2	40.4	45.6	70.5	73.5	56.8	57.4	8.7	11.9	13.9	27.0	2.7	2.9	35.6	35.3
Middle East	8.5	8.0	6.4	6.7	2.0	1.0	—	—	—	—	6.2	9.5	8.1	4.6	6.2	6.0
Africa	5.5	5.3	30.1	26.8	11.4	8.7	5.7	5.5	—	—	12.3	11.3	8.1	6.7	10.5	8.6
Asia	13.4	19.1	—	—	0.7	0.5	—	—	47.8	48.5	1.5	1.9	37.8	50.3	9.3	14.5
Oceania	3.2	2.7	2.6	2.5	—	—	—	—	—	—	47.7	27.9	5.4	3.3	5.6	3.5
Latin America	13.2	13.8	8.3	7.2	1.3	1.0	8.0	7.2	17.4	11.3	3.1	2.1	27.0	17.6	9.9	10.1
Caribbean and W.A.I.	10.6	10.3	11.6	9.5	9.4	8.0	2.3	1.0	—	—	12.3	13.6	8.1	10.8	9.7	9.0
	100.0	100.0	100.0	100.0	100.0	100.0	100.0	100.0	100.0	100.0	100.0	100.0	100.0	100.0	100.0	100.0
Developed market economies	49.4	47.0	10.0	47.3	76.5	81.0	83.0	86.4	43.5	40.0	41.5	48.2	5.4	6.7	52.6	52.5
Developing countries	50.6	53.0	90.0	52.7	23.5	18.2	17.0	13.6	56.5	60.0	58.5	51.8	94.5	93.3	47.4	47.5

Note: H = Hotels; R = Hotel rooms.
Source: Hotel directories and field data.

distribution of hotels more akin to the geographical distribution of foreign trade and investment *as a whole*. The very marked country variations in the distribution lend further support to the hypothesis that the hotels are not homogeneous at a given quality level and that there are marked differences between the hotels operated by French, 'Anglo-Saxon' or Japanese MNEs, as well as variations in the hotels of MNEs of the same nationality.

Within the broad picture, *firm-specific* variations occur. For example, there is some reason to suppose that the airline-associated MNEs chains favour countries, and locations within countries, served by the parent company airline. Indeed the airlines' international hotel operations may be regarded, at least in the initial stage of development, as an important part of the 'development arm' of the airline, consolidating market shares on particular routes or indicating commitment to a particular country, thereby increasing the chance of being offered traffic rights on new and potentially lucrative routes. This was certainly the case in the early years of Inter-Continental Hotels (operated by Pan-Am) and Hilton International Inc. (operated by TWA) and appears to be currently so for Japan Airlines, Continental Airlines and, to a lesser extent, British Caledonian and Air France (Meridian Hotels).

Internalization Advantages

International tourism would appear to offer substantial benefits from the vertical integration of airlines, hotels and tour operators (wholesalers) and indeed all the major international airlines have tour operating interests, many have hotel interests and some of the largest European tour operators have close associations with charter airlines and operate hotel subsidiaries. However, these linkages are, with the exception of some tour operator-charter airline links,[5] generally not significant. For example, although Hilton International is wholly owned by TWA and Inter-Continental Hotels (ICH) by Pan-Am,[6] these hotel groups are in fact largely operated as separate professional and specialist hoteliers in their own right and while at first there was a close complementarity between the airline's routes and the location of hotels, this is no longer the case. Only 22 per cent of Hilton International hotels and 60 per cent of ICH are at or near destinations served by the parent company airline. Some major airlines, for example British Airways, do not operate any hotels,[7] while the other airlines[8] have disposed of some or all of their interests. The only exception we have found is

Japan Airlines which owns or manages seven hotels outside Japan and has developed marketing or referral arrangements with 48 others.

The principal form of internalization is within the hotel industry itself. Each of the 81 MNEs with operating interests in two or more countries, was requested to classify their foreign affiliated hotels according to four main forms of involvement:

(i)   those in which they had an equity interest sufficient to ensure that they had some *de facto* if not *de jure* management control;

(ii) those in which they operated some kind of leasing arrangements;

(iii) those in which the main form of association was a management contract;[9]

(iv) those in which the main form of arrangement was a franchise or some form of marketing agreement, over and above that which might normally be involved in a referral or reservation system.

This task was complicated by the fact that, in several instances, MNEs has more than one type of association with the same foreign hotel. For example, a number had a small equity stake interest in a foreign hotel while operating a management contract or a franchise; others had a majority equity interest but had a shared managerial responsibility with other MNEs. Some leasing arrangements also involved either equity capital or a marketing or managerial agreement. In such cases, we had to classify a hotel to that category which, in our opinion, best reflected the nature of the association between itself and an MNE.

Not all the enterprises approached provided all the information requested, but our coverage, which varied slightly according to the degree of detail of data asked for, was between 75 and 80 per cent of the hotel rooms of the 1,025 hotels presented in the earlier tables.

Tables 5.3 and 5.4 present the broad picture. Including hotels which at the end of 1978 were being constructed, about one-third of the foreign hotels had equity capital invested in by the MNEs with which they were connected, and two-thirds had some form of contractual arrangement with them. Of the non-equity transactions, the management contract was the most preferred form, accounting for at least two-fifths of all forms of involvement by MNEs. Management contracts may embrace the development, design and construction of a hotel as well as its day-to-day operations.

There are noticeable differences in the mode of involvement as between developed and developing countries. About 48 per cent of the

Table 5.3: Percentage of Rooms of Transnational Corporation-associated Hotels Abroad by Type and Date of Involvement, 1978

	Ownership (or part-ownership)[a]	Leasing arrangements	Management contract[b]	Franchising	Total
Developed market economies					
Before 1964	41.0	28.1	30.9		100.0
1965–1974	60.1	10.5	29.5		100.0
1975 + after	25.7	8.8	65.4		100.0
All periods	47.8	11.9	23.5	16.8	100.0
Developing countries					
Before 1964	21.8	45.0	33.2		100.0
1965–1974	22.2	22.2	56.8		100.0
1975 + after	6.7	2.7	90.6		100.0
All periods	17.6	10.3	63.1	9.0	100.0
All countries					
Before 1960	19.0	38.0	33.8	9.3	100.0
1960–1964	31.7	21.1	47.2	. . .	100.0
1965–1969	42.2	21.8	29.0	6.9	100.0
1970–1974	38.0	14.9	36.8	10.3	100.0
1975–1978	21.4	10.3	52.2	16.0	100.0
1979 + after	3.3	1.2	87.1	8.3	100.0
All periods	31.4	12.2	44.7	11.7	100.0

Notes: a. Where accompanied by some operating participation. b. Including technical assistance agreements.
Source: Hotel directories and field data in respect of 491 foreign hotels with a total number of 156,869 rooms.

Table 5.4: Percentage of Rooms of Transnational Corporation-associated Hotels Abroad by Form of Involvement of the Corporations, 1978 (regions and main countries)

	Ownership (or part-ownership)		Leasing arrangements		Management contract		Franchising		Total
North America	24.1		15.5		41.0		19.5		100.0
of which United States		16.3		20.0		44.2		19.7	
Europe	53.7		13.3		20.5		12.6		100.0
of which United Kingdom		62.0		3.0		20.3		14.8	
France		21.6		0.5		73.1		4.8	
Middle East	4.5		11.6		74.5		9.7		100.0
Africa	18.4		8.1		72.2		16.0		100.0
Asia	14.9		1.9		59.5		23.2		100.0
of which Japan		36.2		7.9		55.9		—	
Oceania	31.4		21.0		32.7		15.0		100.0
Latin America[a]	17.8		19.4		49.1		13.6		100.0
Caribbean + W.A.I.	21.1		21.9		49.1		8.0		100.0
All regions	30.5		11.9		44.2		13.4		100.0
of which developing countries		21.1		4.9		74.2		—	

Note: a. Excluding Holiday Inn hotels.
Source: Based on hotel directors and field data in respect of 619 foreign hotels with a total number of 182,925 rooms. The slight difference in the total proportions of each category between the figures in this table is due mainly to the inclusion of some Holiday Inn hotels in this table which were excluded from the other.

rooms in hotels in developed countries are in hotels which are owned or partially owned by MNEs, compared with only 18 per cent in the case of hotels in developing countries. In no less than 63 per cent of developing country hotels, the form of association is the management contract; the franchise agreement is also less prevalent in the developing world.

Partly these data reflect the age of hotels, and the fact that such a substantial proportion of the hotels now being built is in the developing countries. Table 5.3 shows that since the 1960s, the predominant forms of involvement by MNEs have moved away from equity and leasing arrangements towards mangement contract and technical service agreements. Of the 174 hotels in which MNEs have become involved since 1975, about which we have information, no less than 107 or 61.5 per cent have taken the form of management contracts. Over the period as a whole, the late 1960s and early 1970s saw a resurgence of interest in equity participation; this was mainly because the European hotel chains entering into the international network chose to do so by acquiring existing hotels rather than becoming involved in *de novo* hotels. Later, the tour operators also opted to penetrate the foreign market — in this case, for clients in search of 'sun lust' holidays — by acquiring hotels. Club Mediterranée, on the other hand, has chosen to expand mainly through the management contract route.

Details of differences in forms of involvement by home country of the MNE hotel chain are presented in Table 5.4. The American, French and Japanese and developing country chains appear to favour a non-equity route of participation; they clearly see their role, primarily, though not exclusively, as suppliers of technology and management and market expertise to foreign hotels. By contrast, the other European, including the UK chains seem to prefer at least some ownership stake — although they too are increasing their management contracts.

Received theory tends to assume that the extent of internalization (which is provided by the degree to which the transferor of resources continues to exercise control over the use of these and complementary resources owned by the transferee) and ownership stake are closely correlated with each other; a 100 per cent equity stake being necessary to ensure complete control, a zero equity stake implying no control, and anything between depicting various degrees of control — with the crucial stake being 51 per cent. Little attention has been given in the literature to alternatives to equity investment as a means of retaining control over the use of an intangible asset.

From a legal viewpoint, a *de jure* control is a function of ownership, and remains until the owner wishes to relinquish his rights, or he is forced to divest. However, it is quite clear that some equity investments in foreign hotels have the characteristics of portfolio rather than direct investment. The investment is in the assets acquired and the return, through income or capital appreciation, is assumed to be dependent on those assets being profitably utilized without any direct intervention by the owner. The purchase by the Arabs of some hotel properties in London and elsewhere are examples, but one suspects that the expectation of gain on property values has influenced the recent wave of purchases by some UK hotel companies, notably Grand Metropolitan and Trusthouse Forte in European and US hotels. Here the question is whether the purchaser is providing services to design and operate a hotel; or those of expertise in property development and/or speculation.

It is equally apparent that some MNE involvement in foreign hotels through the non-equity route has the characteristics usually associated with direct investment in the sense of providing *de facto* control. A very great deal of influence is exerted on the day-to-day operation of some hotels and on their long-term production and marketing strategy, through the management contract. The period of the management contract is normally between 10 and 20 years with the right to renew the agreements for a further period on the same terms and conditions, except if the option to renew is deleted. According to one US-based TNC we visited, its contractual terms authorized it to:

Supervise, direct and control the management and operation of the hotel and render, supervise and control the performance of all services and do or cause to be done all things reasonably necessary for the efficient and proper operation of the hotel.

In this particular case, control over the day-to-day organization and operation of each hotel was detailed and complete. It included the setting of all room and other prices for the hotel, the negotiation and execution of contracts for the operation of the hotel and the provision of technical consultants and other specialized experts for non-routine services. The structure of the remuneration of the management usually combines a basic fee irrespective of profitability of the hotel with an incentive fee plus charges for various services (e.g. technical consultants, reservations systems, sales promotion, administrative expenses, etc.).

Apart from financial questions, other decision-taking procedures are written into the contract. In most cases, the TNC will reserve the right to make such alterations, additions or improvements in or to the hotel as are customarily made in the operation of modern international hotels. Major alterations usually require the consent of the owners of the hotel but there is usually a clause in the agreement that this should not be 'unreasonably' withheld.

Most agreements also have escape clauses for the TNC. For example, agreements may be terminated if the TNC is prevented from, or materially restricted in, obtaining foreign currency or in remitting foreign and/or local currency out of the country in which the hotel is located. It may also be ended by circumstances constituting *force majeure* which has a substantial adverse effect upon the operation of the hotel. Terms of compensation are also laid down in the event of compulsory purchase.

Finally, the contracts usually stipulate an arbitration panel, a court in the home or host country under the rules of Arbitration of the International Chamber of Commerce and settled by one or more arbitrators appointed by the Chamber.

These different forms of involvement suggest that international production might be considered as a matrix in which each cell represents a combination of degrees of control and equity involvement, which ranges from high/high to low/low; but in the hotel sector, at least, with a low ownership but high control being quite a common form. Internalization in this sense applies whenever a firm of one nationality has any form of control or substantial influence over production located in another country, other than by an arm's-length or 'spot' transaction. It ranges from subcontracting right the way through to 100 per cent ownership. To determine whether and how much internalization is *de facto* practised, one therefore needs to look at the control procedures of equity-based control and the terms of the contract of contract-based control.

There are three main reasons why a firm may wish to retain control or influence over resources transferred to another firm. One is that it believes it knows better than the management of the recipient firm how these resources should best be used (i.e. it can operate on a superior production function) and that this particular form of knowledge (what Peter Gabriel (1966) refers to as organization skills) cannot be marketed, at least not on an off-the-shelf basis. The second is that the goals of the parent firm seeking to maximize worldwide profits or growth may not always be consistent with those of any particular affiliate or associate whose interests are more likely to be directed toward local profits or growth and hence the need by the parent company to integrate decision-taking in the affiliate with other parts of the enterprise. The third is the appropriability problem (Arrow, 1975) in that once 'know-how' is transferred to a second party this reduces the private return on the information created by the first party. With regard to the second reason, it is our reading of the situation in the hotel sector that, in general, control is not necessary to advance the benefits of global integration and to ensure that the best interests of the parent company are promoted.

It is worth elaborating on this latter point. Unlike many other activities of MNEs, international hotel chains cater for customers physically present at the point of production; they earn foreign currencies from foreign visitors but they do not export, or practise market allocation. Nor is there any product specialization. Although the hotels within a chain do differentiate their products there is no intra-group trade (not, at least, as far as the final product is concerned), nor is there any process specialization, although the extent to which individual hotels import equipment, and current inputs (e.g. food and furnishings) may differ. Moreover, even where they are owned by foreign capitalists, most hotels are geared towards self-contained goals and are operated as independent entities. Control is exerted primarily to ensure these goals are met rather than because of any difference in objectives between affiliate and parent companies, although such differences may occur between host governments and the companies, e.g. with respect to the employment of local personnel and sourcing of inputs. The major *possible* exceptions are in the recruitment of top management and professional staff, which may be moved around at the discretion of the MNE; and the purchase of some items of equipment and current inputs, which may be controlled by a central purchasing department (although we found little evidence of this in our study).

Given this absence of potential conflict between the objectives of the individual hotel and the MNE, *ownership* of the hotels is not required. Control over the quality of operation of the hotel can be effected through contracts reinforced by regular overt and covert inspection of the hotel or by a resident representative of the MNE (as practised, for example, by Sheraton). The appropriability problem creates separate issues. However, we would explain a preference for non-equity control in the following way. Firms will seek to minimize the costs and maximize the returns from control, while, as Mason (1980) has pointed out, the degree of control considered necessary will be positively related to the size of the appropriable economic rents inherent in the technology. The prevalence of contract control, particularly in developing countries, can be explained in the hotel industry in the following way. MNE hotels create appropriable economic rents through their superior knowledge of market inputs and in their ability to co-ordinate a large range of complementary activities to produce a superior product to that of most individual indigenous hotels. Since these ownership advantages take the form of human capital rather than superior technology embodied in physical capital (where the disclosure involved in licensing or joint ventures would effectively destroy the ownership advantages of the MNE), it may be presumed that the economic rent can be effectively protected through contracts which protect the name of the hotel chain and, in the case of managerial contracts, ensure that the operation of the hotel is vested with the MNE, without the need to engage in equity control with its associated costs and risks.

It is true that the use of contracts has its own transaction costs. For example, Williamson (1979) emphasizes the risks involved in investment in physical and human capital which is specific to a particular transaction. In the case of hotels, for example, this might take the form of resources devoted to the design, development and marketing of a particular hotel, and the specific training of staff concerning local laws, customs and language. Such investment by the MNE will only be undertaken on the assurance of a continuing relation with the hotel. The problem, as Williamson points out, is that long-term contracts are necessarily incomplete since all future eventualities cannot be foreseen and adaptions to changing market conditions will have to be made over the life of the contract (typically 10/15 years in the case of hotel management contracts). Either side may therefore seek to shift the distribution of benefits or costs arising from the change in market conditions. To a certain extent this risk can be reduced by specifying certain provisions in the contract, for example — compulsory arbitration by a third party and compensation for *force majeure*, but such safeguards cannot at the same time provide complete insurance and be sufficiently precise to leave no problems arising from different interpretations, while they may also be unenforceable.

The use of contracts may also lead to a greater diffusion of knowledge (and hence loss of competitive advantages) to the host country's hotel sector.[10] However, our understanding of the international hotel industry is that such transaction costs are not large. Opportunistic behaviour of a hotel owner will be inhibited by the knowledge that the MNE will probably react by, for example, reducing the long-term transference of 'know-how', reducing the promotion of the hotel through its reservation system, etc. Also, a large proportion of the investment in physical and human capital by the MNE will not be specific to a transaction but will have alternative uses. Regarding the diffusion of knowledge, we would expect a significant proportion of the intangible assets transferred, particularly in operating hotel chains, to reside within the organization as a whole and thus for the MNE to continue to retain an important element of its ownership advantages. This arises partly from the economies of scale associated with size and partly from the international operation of the MNE which increases the collective knowledge and experience of the group. The nature of the ownership advantages of the MNE enables the economic rent to be appropriated through contracts for the use of the hotel's name, the marketing and reservation system, and physical inputs supplied by the central purchasing unit of the chain. Also, while the collective knowledge and experience of the MNE will be codified as far as possible in operational and instruction manuals, it is inevitable that an important element will be tacit, and therefore require personal involvement and demonstration. This not only helps to protect the appropriable economic rents of the MNE, but also enables it to extract some of the rent through fees charged for supplying this personal knowledge.

Naturally, the element of contract-based control varies with the type of contract, which, in turn, one would expect to depend on the particular ownership-specific advantages of the contractor. These also may be country or firm specific. Thus, where the advantages are to do with the actual day-to-day running of a hotel (as in the case of hotels in some developing countries with little or no hotel experience), the management contract may be the favoured form of involvement; where some specific help is needed, e.g. on the provision or catering side, or housekeeping, a technical service agreement may be appropriate; where the advantage primarily lies in marketing and attracting and retaining foreign visitors, then a franchise agreement and/or reservation may be sufficient.

Ownership of a hotel can be generally viewed as more in the nature of portfolio investment where the objective is to maximize the capitalized value of a future stream from the asset required. This might be done by reading the market correctly and taking advantage of differences in capitalization ratios and exchange rate expectations; this is Aliber's explanation (Aliber, 1970, 1971) for movements in direct investment between different currency areas[11] and would seem borne out by the marked rise in net inward investment into the US hotel industry in the late 1970s.

The marked prevalence of contract-based control may also be limited to the rapid post-1960 expansion of international tourism and with it, the expansion of the international hotel chains into these new makets. Pressure for expansion may arise from a number of considerations. The market for international class hotels may be viewed in the context of oligopolistic behaviour where the leading MNEs recognize their interdependence so that when one enters a new market, for example the Middle East, others follow. The problem is that the consequent bunching of supply of hotel accommodation may lead to excess capacity and depress rates of return on investment, and non-equity forms of involvement will substantially reduce the cost of this to the MNE. Expansion may also be required to defend the unpatentable proprietary knowledge of the MNE, while the substantial investment in training will carry its own momentum for continual expansion. Expansion via direct investment would involve raising large sums of money for widely-spread projects in a relatively short period of time. Moreover, it would involve detailed knowledge of a wide variety of local conditions involving land, labour, contract and fiscal law, and the operation of local goods and factor markets involved in the construction industry. Contract-based control avoids these costs by enabling local investors, who probably have an absolute advantage in their knowledge of local conditions, to finance the hotel, leaving the MNE free to meet its own objectives through contract-based expansion and control.[12]

Country-specific Characteristics of Internalization Advantages

It can readily be seen from Table 5.4 that some of the factors determining the form of involvement of MNEs may be influenced by home and host country specific variables. For example, the lack of indigenous hotels-trained staff and the very fast rate of growth of hotel construction (with the attendant risk of excess capacity) in the Middle East, coupled with the plentiful supply of local finance capital, explains why foreign-based companies of all nationalities prefer to be involved in hotels in these countries via the management contract rather than the equity investment or franchising route. On the other hand, in India, government regulations coupled with a strong indigenous hotel sector and the need to gain and maintain an entry into the main tourist generating markets, explain why few hotels are now either owned or managed by foreign companies, although links to international chains via the franchising or reservation/referral route are still important. In the more advanced developing countries, like Mexico and South

Korea, general management contracts are gradually giving way to marketing-oriented and/or specific technical assistance agreements, as indigenous hotel skills and experience increase.

We must also bear in mind, however, that market analysis assumes that buyers have complete knowledge of the economic rents accruing from the advantages conferred by the MNE and the costs incurred by the MNE in generating these rents. In practice, this condition is unlikely to be met, particularly in developing countries. Given that risks of variations in demand, expropriation, etc., may be higher in developing than in developed countries, the MNE may prefer, and be able, to extract the full economic rent through contracts without the risks involved in ownership. Conversely, in developed countries, information flows and the expertise of investors may well be greater and hence rents may only be fully captured through ownership. Certainly Table 5.4 suggests that in Europe, MNEs own, or partly own, about half of all affiliated hotels while in most developing countries the corresponding proportion is under one-fifth and in the Middle East it is less than 5 per cent. Conversely, management contracts prevail in only 11 per cent of European affiliated hotels, compared to 66 per cent in the Middle East, 72 per cent in Africa, 68 per cent in Asia and 44 per cent in Latin America. A small sample of hotels affiliated through management contracts and covering 5 developed and 13 developing countries also indicated that the fees and payments accruing to the MNE absorbed a considerably higher proportion of the gross operating profits of the hotels in developing countries than in developed countries, despite very similar occupancy rates, lending further partial support to the hypothesis of unequal access to information and bargaining power as between MNEs and host developing countries.

From the viewpoint of home countries, Table 5.4 has shown that the form of involvement does vary, but closer inspection reveals that this reflects a different type of MNE and/or differences in countries in which the companies are involved. For example, UK and Scandinavian firms tend to own a higher proportion of their hotels than do other nationalities. In part, this reflects the higher proportion of tour operators among the MNEs involved in foreign hotels. In the case of the UK in the late 1970s, it also reflects the attractiveness of property investments in countries with weaker currencies than sterling and/or with lower interest rates than in the UK.[13] Finally, countries whose entry in the foreign hotel business is most recent (e.g. Japan) tend to involve themselves through ownership or management contract; franchising is mainly the preserve of MNEs which are well established, from countries which generate a great deal of tourist traffic and are hosted by countries with a strong indigenous hotel sector.

Firm-specific Internalization Advantages

The choice between the equity and non-equity route of involvement will, according to the eclectic theory, be influenced by the type of activity engaged in by the parent MNE. For example, hotels associated with MNEs with interests in related tourist activities are more likely to wish to have some equity participation so that they can capture the full benefits of integration of these activities. On the other hand, specialist hotel companies which regard their expertise as extending to property development and speculation may seek an ownership stake for different reasons. Others, which regard their main ownership advantage as the maketing of the end product, may be content with a franchise agreement.

Conclusions

The eclectic theory of international production provides a useful framework in explaining the reasons for, and patterns of, foreign involvement in the international hotel industry. Ownership advantages have been found to derive from the nature of foreign hotel accommodation as an 'experience good' often consumed in an unfamiliar environment, where the trademark of the MNE hotel chain guarantees a standard of service with certain characteristics demanded by the tourist (principally business tourist). International hotel chains may also operate on a superior production function to local hotels, partly because, being multinational, there is a wider learning process derived from operating in different economic environments and a wider sourcing of inputs, improving both quality and competitiveness. Fundamentally, there are significant economies of size and logistical skills which enable the knowledge and expertise developed by the organization as a whole to have many of the characteristics of a public good within the organization, that is the human and physical resources and co-ordinating ability of the MNE may be supplied to a newly associated hotel at a much lower marginal cost than that of a new entrant into the market.

An important element in maintaining the knowledge and trademark of the MNE, and thereby consolidating and improving market share, is investment in training, which we have likened to the importance of research and development to MNEs in certain areas of manufacturing.

Knowledge acquired by first servicing the home market combined with meeting the needs of foreign business tourists explain the correlation between the country distribution of foreign hotels and foreign direct investment, while the nature of the ownership advantages explain the predominance of MNE hotels in developing countries compared with developed countries. As the eclectic theory suggests, however, these general patterns are modified by country- and firm-specific characteristics. Of the latter, experience in operating domestic hotel chains would appear to be important while the former includes the particular objectives of the MNE parent company, especially where this is an airline or tour operator (wholesaler).

Location-specific advantages are not of the same order as in manufacturing because there is no choice between servicing the market by exports or by establishing an affiliate. However, given limited resources, MNE hotel chains do have to decide between alternative countries, and locations within a host country, and in this sense the decision is no different from other forms of foreign investment.

Of particular interest in analysing MNE hotels is the choice between alternative forms of involvement. Previous analysis of this in the context of the manufacturing and extractive industries has regarded ownership and control as being synonymous with an absence of equity participation employing no control over the enterprise. Our reading of the international hotel industry, however, clearly shows that the two elements should be analysed separately. In the case of hotels, ownership of a hotel often has the characteristics of portfolio investment in an asset which, given exchange rate expectations, may be regarded purely as maximizing the capitalized value of the factor income stream from the hotel. The owners of the hotel may have little knowledge of hotel operations and employ a professional management company to operate the hotel. The management company in turn will only become involved if they can protect their ownership advantages and in practice this may require a large degree of control of the assets. The hotel management company, however, may be unwilling to invest in the ownership of the hotel either because it regards itself as having little expertise in property development, or because it regards ownership as a high-risk venture, or because expansion would be reduced by the need to borrow large sums of capital. We therefore often find that it is to the mutual advantage of both parties for *de jure* control to be with the hotel owners but *de facto* control to be established through contracts. These contracts are more easily arranged because of the characteristics of the industry, in the sense that unlike manufacturing, these is no need for a policy of market sharing by the affiliates to maximize the global profits of the MNE, nor is there any production specialization, while there exist ample opportunities to appropriate the economic rent from the MNEs' activities. Again, the actual pattern of forms of involvement is modified by country-specific characteristics, both in terms of host government policy and the local supply of factor inputs (capital, skilled labour, etc.) and by firm-specific factors (e.g. where the parent company is a tour operator). Analysis of the international hotel sector therefore extends our appreciation of the possibilities for contract-based control as compared to the more traditional equity-based control of a foreign enterprise.

Space does not permit us fully to explore the policy implications, particularly for developing countries, of our analysis. Governments, however, should be aware that probably even more than in manufacturing industry, alternative forms of involvement of MNEs are possible and host governments should be aware of the costs and benefits of each in relation to the country's social and economic objectives. They should also be aware that existing laws which control foreign direct investment may be inadequate to control non-equity forms of foreign involvement and that local investors may have inadequate information and expertise when negotiating such contracts. The MNE may also introduce the sophisticated technologies associated with large hotels rather than the simpler technologies of small-scale hotels (which may be more appropriate, particularly for resort tourism) in order to reduce the appropriability problem and increase the returns to the MNE. Finally, if our analysis of the industry is correct and in particular the MNE hotels do not simply produce a 'quality' product but a differentiated one as well, then investments in training by the government will be a necessary but not sufficient condition for a successful indigenous hotel section. Cooperation with an established MNE will also be required both to impart proprietary knowledge and to enable effective marketing of the hotel.

Notes

1. These data *exclude* the 474 US Travelodges operated by Travelodge International Ltd, which is owned by Trusthouse Forte, but operated independently of them.

2. These include the location of the hotel, entertainment, leisure, shopping, conference and business facilities, the extent and quality of housekeeping and restaurant services, the decor and furnishings of public rooms and the general amenities of the hotel, e.g. gardens, provision for children, TV in bedrooms, etc.

3. Hilton International, *Management Path to Profit*, p. 19.

4. E.g. as in the case of tourists wishing to visit East Germany who might stay at West German hotels or tourists wishing to visit China who might stay at Hong Kong hotels.

5. E.g. Thomson (the largest UK tour operator organizing over three-quarters of a million inclusive tour holidays) and Britannia Airways are both part of the International Thomson Organization.

6. Acquired by Grand Metropolian Hotels in August 1981.

7. Although it does have some minor equity participations and participation with some other European airlines in the Penta Group of hotels.

8. E.g. KLM, American Airlines.

9. Including *ad hoc* technical assistance agreements. These appear only to have been concluded in the last two or three years, but from conversations with hoteliers in developing countries, they seem likely to become one of the main forms of involvement in the 1980s — mainly because they do not involve the extent or the continuation of control over decision-making implied in a management contract.

10. Indeed this is one important potential advantage of MNE involvement in the hotel sector and particularly in developing countries.

11. More particularly, deviations of such movements around what might be predicted if the countries were within the same currency area.

12. The best example of which is Holiday Inns.

13. Which *inter alia* prompted the purchase of the Howard Johnson chain of hotels by the Imperial Tobacco Co.

6 REGIONAL OFFICES IN MULTINATIONAL FIRMS

Robert E. Grosse

Introduction

Regional offices are administrative centres for business activities of multinational enterprises (MNEs) in several, usually geographically proximate, countries. During the past two decades, firms in all major industrial categories have reorganized their management structures and delegated some (usually increasing) responsibilities to such geographically dispersed administrative locations. These regional offices are used to centralize information and to make some types of decisions at the multi-country, i.e. regional, level. Then information is filtered back to the home office, where other types of decisions are made. Stratification of the decision-making process allows the firm to treat some problems at the local level, others at a more central, regional level, and finally others at the home office — thus avoiding an increasingly overwhelming direct inflow of information into the home office.

Organizationally, the typical corporate structure appears as some variant of Figure 6.1, with direct control (solid lines) or just co-ordination of information (dotted lines), assigned to various regional offices.

Thus far in the histories of most MNEs, regional offices are assigned responsibility for control of a few specific functions, such as sales and promotion, while many functions remain under the control of the home office. The rationale for these developments and an economic strategy for using regional offices can be seen through the theory of the multinational firm.

On the Theory of the Multinational Enterprise

The theory of the multinational firm has progressed a long way since Stephen Hymer wrote his analysis of the international activities of large US-based firms in 1960. Both company and industry studies have given us a better understanding of the monopolistic advantages possessed by these multinational enterprises, their abilities to internalize markets and market segments in different countries, their financial structures and strategies, and finally their significance to the countries in which they operate. We have gone from attempts to develop a special theory for MNEs to efforts to integrate them into existing theories of the firm or

107

Figure 6.1: Common MNE Organizational Structure, 1970s

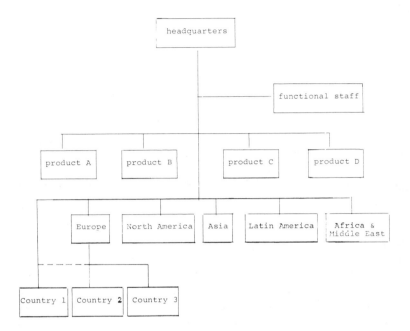

theories of industrial organization.

This chapter accepts the multinational firm as an extension of the standard firm in microeconomic theory. It diverges from pure neo-classical theory by assuming the existence of proprietary knowledge (i.e. imperfect information and/or non-standard technology) and of international movement of some production factors, especially skilled labour and capital. These assumptions allow firms the capability to internalize parts of the production and distribution process (or to sell their proprietary knowledge), not just domestically but also across national boundaries. By proceeding along these lines, it is possible to show that regional offices are an economically justifiable development in the structure of MNEs.

In the present analysis the MNE should be viewed as an organizational structure of economic activity. That is, in the economic continuum from search for raw materials and transformation of materials into production inputs and products all the way to purchase by final consumers, MNEs organize various parts of the process. The firm's participation may amount to absorption of some markets into its own operations (e.g. vertical integration) or 'market-making' by serving as a broker between buyers and sellers of products or services, or a mixture of the two. As clarified below, regional offices serve the goals of market-making and internal (to the firm) control of operations at the international level.

On Internal Markets

As Rugman has shown earlier in this volume and elsewhere,[1] internalization of markets or transactions previously external to the firm is a necessary condition for existence of a multinational firm. In fact, as Casson points out above, this condition really should be stated as part of the definition of the MNE. A multinational enterprise is a firm which, at a minimum, owns some kind of facilities/resources in at least two countries – and thus internalizes the use of those facilities or resources across national boundaries.

Still following Casson, it can be argued that from a standpoint of economic efficiency, a firm should internalize those transactions which it can carry out at a lower social opportunity cost than could the free market or any other external market. This reasoning supports the use of backward vertical integration by firms that want to reduce the riskiness of external sources of supply. Equally, it supports horizontal or forward integration across national borders by firms that need international markets to sell minimum optimum scale (i.e. least cost) quantities of production.

Regional offices in MNEs are intended to reduce the *internal* transactions costs of moving information and making decisions within one firm, as well as to internalize some functions (such as selling) in some national markets of a region. The former goal relates directly to the firm's own ability to manage information efficiently. Very often this aspect of a firm's activities is ignored in microeconomic theory[2] and even in the discussion of internalization – but internal markets and transactions costs are central to the economics of a regional office.

On Monopolistic Advantages

In addition to emphasizing the firm's expansion to internalize markets and transactions, the economic theory of multinational enterprises points out the necessity of some competitive advantage(s) in order for an MNE to compete successfully with local firms in foreign markets. A few authors have pointed to strictly financial advantages such as international diversification of assets and preferential real discount rates for firms in countries with revaluing or devaluing currencies.[3] Most of the emphasis, however, has been on firm-specific advantages resulting from proprietary technology, international sources of supply and distribution, economies of scale in production, and managerial know-how.

The main significance of this aspect of the theory of MNEs in the present context is that it underscores the inter-industry differences in competitive advantages. Economies of scale in production are vital to automobile manufacturers but generally rather unimportant to firms producing cosmetics or drugs. Possession of proprietary technology is central to competitiveness in the chemical and pharmaceutical industries, but relatively unimportant in tyre production or in making many electrical household appliances. By comparing groups of firms from various industries for their relative propensities to use regional offices, industry characteristics can be linked to office functions. Thus the economic rationale for regional offices differs across industries according to the structure of firms' internal markets.

On the Empirical Base

While the theoretical aspects of this analysis are not confined to any individual country or industry, empirical evidence is drawn primarily from companies/banks with regional offices in Miami or Coral Gables (for Latin America), London (for Europe) and Honolulu (for Asia). Primary evidence was obtained from 55 Latin American regional offices through interviews and mailed questionnaires during 1978–81. Evidence concerning European and Asian regional offices comes from 15 home office interviews and both published and unpublished findings of Heenan and Dunning, all collected during 1977–80.[4]

The companies are predominantly US-based in each sample, though a substantial number of European firms are included as well. Figure 6.2 presents some of the important characteristics of the firms.

A Conceptual Framework for Regional Office Location and Functioning

This section elaborates the 'fit' of a regional office within a global firm, according to the two primary functions of (1) regulating part of the firm's internal market and (2) providing contact with customers or suppliers external to the firm in the region. The interesting and related

Figure 6.2: Characteristics of MNEs in the Empirical Samples

Sample	Industry	SIC #	Average annual global sales per firm, 1980 ($ million)	Number of firms
Latin America	chemicals	28	4,397	12
	food processing	20	n.a.	4
	machinery	35	3,235	10
	transport equipment	30	4.306	8
	mining and petroleum	29,33	37,020	4
	banking	60,61	n.a.	36
Europe	chemicals	28	8,019	4
	food processing	20	n.a.	2
	machinery	35	5,892	10
	mining and petroleum	29,33	n.a.	3
	banking	60,61	n.a.	2
Asia	airlines		2,954	5
	food processing	20	n.a.	1
	machinery	35	10,277	4
	transport equipment	30	1,692	3
	hotels		n.a.	2

Note: In all tables, when data for only one firm in a category are available, then that information is *not* presented, to avoid reference to a specific firm.
Source: University of Miami MNE databank; Dunning and Norman (1979); University of Hawaii regional office listing (1981).

question of choosing the city of location for an office has been discussed elsewhere.

As already established, regional offices are used by multinational enterprises either to co-ordinate internally the firm's affiliates in some geographic area (e.g. Latin America, Europe or Asia) or to serve as a branch of the firm offering sales/services to unaffiliated customers in the region. From a management perspective, the former function implies some degree of control over affiliates' operations in the region, while the latter function implies responsibility for serving customers' needs, rather than the firm's internal needs. Also, the co-ordination or headquarters' function implies a new level of administration between the home office and foreign affiliates in a region, while the branch function places the regional office in a similar position to other domestic and foreign branches. (For example, the regional branch can be assigned profit centre responsibility if it carries out the sales function. The regional headquarters can oversee profitability in affiliates, but it will not carry out the sales function directly.)

The *regional headquarters* gained substantial popularity among MNEs in the 1970s for co-ordinating activities in Europe (typically from Paris, Brussels or London), Asia (especially from Hong Kong, Singapore or Honolulu), and Latin America (usually from Miami). The primary 'function' of a regional headquarters is to be a major link between the home office of an MNE and its affiliates located in some region possessing relatively homogeneous conditions (e.g. level of economic development, language, simple geographic proximity, etc.). Conceptually, at least, the regional headquarters is an inside-the firm operation, without direct responsibilities towards final customers or suppliers. Specific control and oversight functions over affiliates' operations are delegated to this arm of the home office — which benefits from proximity to the affiliates and avoidance of home-office distractions on issues unrelated to the region. This kind of office will necessarily maintain a difficult balance of functions among (1) those pulled away to the (regional) office and (2) other functions — such as major capital budgeting and diversification of products — retained at the corporating headquarters.

The *regional branch office* traditionally has been used by firms as an outlet for production from other affiliates in markets judged too small for local production. That is, the typical regional branch office has responsibility for one or a few major functions, especially sales, in a group of countries where the firm has no producing affiliates. Manufacturing firms also may assign the warehousing and distribution function to a regional branch office, which may serve both customers and affiliates as a parts depot. Multinational banks operating in the United States may use the regional branch office to carry out international business activities in cities outside of the home state — thus attaining inter-state branching, though only for international business.[5] The regional *bank* office (i.e. Edge Act Corporation) may in fact carry out most of its business with *domestic* firms, whose borrowing or deposits relate to these firms' international transactions. In general, the regional branch office deals directly with customers/suppliers and acts as the MNEs main link to these outside groups.

Figure 6.3 demonstrates that, at present, most Latin American regional offices in Dade County, Florida, act as functional branches for the firm, not as regional headquarters. (This general finding holds for Asian offices as well, but not as clearly for European offices, which serve more frequently as headquarters.)[6] As far as major responsibilities are concerned, sales to customers are the main function for all types of office except the manufacturing firm's regional headquarters, which generally balances this duty with control and co-ordination of affiliates in the region.

Figure 6.3: Distribution of Latin American Regional Offices, Headquarters vs. Branch

Type/role of office	Manufacturing firms	Business service firms
regional headquarters (number)	11	3
(MNE co-ordination ÷ outside sales) as the role of the office	50/50	25/75
functional branch (number)	32	9
(MNE co-ordination ÷ outside sales) as the role of the office	10/90	10/90

Source: Interviews at 55 regional offices during 1978–81.

This situation is shifting to some extent, as firms assign additional regional co-ordination responsibility to these offices.[7]

The rationales behind regional headquarters and regional branch offices differ substantially in concept (though they appear to converge in their solutions for optimal location).

Regional Branch Office, Location and Functions

Consider first the use of a regional branch office as seen from classical location theory. Alfred Weber reasoned that, 'for any region or area, the normal and fundamental situation . . . is an even distribution of production over the whole area, and international division of labor is a deviation therefrom' (if natural resources and population initially are dispersed evenly in the area).[8] This statement implies that free competition would lead to production and distribution locally in each area's market. Given the existence of trade barriers, scale economies in production, and uneven distribution of population and natural resources, we see a 'bunching' of production in low-cost locations, and of distribution in locations with favourable access to the market(s). In this context, a regional branch office would only be justified if it were located at a transportation hub for the relevant region, and if the costs of centralized distribution were lower than the cost of distributing from multiple locations within the region.

In addition to the transportation costs which partially determine distribution points, there are also 'agglomeration economies' that may reduce the cost of a centralized distribution (or production) point. These include:

(a) large-scale economies within a firm, consequent upon the enlargement of the firm's scale of production (or operation) at one point;

(b) localization economies for all firms in a single industry at a single location, consequent upon the enlargement of the total output of that industry at that location;

(c) urbanization economies for all firms in all industries at a single location, consequent upon the enlargement of the total economic size (population, income, output or wealth) of that location, for all industries taken together.[9]

This theory in its basic form stops after considering the cost problems involved in location, though recent theorists have recognized that the demand side (i.e. proximity and visibility to customers) is a significant factor as well.[10]

Specifically, they recognize that the physical presence of a firm often raises aggregate demand for a product which otherwise would be sold through agents or distributors. Customers often prefer to deal directly with the supplier, rather than to operate through intermediaries. There is some reason to believe, then, that by 'internalizing' this part of the sales and distribution functions (as compared to selling through agents), the MNE may generate an increase in demand for its product or service.[11] In the Latin American case, at least, several of the regional branch offices were established after unaffiliated agents' sales grew to sizeable volumes in the region. Thus, the regional market initially was fully external, until the MNE brought regional marketing responsibility into the regional branch as a reaction to growing demand.

The regional branch office could serve as well in the form of a central purchasing site, for obtaining products or raw materials from suppliers in the region. In this manner the office would seek to gain access to desirable sources of products/materials that the firm may wish to purchase from various suppliers in the region. The function in this case is purchasing, but it again accomplishes the liaison task between the firm's home office and unrelated firms in a region.

Finally, the regional branch office may serve as a central service location for customers. The MNE can store replacement parts and extra supplies of machines, chemicals, etc., as well as maintaining a technical staff to be dispatched to assist customers in need of repairs. Both the spare parts depot and the centralized service facilities are organizational forms used domestically, and which can be used at the international level also.

From the theory regarding location of economic activity and the concept of the regional office, it is expected that a *regional branch office* may provide a net benefit to the multinational enterprise by:

(1) reducing travel time of executives/salesmen/technicians, who frequently visit customers/suppliers in the region;
(2) placing the personnel in a location with excellent communications, both to the home office and to the suppliers/customers;
(3) creating a focal point, divorced from the home office, for managing and promoting the firm's business in the region (agglomeration economy (a));
(4) gaining access to a pool of talented potential managers and staff, who are familiar with the language and culture of the region (agglomeration economy (b)); and
(5) gaining access to new business, resulting from the concentration of many firms' regional offices at one location[12] (agglomeration economy (c)).

Thus, the functions of a regional branch office are mainly sales and distribution of products or services in countries of that region, and its location is primarily a function of product and passenger transportation and communication with the region.

Regional Headquarters, Location and Functions

Next, consider the case of a regional headquarters. Classical location theory ignores this problem completely, though one can easily extrapolate the cost-minimizing strategy to this type of office. Here, the main question is whether or not the new layer of management, between home office and affiliates, can justify the expense of its operation. If the regional headquarters can either reduce global costs to the firm or raise revenues by providing faster or otherwise better help to affiliates, then its cost may be outweighed by these other gains.

Evaluation of the regional headquarters' success will be far more difficult than a similar evaluation for a branch office, because all of the headquarters' activities are internal to the firm. This means that either the activities are priced artificially (with 'transfer prices') or that they are unpriced (i.e. externalities). For this reason, conclusions about the cost-effectiveness of a regional headquarters necessarily will be qualitative, though some numerical information can be included.

As discussed below, the main functions of a regional headquarters typically relate to overseeing the marketing activities of affiliates in the region. That is, they operate in the same general areas as do branch offices, but they are one step removed from actual customers or suppliers. (In the European case, much more often the office also has responsibility for manufacturing affiliates in the region.) The regional headquarters evaluates performance by affiliates and serves as a conduit for information in both directions between home office and affiliates.

Looking, then, at the *regional headquarters*, it is expected that the whole MNE will receive a net benefit from:

(1) reducing travel time of executives who frequently visit affiliates to monitor their operations and potentially to develop regional strategies;

(2) placing the managers of the regional headquarters in a location with excellent communications, both to the home office and to affiliates;

(3) centralizing information at a manageable (i.e. regional) level, rather than overwhelming the home office with it, and rather than allowing excessive autonomy to each affiliate by not centralizing information at all (agglomeration economy (a));

(4) gaining access to a pool of talented potential managers and staff, who are familiar with the language and culture of the region (agglomeration economy (b)).

In summary, the functions of a regional headquarters are mainly co-ordination and oversight of affiliates in a region, and its location is primarily a function of passenger transportation and communication with the region.

Overall, classical location theory would lead the firm to locate functions or operations in places where the total cost to the whole firm is minimized, so that the firm can minimize the delivered cost of its product/service to customers. The theory concludes that regional offices would only be justified if they offer the firm a lower-cost alternative to locating the same functions at the existing home office or at a production facility, or in the specific local market to be served. As noted before, recent location analysts have added that the *net benefit* to the MNE is what should be measured; so regional offices should be evaluated for both their reductions in cost to the total enterprise *and* their additions to revenues of the total enterprise.

The Economics of a Regional Office

As Foreign Direct Investment

A simple way to evaluate the economic worth of a regional office is to isolate that unit from the multinational firm and measure the costs and benefits associated with its operation. As already shown, from the firm's standpoint, the office is justifiable if its addition to the full enterprise's revenue and its reduction of the full enterprise's costs outweigh its cost of operation. From a social standpoint this must also be true, plus it must be less costly (in social opportunity cost) to use resources in this employment, rather than to have a separate firm carry out the same functions.

This says that in terms of capital budgeting for the firm, if:

$$\sum_{i=1}^{n} \sum_{t=1}^{m} \frac{Bit}{(1 + k_i)^t} + \sum_{t=1}^{m} \frac{Bn + 1, t}{(1 + k)^t} > \sum_{i=1}^{n} \sum_{t=1}^{m} \frac{Bit^*}{(1 + k_i)^t}$$

where

Bit   = net-of-tax earnings from affiliate i in period t
ki   = the cost of capital for the ith affiliate
Bn + 1   = the regional office's net after-tax earnings
k   = the MNE's global weighted average cost of capital
Bit*   = Bit without existence of the regional office,

then the regional office is justified.

Using this kind of model, a potential regional office can be evaluated similarly to any other foreign or domestic investment project. If the office location happens to be within the home country, then it is strictly incorrect to view it as a foreign direct investment. However, typically domestic and foreign sites are considered for office location, and thus the model is capable of measuring both types. Note that the appropriate cost of capital, k, should be the firm's global weighted averaged cost of capital, since the regional office can be financed from any source,[13] and profits can be shown anywhere (through appropriate transfer pricing). This is different from the usual foreign investment evaluation, where a host-country cost of capital is appropriate for evaluating a project.[14]

Unfortunately, this presentation does not focus on the key costs and revenues involved in the actual measurement. To achieve that focus, a survey of Latin American regional offices was carried out in 1980. Its results show that for the median non-bank office of seventeen employees, annual costs associated with the office were $1.2 million distributed among:

| | Costs | |
	with regional office	before regional office
1. salaries and wages	40%	same
2. transportation to the region and the home office	25%	much higher
3. office rental and utilities	20%	~ 0
4. telephone, telex and correspondence	10%	a little lower
5. other expenses	5%	a little lower
total	100%	?

Source: mailed survey of 15 Latin American regional offices in 1980.

Now the problem is to compare these costs to analogous expenses when the firm operated without the regional office. Though full empirical evidence for the comparison is not available here, the principle is clear, and firms can readily perform the calculations. Notice that the costs of salaries and wages, at least initially, are not much higher than what the MNE has been paying, since over 80 per cent of the managers are brought to the regional office from elsewhere in the firm.[15]

On the revenue side, estimates of new business generated by the regional offices varied widely, and it is not clear how much of that same business would have been generated anyhow, with the same managers travelling from the home office or from existing subsidiaries. So rather than attempt a counter-factual, 'what if?' scenario, let us simply investigate the cost side — and argue that whatever the addition to the MNE's total costs from use of a regional office, this needs to be at least offset by incremental revenues generated by the office.

Clearly, in the case of the pure regional headquarters, operating entirely internally within the MNE, no new revenues wiill be generated directly by the office. So, either costs will need to be reduced overall or some calculation of indirect generation of new revenues wiill be needed.

Given the extremely low cost of maintaining a regional office, relative to other costs incurred globally by the MNE, it is likely that even a substantial percentage reduction in these costs will be unimportant overall. It remains, then, to analyse precisely what improvements in the firm's internal markets are created by regional office operations.

In Terms of Internal Transactions Costs

Probably the single most important function of a regional office is

Figure 6.4: Main Responsibilities/Goals of Regional Offices (excluding banks)

- sell the firm's products/services to customers (including unaffiliated distributors/agents) in the region
- co-ordinate the sales activities of affiliates in the region
- develop an overall regional strategy for the firm
- pass requests for products/services *within* the MNE
- collect and report financial information from regional operations to the home office
- visit affiliates to 'keep an eye on' their activities
- disseminate internal information about new products and services that are available within the firm
- provide technical (e.g. scientific or legal) service assistance, either directly or through requests to the home office
- train managers in the company to deal with regional business, thus preparing them for assignments in the region
- take full responsibility for operations of affiliates in the region

Sources: 10 regional office interviews in 1981; Dunning and Norman (1979); Heenan (1977, 1979).

communication. That is, gathering of information from customers, suppliers and affiliates in a region and communicating it to the firm's highest-level decision-makers, and vice versa. These decision-makers may include the regional office manager among them; the idea is that a better understanding of regional business conditions can be obtained through the regional office, and so home-office decision-making can be done by a reasonably manageable number of executives using already-screened information.

When questioned about the key kinds of information and activities for which they are responsible, Latin American regional office managers responded as shown in Figure 6.4. If these, then, include the central parts of the MNEs' internal market in which regional offices play a role, it should be possible to measure the improvements in efficiency that result. (Note that this discussion relates *only* to the internal transactions of the firm, not to external relations with customers or suppliers.)

In the present study it was not possible to obtain profitability data for regional operations, so no numerical conclusions of that type are available. In any firm, however, the calculation of improvements in each function assigned to the regional office (comparing pre-regional office and post-regional office data) should be feasible.

In terms of one readily-visible and measurable function — visits to affiliates in the region — it is possible to draw up a basic cost calculation. Rather than estimating the cost savings in dollar terms, the number of hours of executive time is used. The approximate saving for an average MNE with headquarters in New York and 17 managers and staff in the Latin American division would be as follows. Assume that five of the regional office employees spend 30 per cent of their time travelling to affiliates in the region. The same business trips would require a 2½ hour flight from New York to Miami, plus layover before the Latin American flight(s), plus return flights, plus the extra time spent getting to and from the airport in New York. These extra hours are very fatiguing, from traffic to the airport to extra 'jet lag' in each trip. A conservative estimate of extra time required from New York would be 1½ work days (12 hours) per trip. At an average of twenty trips per year, this totals 1,200 extra hours for the five regional office employees. (Of course, it is necessary to subtract from this savings any additional time needed for communication between the home office and the regional office, which previously were located together.)

Time spent in travel to the region is only one of the half-dozen major costs to be considered in evaluating the regional office's effectiveness in the MNE's internal market. (Others include, for example, the costs of: telecommunications, support services, maintaining expatriate staff; and the 'cost' of political riskiness.) Specific, higher costs to be expected when creating a regional office (as compared with previous costs when regional executives were in the home office or just in local affiliates) include: (1) wages/salaries to any *new* staff/executives hired; (2) reduced access to internal resources such as the firm's lawyers, scientists and other managers; and (3) costs of travelling to and communicating with home office personnel.

This same kind of calculation of transportation costs can be used to evaluate the regional branch offices. They then have the added benefit of increasing regional sales revenues (in most cases).

Latin American, European and Asian Regional Offices

The Latin America Case

Two features of regional offices for Latin America strike the observer. First, they are almost all located outside of the region, in the United States.[16] While a handful of regional branches and headquarters exist in

Caracas and Mexico City, over 100 are located in Miami, several dozen in Houston and some as well in Atlanta. Second, the number and responsibilities of offices vary widely by industry. Every US-based multinational bank in the top 16 has a regional office in Miami, as do half of the top 15 chemical companies; no automobile manufacturers have offices and only one mainframe aircraft manufacturer has one. Figure 6.5 gives some idea of the relative concentrations of US-based firms using Latin American regional offices in 11 industries.

Multinational banks have established regional offices (i.e. Edge Act Corporations) to pursue new international business through major 'gateway' cities in the US, which allow rapid transportation to/for foreign customers. Thus Miami, New York, San Francisco and Houston have attracted dozens of these offices. At the same time, under US banking law, Edge Act Corporations may serve the international needs of *domestic* clients — so they are widely used for that purpose as well. Since almost no banks have many affiliates in Latin American or Asia, and only a few banks have European branches/subsidiaries, their regional offices are used almost exclusively as *branches* dealing with outside clients. The Edge Act Corporation may add *domestic* functions if US banking laws change to permit inter-state banking, as appears reasonably likely today.[17]

Among manufacturing industries, the assignment of responsibilities to each office, between headquarters and branch activities, appears to follow the pattern of technology intensity. That is, the more R and D-oriented the firm, the more likely it will use the office as a regional headquarters; and the less technology-intensive the firm, the more likely it will operate a regional branch. Firms using regional headquarters averaged 2.78 per cent in their R and D expenditures, while firms using regional branches averaged only 1.93 per cent of sales in R and D spending. It is possible to argue that this result should be expected, since high-technology firms may try to integrate their global (or regional) production and avoid producing the same products in each country; more standardized products are often produced in each national market. Thus, technology-intensive firms may benefit more than the others from the use of a regional headquarters. While this argument may be appropriate for explaining global patterns of MNE production, it receives only insignificant support in Latin America, where the firms do not trans-ship much output within the region. (A t-test for no difference in mean technology intensity between firms using regional branches and regional headquarters, however, yielded only $t = 1.54$ with $t_{critical\ .05,29} = 2.045$; $H_0 : u_1 = u_2$.)

Figure 6.5: Industrial Diversity of Latin American Regional Offices

Industry (SIC #)	# of firms with a regional office of the top 10 firms in the industry, US	4-firm concentra-tration ratio, US (based on sales)	R & D expenditure as a percentage of sales (%)	Main function of the office
banking (605)	10/10	.29	n.a.	fin, mgt.
chemicals (281, 2, 7)	4/10	.45	2.4	mgt.
drugs (283)	2/10	.32	4.9	mgt.
electrical appliances (363)	2/10	.80	1.8	mktg.
engines and farm equipment (351, 2)	6/10	.80	1.9	mktg.
food processing (203, 4, 7, 9)	4/10	.29	0.6	mgt., mktg.
industrial equipment (353)	6/10	.31	1.6	mktg.
metals (33)	3/10	.61	0.9	mgt., mktg.
telecommunications (366)	2/10	.98	1.2	mgt., mktg.
oil (291)	2/10	.60	6.6	mgt.
tires (301)	4/10	.81	1.8	mktg.

Sources: Univ. of Miama MNE databank; *Business Week*, 14 March, 1981; 6 July 1981.

Another problem with the integrated concept for explaining regional office usage is that it leads to the conclusion that producing affiliates need to be co-ordinated — but this does not necessarily imply co-ordination from a regional office. Many technology-intensive firms that produce computers, other electronics products, and even chemicals and pharmaceuticals do not use regional offices for Latin America at all. None the less, among the offices which do exist, chemicals-related industries (i.e. petroleum, chemicals and drugs) account for three-quarters of the regional headquarters.

Perhaps a better rationale for the observed pattern of headquarters and branches across the sample of firms is simply that firms with more assets at stake in Latin America will be more prone to use a regional office to oversee, support and protect those assets. This hypothesis can be tested by comparing the average number of manufacturing facilities in the region for headquarters v. branches. A simple t-test comparing the mean number of manufacturing affiliates per head-quarters with the mean number per branch shows $t = 4.22$, and $t_{critical\ 24,.025} = 2.060$. (The variances of each subsample were compared to ensure equal distributions.) Thus the null hypothesis, $\mu_1 = \mu_2$, is rejected, and it appears that headquarters are used significantly more often when the firm has many manufacturing affiliates in Latin America. This result leads us to believe that, as more firms develop manufacturing affiliates in the region, more regional headquarters will be established. (In the European case, this appears to be exactly what is happening.)

The difference could also be a historical development, i.e. as firms grow in size and experience within a region, they may evolve into structures which include the regional headquarters. The longer an MNE operates in Latin America, then the more likely it will use a head-quarters to control its business there. Using the date of establishment of the first Latin American affiliate, and a Mann-Whitney U-test to compare dates for firms using headquarters v. firms using branches, $U = 33$. This cimpares with $U_{critical\ .01} = 49$. (These results imply a 99 per cent confidence level that firms using headquarters establish affiliates in Latin America earlier than the others.) Once again, a significant difference exists — regional headquarters are used more widely by firms with greater experience in the region.

Other hypotheses that could explain a firm's propensity to use a regional headquarters rather than a regional branch include:

(1) the degree of decentralization of the firm [evidence unavailable]

(2) the degree of turmoil in the home office (i.e., the more stable the organization, the more likely that decision-making power could be assigned to an executive working away from the home office) [evidence unavailable]

(3) the firm's dependence on Latin American sales relative to global sales (All firms derive less than 10 per cent of global sales from Latin America. No test was performed.).

A final aspect of organizational structure that may help to explain the preponderance of regional headquarters in a few industries is the firm's orientation towards functional, regional or product divisions at the top levels of management. First, managers were questioned about the issues presented in Figure 6.4, which attempts to clarify the balance of authority within firms on specific decisisons. Many firms manage different decisions in different chains of command in the management hierarchy; for example, it was discovered that a clear majority of chemicals and related products firms use a 'dual reporting scheme'. Top management divides responsibility for a set of regions (e.g. US, Europe, Latin America, Far East) worldwide, such that each subsidiary's general manager reports to a regional general manager, who reports to an international general manager at the home office. Product managers in a subsidiary report to their general manager and to product managers at the regional headquarters; those managers in turn report to a regional general manager and a home office product manager. Thus two lines of authority exist, with priorities following different routes for different decisions.

The dual reporting scheme allows for close communication among managers in each product group — a very desirable plan since new products and applications arise frequently in these high-technology firms. At this point no conclusions can be drawn as to the net benefit of using a dual reporting scheme; in fact, such a scheme may be the result of firms' strategies of production location.

Next, consider the specific functions which are assigned to regional offices, regardless of branch of headquarters designation. Figure 6.6. presents results of a survey of 25 of the regional office managers.

It should be clear from these results that the *marketing* function, defined broadly to include sales, communications, exports and overall strategy, is the main responsibility of the offices. In this combined sample of regional branches and headquarters, management responsibility for affiliates in the region is divided between home and regional offices. Comparison with European offices appears below.

Figure 6.6: Decisions which are the Primary Responsibility of Managers in Each Location (responses by Latin American regional office managers)

Decision variable	Location	Primarily Miami or Coral Gables	Regional/ home office	Primary home office	Primarily subsidiary	Not relevant
1.	choosing support staff	93*	—	4	4	—
2.	communicating with Latin American affiliates	88	—	8	4	—
3.	setting marketing strategy for Latin America	78	—	8	15	8
4.	selling in Latin America	72	—	—	20	8
5.	exporting to Latin America	48	12	8	—	8
6.	managing Latin American subsidiaries	44	—	33	7	15
7.	choosing managers for Latin American responsibility	43	14	43	—	—
8.	accounting for Latin American operations	43	—	47	4	7
9.	providing financial services for Latin American affiliates	37	11	37	11	4
10.	transporting products to Latin America	36	4	21	11	29
11.	major capital budgeting	32	14	46	—	7
12.	supplying legal services to affiliates	25	11	58	4	4
13.	advertising to Latin America	21	14	32	11	21
14.	inventory levels in Latin American affiliates	19	11	15	15	41
15.	insuring shipments to Latin America	18	7	50	4	21
16.	supplying funds	18	14	61	4	4
17.	supplying scientific and technical services	15	4	56	—	26
18.	choice and supply of raw materials	14	7	7	21	50
19.	importing into the US	7	4	11	—	79

* Percentage of firms in the interview sample which place primary authority for the decision in each location.
Source: Grosse (1981a) p. 53.

Figure 6.7: Regional Headquarters of Multinational Enterprises in Europe, 1976

European location	Parent country other	United States	Japan	Sweden	United Kingdom	Canada	UK/ Holland	Germany	France	Italy	Belgium	Other	Total
1 UK	London	72	11	–	–	2	–	–	–	–	–	–	85
	Other	35	1	–	–	2	–	–	–	–	–	1a	39
2 Belgium	Brussels	70	3	–	–	1	1	–	–	–	–	–	75
	Other	7	–	–	–	–	–	–	–	–	–	–	7
3 Denmark	Copenhagen	16	1	–	–	–	–	–	–	–	–	–	17
4 France	Paris	43	–	–	–	–	–	–	–	–	–	–	43
	Other	10	–	–	1	–	–	–	–	–	–	–	11
5 Germany	Dusseldorf	20	26	3	1	1	–	–	2	–	1	–	54
	Frankfurt	29	–	3	1	1	2	–	1	3	1	–	40
6 Italy	Rome	14	–	–	–	1	1	–	–	–	–	–	15
	Milan	23	2	5	3	1	1	–	–	1	–	–	35
7 Netherlands	Amsterdam	14	3	1	1	–	–	–	–	–	–	–	20
	Other	16	1	1	1	–	–	–	–	–	–	–	19
8 Spain	Madrid	17	2	7	2	–	–	1	–	–	–	–	29
	Barcelona	4	–	1	1	–	1	2	–	–	–	–	9
9 Sweden	Stockholm	8	–	–	1	1	1	3	1	–	–	–	14
10 Switzerland	Geneva	37	–	1	–	1	–	–	–	–	–	1b	40
	Other French	13	–	–	2	–	–	–	–	–	–	–	15
	Zurich	23	1	–	–	1	–	–	–	–	–	–	25
	Other German	22	1	–	–	1	–	–	–	–	–	–	24
Total		493	52	22	13	12	6	6	4	4	2	2	616

Notes: a. South Africa. b. Australia.
Source: Dunning and Norman (1979) p. 75.

Figure 6.8: Major Products of Respondent Firms, European Headquarters

Product area	Number of firms	Average annual sales ($ millions)	R & D as a % of annual sales
computer products	4	9,856	5.17
chemicals	4	8,019	3.58
machinery	3	4,150	2.23
electronics	3	1,999	3.93
food products	3	n.a.	n.a.
oil	3	70,747	0.32

Source: adapted from Dunning and Norman (1979) pp. 80, 96.

The European Case

Data available on European regional offices relate only to headquarters operations, so no comparisons can be made between these and branch offices. This is especially unfortunate, because it would be valuable to compare the MNEs structures in Europe with those in Latin America (and Asia). The (currently untestable) hypothesis is that European offices, located in a market (i.e. the European Economic Community) as large and developed as the United States, would function very differently from LDC offices in the smaller markets of Asia and Latin America. Given only information about European regional headquarters, it appears that they function quite similarly to the Latin American headquarters.

Figure 6.7 lists the number and locations of European regional headquarters as found in a Business International Corporation survey in 1977.

United States-based MNEs constitute about 80 per cent of the total, and most of the European headquarters are within the Common Market, with the exception of 95 offices in Switzerland. The reasons for such a wide dispersion of office locations within Europe are explored anecdotally in Dunning and Norman (1979).

Dunning and Norman found, in their survey responses from 29 firms, the group of industries represented in Figure 6.8.

Unfortunately, the very small size of the sample, relative to the 616 total offices in the region, does not allow any possibility to analyse the distribution of industries in detail. Broadly speaking, these industries appear to be the same as those in the Latin American sample.

As far as specific responsibilities of the offices are concerned, Dunning and Norman found that marketing *and* production were central functions, as shown in Figure 6.9. Responsibility for acquiring and generating financial data about affiliates' operations for use by the

Figure 6.9: Functional Responsibilities of European Headquarters

Functions	Number of firms ranking the function at:						Average rating	
	5	4	3	2	1	0	mean	std. deviation
	(5 = most important)							
1 choice of markets & market development	16	2	3	0	0	2	4.22	1.51
2 product & production mgt (choice of sites, processes & products)	11	3	2	4	1	2	3.57	1.73
3 sourcing of materials, quality control, etc.	2	5	4	5	2	5	2.35	1.67
4 industrial relations and wages policy	3	2	3	7	2	6	2.09	1.70
5 dealing with governments	2	4	2	9	1	5	2.22	1.60
6 acquiring & generating financial information								
(a) for home office use	9	4	6	4	0	0	3.78	1.67
(b) for local affiliates	7	2	4	4	0	6	2.74	1.98
7 acquiring & generating other business service info								
(a) for home office use	5	5	6	2	3	2	3.04	1.61
(b) for local affiliates	2	4	5	4	3	5	2.26	1.66
8 identifying investment & licensing opp'ties	6	4	3	5	0	5	2.83	1.87

Source: Adapted from Dunning and Norman (1979) pp. 83, 97.

home office also ranks high among the priorities of these offices. This issue was not raised directly in the Latin America survey, except within the general category of 'communication' between home office and affiliates in the region. The main difference between European and Latin American office responsibilities appears to be the emphasis on 'product and production management'. European (headquarters) offices ranked this third highest among the activities discussed, while Latin American (headquarters *and* branch) offices ranked a variety of product/production variables between sixth and eighteenth of 19 total decision variables. Even this apparent divergence may be superficial, if only Latin American headquarters were compared to the European offices, all of which are headquarters.

Figure 6.10: Characteristics of Asian Regional Offices in Honolulu

Industry	Number of firms	Global annual sales, (in millions) av.	Average # of employees/ office	Main function
aircraft manufacturing	3	1,692	3	sales & service to customers
airlines	4	2,954	2	sales to customers
engineering/ management services	2	n.a.	n.a.	services to customers
food processing	1	n.a.	n.a.	sales & service to customers
hotels	2	n.a.	n.a.	supervise hotels
office machines, computers	3	10,277	30	sales & service to customers
other machinery	2	n.a.	n.a.	sales & service to customers

Source: Amended from 'Asia/Pacific Regional Offices in Hawaii' (November 1981) xerox.

The Asian Case

Far less evidence is available concerning the regional offices for Asia. Because they are located in a variety of cities, including Honolulu, Singapore, Hong Kong and Tokyo, it is difficult to generalize very much without information from a group of the cities. At present, we only have information related directly to the offices in Honolulu, plus anecdotal evidence from Latin American and European managers concerning their Asian offices.

The Honolulu offices primarily serve as regional *branches* for the MNEs' sales in all or part of Asia. Figure 6.10 presents some characteristics of the firms using such offices.

The small amount of information available here appears to show that Asian offices in the sample are quite similar to the Latin American branch offices. That is, they provide direct sales to clients in the region, and they offer after-sales service to these clients. Only two or three of the offices have management responsibility for affiliates in the region. Similar findings come from interviews of managers elsewhere in MNEs, commenting on their firms' Asian offices. It remains to be seen whether the relatively small number of Asian regional headquarters serve the same functions as headquarters' offices for Europe and Latin America.

Conclusions

Regional offices would be a puzzling phenomenon, if viewed from the standpoint of neoclassical economics or traditional industrial organization. When perceived as a part of the internal market of a multinational enterprise, they appear as an almost obvious aspect of the global expansion of these firms.

The main functions of regional offices currently are (1) to oversee especially the marketing function of affiliates and to carry out that function in countries where the firm has no affiliates; (2) to serve as a conduit of information from customers/suppliers in the region to the home office; and (3) to co-ordinate the flows of information and products within the MNE, between the home office and regional affiliates.

According to location theory, the functions of a regional headquarters office should be those which can reduce costs to the total MNE, or which can raise revenues to the total MNE, relative to the same functions being carried out in the home office or in the affiliates. The regional branch office, on the other hand, interacts directly with customers/suppliers, and thus may justify its existence through this additional function.

Managerially, these offices can be justified if they improve the functioning of the firm's internal market for information flows between the region and the home office (or if they increase revenue to the MNE by offering direct sales to customers). The costs and benefits of the offices can be calculated in terms of salaries and wages, rentals, transportation, communication, etc., but a key measure that remains is the effectiveness of intra-firm communication. That is, improvement in decision-making on regional issues is ultimately a major aspect of the office's justification. Measurement of that improvement will probably prove elusive, since internal markets of this type are complex and difficult to quantify. Even so, the regional offices often appear justified on the previously-meaured cost grounds alone.

The regional office is a very 'footloose' affiliate itself, requiring only a location with good transportation and communication between the region and the home office. Similarly, the regional office may be transitional between a time of very centralized control from the MNE's home office to a later time of substantial decentralization of control to affiliates in individual countries. Certainly, it appears that national governments would prefer to see more decision-making autonomy of MNE affiliates in their jurisdictions. So, regional offices, either head-quarters or branches, may decline in use as transportation and communication costs fall, as MNEs grow in each national market, and as governments attempt to limit MNE's transnational powers.

For the moment, however, it appears that regional offices are increasing in numbers and in the functions that they perform. The growth of an MNE's business activities in a region such as Europe, Latin America or Asia, very frequently leads to the use of a regional co-ordinating office. No trend has developed to lead away from this organizational structure — and indeed there are hundreds of MNEs which have not yet utilized regional offices. All evidence uncovered in this study leads to the conclusion that regional office use will continue to grow through the 1980s.

Notes

* The author thanks Hossein Kazemi for research assistance on this project.
    1. See Alan Rugman, *Inside the Multinationals: The Economics of Internal Markets* (Croom Helm, London, 1981).
    2. However, it is not always ignored — as shown by the awarding of the 1980 Nobel Prize in economies to Herbert Simon, who has been investigating the internal efficiency of the firm for many years.
    3. On diversification see Rugman, *International Diversification and the MNE* (Lexington Books, New York, 1979); and Jacquillat and Solnik, 'Multinationals are Poor Tools for Diverisifcation', *Journal of Portfolio Management* (Winter 1978). On preferential discount rates, see Robert Aliber, 'A Theory of Direct Foreign Investment', in Kindleberger (ed.), *The International Corporation* (MIT Press, Cambridge, Mass., 1970).
    4. See David Heenan (1977) and Heenan and Perlmutter (1979) for a view of the implications of regional headquarters to firms and to the cities of location, especially Honolulu. See also Dunning and Norman (1979) for a detailed examination of the London regional offices.
    5. This issue of inter-state branching has been the subject of intense debate during the last few years. See, for example, Foorman (1980) or Cobb (1980). Edge Act Corporations clearly could be the forerunners of full-service inter-state branches.
    6. Unfortunately, a numerical division of the Asian and European offices between headquarters and branches was not available. See Dunning and Norman (1979), Chapter 5, for a discussion of the European case, where regional head-quarters appear to be more common.
    7. Only a few companies and banks in the 55-firm sample have added specific major functions to the regional office responsibilities, so the trend is not yet measurable.
    8. Alfred Weber (1958), p. 138.

9. Walter Isard (1977), p. 161.

10. E.g. Dunning and Norman (1979), Schollhammer (1974).

11. Even with the regional office, an MNE may operate through agents/distributors in individual countries. The office just moves the MNE one step closer to full local presence in each country of the region. Thus the office may not internalize any more of the sales function, if agents are still used – but it does improve the information flow between agents and the home office.

12. An additional benefit is gained by firms which use the branch to co-ordinate unaffiliated distributors and agents as well as serving directly customers abroad. In that case the firm/bank may be able to *internalize* information and service flows to the foreign markets, where formerly such functions were left to the unaffiliated firms or competitors.

13. In the Latin American regional offices, frequently payroll checks are issued directly from the home office, rather than from a local account, which presumably would obtain funds from sales and services. This is to say that many firms find it more useful to centralize the financial flows in the home office, and then 'create' accounts for the regional office to evaluate its performance.

14. For example, see Alan Shapiro, 'Capital Budgeting in the Multinational Corporation', *Financial Management* (June 1978).

15. This calculation uses data from the Miami MNE databank.

16. Though some people would argue that Miami, the centre for these offices, is more a part of Latin America than of the United States.

17. Edge Act Corporations are analysed in greater detail in Grosse (1981b). They may add substantially to the multinational banks' internal functioning, since they were allowed to handle eurocurrency deposits/loans beginning in December 1981. Clearly, the functions of an Edge Act Corporation are largely determined by US banking laws, and not only by banks' desired strategies.

7 INDUSTRIAL CO-OPERATION, JOINT VENTURES AND THE MNE IN YUGOSLAVIA

Peter F. Cory

Introduction

In the theoretical paradigm that has emerged as dominant in the 'international investment' literature in recent years, the MNE is treated as a phenomenon of internalization within flawed or imperfect markets. The basic analytics are derivative of the Coasian theory of the firm, and of Williamson's analysis of markets and hierarchies. The argument, reduced to the simplest of terms, is that when transactions costs associated with market contracting tend to be high, internal, hierarchical decision-making processes may be both cost-effective and revenue-enhancing mechanisms for resource allocation.

Attempts to validate and substantiate this line of analysis, and to specify the precise circumstances under which it might apply, have been quite numerous. Teece (1976), Buckley and Casson (1976), Casson (1979), Rugman (1980a, 1980b, 1981a), and Calvet (1980) immediately come to mind. A particularly comprehensive framework is offered by the so-called 'eclectic' theory of international production, discussed by John Dunning in a series of papers (Dunning, 1977, 1979, 1980).

The eclectic theory considers the MNE's strategic decision-making — between the export/subsidiary production/licensing options that are available to it — in terms of a three-stage analysis. These cover the nature of the 'ownership-specific' advantages possessed by the firm; trade and location theoretic considerations (that determine whether the production activity exploiting these advantages should be 'at home' or 'abroad'); and the character of market failures that suggests advantages to internalization (and which are, of course, associated with the exact nature of the firm's ownership-specific advantages).

It is impossible to do justice to a huge literature in a brief few paragraphs. But it probably can be said that a rough consensus does exist that three sets of circumstances are most likely to produce internalization of resource transmissions, production activity and trade flows. These are: (i) When market failures in information or technology markets are severe. The problem of appropriability of valuable proprietary technology is one of the important considerations here, but far from the only one. Information asymmetries; the embodiment of technology in complementary inputs; public good characteristics other than the question of 'exclusivity' are all potentially important factors; (ii) When strategic considerations involving oligopolistic penetration and control of markets, including scale and product differentiation (based on technology and/or advertising and brand identification), are important for maximization of returns; (iii) When international production rationalization places special demands on supplier-user relations (when stringent quality control, precise production scheduling, and so on are critical for user profitability). Indeed, high levels of foreign subsidiary activity out of home countries, and penetration into host countries, do tend to be associated empirically with concentrated market structures, industry technology- and advertising-intensity, and large scale of plant and size of firm. And intra-firm international trade does appear to be most characteristic of technology-intensive industries or products.

The emphasis on foreign subsidiaries has not, however, been exclusive. It is well known that joint-venture (JV) arrangements are widely utilized by MNEs, especially those from Europe and Japan, and that licensing agreements (LAs) have been contracted extensively. Both these phenomena have been the subject of considerable scrutiny, and today we have a much better understanding of the circumstances under which an MNE may accept, or even prefer, such arrangements — thanks to the work of, amongst others, Franko (1971, 1974), Berg and Friedman (1978, 1979), Buckley and Davies (1979), Giddy and Rugman (1979), and the numerous contributions to the internalization theory of the MNE cited above.

Yet there has also been a growing interest in these and other alternatives to the majority- or wholly-owned subsidiaries from a different perspective. Beginning in the late 1960s and early 1970s, there has been a substantial growth in MNE involvement in the socialist countries, and particularly in Eastern European countries such as Hungary, Poland, Romania and Yugoslavia. This involvement has taken a variety of foms, ranging from arm's-length licensing, to equipment and technology purchases with 'compensating exports' of the resultant product, to more complex 'industrial co-operation agreements' (technology transfer plus co-production, subcontracting, or inter-firm specialization in the production of parts of components), and/or joint ventures with MNE equity participation.

In this context, several authors have carefully explored the nature of these contractual arrangements, the more complex of which are seen to be a significant set of inter-corporate commercial relations that are intermediate to, and in important ways distinct from, *both* straight licensing and parent-subsidiary relations. Carl McMillan's (1977a, 1977b, 1980) and Josef Brada's (1981a) work in this area deserves special mention. For the purposes of the present paper, the crucial question that arises can be posed in the following manner.

The internalization theory of the MNE analyses the factors under-lying the use of non-market mechanisms in the international transmission and utilization of resources. In Eastern Europe (and, increasingly, in LDCs) however, foreign ownership is severely restricted, if not dis-allowed completely, thereby constraining the MNE's strategic options. If the MNE's preferred option is eliminated, the quantity and/or quality of resources transmitted, and the manner of their utilization, will be affected. Yet given the set of 'intermediate' contractual relations that industrial co-operation agreements (ICAs) and joint ventures (JVs) represent, precisely how great will this effect be? The question that arises, then, is 'To what extent might these intermediate contractual relations provide some of the benefits of full internalization (with respect to the maintenance of decision-making authority and control and the lowering of transactions costs) that arm's-length licensing fails to ensure?'

The argument that these intermediate contractual relations may be distinct from arm's-length licensing agreements, that they might involve in some circumstances a *de facto* internalization, follows from the long-term, continuing, mutually dependent, intimate relations in technology transfer and joint production that *can* emerge between the parties to such agreements. Over time, mutual familiarity, understanding, trust and sense of purpose may develop. Important decisions on resource allocation, utilization and reward are, of course, subject to negotiation and bargaining, and are embodied in long-term contractual agreements. But over time, as the nature of relations between the parties changes, the transactions costs associated with negotiating and enforcing such agreements, and adapting them to changing circumstances, may decline substantially. Within the new relationship control may also be attained through the 'exercise of influence', rather than exclusively via the 'exercise of authority' through specified contractual terms (the language follows Neuberger and Duffy, 1976).

In fact, just as equity ownership does not preclude market-based relations between wholly-owned affiliates, the absence of full equity ownership does not preclude non-market, or quasi-market, or quasi-internal, resource-allocation mechanisms betweeen non-affiliates. To cite Brada (1981a) in his discussion of the industrial co-operation agreement between International Harvester and Bumar of Romania in the production of heavy earth-moving machinery, 'the intimacy of the relationship represents an internalization of market transactions by the two participants'.

The gist of the argument, then, is that ICAs and JVs may under some circumstances be somewhat closer in content to the parent-subsidiary spectrum of relations than they are to straight licensing agreements. These intermediate forms are a significant, and not at all uncommon, form of inter-firm arrangement which the analytical literature on the MNE needs to integrate more thoroughly. They can, when successful, be considered as a form of international production, with the local firm's activity effectively determined by/in conjunction with the foreign firm, which also has a lasting interest in the value created.

Perhaps unwisely, we shall not at this juncture attempt to follow up on the analytics suggested by this line of reasoning. The reader is referred instead to the papers of Carl McMillan and Josef Brada cited above, as well as the recent paper by Cory and Dunning (1982), in which many of these issues are reviewed, and upon which some of the preceding discussion is based. The purpose of the present chapter is different. In the light of this discussion, it seems quite clear to this author that empirical investigations of MNE involvement in Eastern Europe are an important source of evidence on the strategic decision-making behaviour of MNEs and also on the nature of the phenomenon of the MNE itself.

In recent years, the volume of such empirical studies has grown substantially. Besides Brada and McMillan's work, that of Marer (1978), Marer and Tabaczynski (1981), Levcik and Stankovsky (1979), and numerous others come immediately to mind. Yet these studies have concentrated on countries whose legislation has, in some instances, been extremely restrictive; and whose economic systems are (except for Hungary) of the command type. Yugoslavia may be a more interesting, valuable and generalizable case study in the present perspective. It is a market, albeit socialist, system; its legislation is rather more conducive to MNE involvement; and the extent of such involvement has, in relative terms, been very much greater.

This chapter's primary objective, then, will be that of analysing the development of contractual relations for the transmission of technology, and for production co-operation on the basis of transferred technology, between Yugoslav enterprises and Western MNEs. An important aim, in doing this, is to improve our understanding of the role of foreign technology in the rather successful (albeit uneven) story of Yugoslavia's post-war industrialization. However, our emphasis in this chapter is, more properly, to provide evidence on the strategic decisions of the foreign corporations themselves. What sort of agreements did they enter, and with what frequency? What did the contracts involve? How did the inter-firm relations develop? To what extent might the ICAs and JVs between Yugoslav and Western MNEs be classified as significant 'intermediate mechanisms' for resource allocation, as *de facto* internalizations? It is our contention that the answers to these questions provide further evidence in support of a broadening of the analytical framework within which the theory of the MNE *as a theory of internalization* is being developed.

In the chapter, we consider first some general, aggregative data on the levels and patterns of the various types of technology transfer contracts between Yugoslav and Western firms. We next consider the development of inter-firm contractual relations within a few major — and some minor — product lines within the 'engineering' industries — motor vehicles, parts and accessories; tractors; household appliances and parts thereof; office and telecommunication equipment; bearings; and razor blades. The focus on these industries (and the exclusion of industries such as chemicals, food processing, wood and paper products, etc., all areas of extensive MNE involvement) is partly a consequence of space limitations, and partly because of a desire to focus on industries where subcontracting and co-production within ICAs and JVs is likely to be more common, given the inherent nature of the products and production processes.

But what can empirical investigations of this sort really tell us? The data, as we shall see, certainly reveal that a very large number of contracts have been concluded in the last few decades, often with MNEs that are very extensive and familiar investors in Europe, North America and the developing countries. We also observe the development of long-term, intimate inter-firm relations, in the manner discussed above, often beginning from import-export or simple licensor-licensee arrangements. Finally, we believe that the technology-transfer and production-co-operation activities are, in a number of cases, truly substantive — they involve the types of activities that the internalization theory would traditionally suggest belong within the realm of parent-subsidiary rather than licensor-licensee arrangements.

Of course, there may be errors in the analysis both in terms of the accuracy of the evidence presented, and in its interpretation. However, if this is not the case, then one is left with perhaps just two alternatives.

One is to conclude that the 'internalization' theory itself has been over-drawn: that other factors explain both the rapid expansion of foreign subsidiary production activity *vis-à-vis* licensing, and the distinct sectoral patterns in that activity which have appeared so consistently from country to country. The alternative interpretation, however, is the one we wish to offer – that the intermediate mechanisms can, and on occasion do, represent a set of viable intermediate, or quasi-internalized, mechanisms for resource allocation. This further suggests the MNEs will be less sensitive – their resource supply responses less elastic – to controls over equity than the more limited analysis suggests. In fact, the MNE is a flexible institution, and this flexibility is observable in its dealings with both the Eastern European countries, and those LDCs that have introduced equity controls in the last decade or so.

Before we proceed, a few notes are in order. In the empirical analysis that lies behind this chapter (but which, due to space considerations, is not fully reported here) we have extensively detailed the timing, nature and content of contracts concluded, where this information is provided in local and foreign press reports. We have also, however, analysed published disaggregated international trade data, for three reasons: (i) a significant aspect of the Yugoslav authorities' focus was on enhancement of exports to Western markets through ICAs and JVs; (ii) the motives of the Western firms in some cases quite specifically related to using local production in Yugoslavia as a means of enhancing their penetration of CMEA and some LDC markets; and (iii) the development of inter-firm trade within production-co-operation programmes is sometimes clearly revealed in the export-import data. The trade data, in other words, may provide some indication of the content and success of the agreements concluded.

Yet there is a further aspect. In recent years, there has been considerable gloominess in domestic and foreign business circles, especially surrounding trade and balance of payments issues. In the late 1970s, Yugoslavia accumulated enormous deficits on current account. The official response was to increase substantially pressure on foreign firms to tie in exports *from* Yugoslavia with their exports of goods and technology *to* Yugoslavia. Foreign resistance to these pressures was, not surprisingly, strong – sales of equipment and licences, and ICAs and JVs were, after all, frequently import-substituting in nature. It is also the case that many of the more 'complex' agreements concluded have, in the past, been motivated more by a desire on the part of both parties to benefit from Yugoslav legislation favouring JVs and ICAs, than to establish meaningful co-operation. Many of the inter-firm agreements are simply 'shells'. Nevertheless, we believe that there have been enough significant, substantive agreements to support the basic conclusion of this study.

The Level and Pattern of Technology Contracts in Yugoslav Industry

By conventional criteria, Yugoslavia's post-war economic development has been rather successful. The fact that it had become, by the 1970s, a significant exporter of 'non-traditional' manufactures in part explains, and in part reflects, this developmental success.[1] Indeed, the period from the early 1960s to the mid-1970s saw a significant shift in the 'structure' of Yugoslavia's exports to developed market economies, undergoing a steady process of 'technological upgrading'.[2]

The process of expansion and technological upgrading of exports — and, of course, of industrial production as a whole, which it reflects — has been intimately tied to the acquisition of foreign technology, and especially Western European and American technology. This technology acquisition has taken place through a variety of mechanisms, including importation of equipment, and also the return of thousands of workers, technicians, engineers and managers from short- and medium-term employment in Western Europe. However our focus shall be on contractual arrangements such as LAs, ICAs and JVs.

Indeed, the rate of contracting of new LAs (for the acquisition of patents, know-how, technical assistance, trade-marks and so on) has increased rapidly. Although there is no complete data available, it is known that 25 to 30 contracts were concluded each year in the mid-1950s, 40 to 45 per annum in the mid-1960s and 125 to 130 per annum in the mid-1970s.

During the 1960s, however, two important new forms of co-operation emerged between Yugoslav enterprises and Western suppliers of technology. In 1959, legislation explicitly recognizing long-term industrial co-operation agreements was introduced, although it was not until 1966 that legislation providing substantial benefits to such agreements was passed. This latter legislation, together with legislation enacted in 1967 permitting joint ventures with minority foreign equity participation, was intimately linked with the 1965 reforms. These reforms envisaged a considerably more decentralized, market-oriented, open and technologically progressive Yugoslav economy. In some ways, the legislation was also a response to considerable dissatisfaction which existed with current licensing practices — it being widely felt that such agreements were quite limited in their benefits, at least compared to the alternative possibilities. In particular, it was felt that the technology involved was generally well behind the most advanced and that restrictions on exports and on the independent development of licensed technologies were proving to be detrimental to domestic development. Technology transfers through ICAs and, especially, JVs were seen as an appropriate solution.

The JV legislation was, in fact, dominated by the technology-transfer issue.[3] Since foreign firms were to establish an equity stake in Yugoslav enterprises, it was expected that Yugoslav firms would gain access to the results of advanced R and D of these countries; that faster and less restrictive transfer of newer, more sophisticated technologies would be facilitated; and that there would be greater interest and effort from the foreign firm in the transfer of other forms of know-how − work organization and managerial technique, marketing skills and so on. A significant emphasis on exports was made necessary by the convertible currency position of Yugoslavia's balance of payments; nevertheless, it was felt that there existed substantial scope for arrangements that took advantage of Yugoslavia's relatively low-wage labour and abundant raw materials, and the prospect of linking Yugoslav enterprises to the established sales and service networks of major European firms was of considerable significance.

In the case of ICAs, apart from technology, the possibility of using increased (international) intra-industry specialization to achieve the more efficient utilization of existing capacities, and to facilitate the construction of larger, optimal-scale capacities, was especially important. With the foreign partner a regular purchaser of the output, it was expected that there would be greater interest on its part in improving the local firm's technology, product quality, and organization and scheduling, on a continuing basis.[4]

Returning to JVs, we should add that in exchange for their contribution of capital, technology, management skills and assistance in foreign markets, the foreign corporation entering a JV was to be offered a secure position for producing and selling on the Yugoslav market and the opportunity to trade on Yugoslavia's 'goodwill' in Eastern Europe and certain developing countries. And, as with ICAs, the possibility existed of establishing operations in Yugoslavia as a low-cost source of supply of parts, components and final products for its own requirements, or for sale to third parties.

Initially, the rate of contracting for both types of agreement rose rapidly once the facilitating legislation had been introduced, although the depressed years of the mid-1970s saw significant declines. As with LAs, data for ICAs are incomplete, but it appears that only 7 or 8 new agreements were concluded each year in the early 1960s; that this had risen to 75 per annum in the late 1960s and early 1970s; and then declined to about 45 per annum by the mid-1970s. In recent years (late 1970s) the rate of contracting appears to have again increased, to about 80 per annum. From 1967 to mid-1978 some 637 ICAs were reported to have been concluded by Yugoslav enterprises.

Joint-venture contracting rose from 5 registrations of agreement in the first year, 1968, to about 25 registrations each year between 1972–4. It then declined to only 15 or so each year for the next 3 years, and probably to an even slightly lower number for the subsequent 3 years (with just 8 concluded in 1980, and perhaps a similar number to September in 1981). From 1968 to 1980 over 200 JV contracts were concluded.[5]

We should now turn to the available data on the *patterns* of contracting for LAs, ICAs and JVs in Yugoslavia; following that we shall have more to say about the foreign firms' attitudes to ICA/JV opportunities available within Yugoslav industry.

Unfortunately, since 1974 the Yugoslav authorities have been reluctant to publish detailed information concerning contracts between domestic and foreign firms. The information that is made available is generally highly aggregated, and the industry classifications are not terribly useful for comparative purposes. The alternative is to collect information as it is reported in domestic and foreign business publications, which is of course very time consuming. We have managed to do this to some extent during the course of the last few years. The basic problem, however, is that there is little that one can do in terms of the accuracy of the reported information (some industrial co-operation agreements are falsely reported as joint ventures, for example, and other reports are quite ambiguous about the specific type of contract involved); and there can be no assurances about the completeness of coverage. The other major problem is that in the period 1965–73, registration of LAs was not compulsory; even the federal authorities seem to have little idea of exactly what occurred during this period. Data on LAs that are published by the authorities are apparently based on surveys, and are almost certainly highly incomplete.[6]

In Table 7.1, we present relatively aggregated data made available to the UN by the Yugoslav authorities: it is useful in that it does permit a broad comparison of the frequency of alternative contractual arrangements across sectors. Unfortunately, it is by now somewhat out of date,

Table 7.1: Contractual Agreements for Technology Transfer, Yugoslavia, 1967 to mid-1976

Sector	Licensing agreements		Long-term production co-operation agreements		Joint ventures	
	Number	Sectoral distribution %	Number	Sectoral distribution %	Number	Sectoral distribution %
Chemicals	132	29.0	10	2.1	32	22.2
Basic metals	35	7.7	18	3.8	13	9.0
Metal-using industries	163	35.8	265	55.4	43	29.9
Transport equipment	40	8.8	50	10.5	8	5.6
Machine tools	55	12.1	57	11.9	20	13.9
Mechanical engineering	68	14.9	158	33.1	15	10.4
Electrical machinery and equipment	26	5.7	48	10.0	18	12.5
Electronic equipment	29	6.4	76	15.9	17	11.8
Agriculture and foodstuffs	23	5.0	4	0.8	7	4.9
Light industry	23	5.0	12	2.5	6	4.2
Other	25	5.5	45	9.4	8	5.6
Total	456	100.0	478	100.0	144	100.0

Notes: 'Mechanical engineering' includes non-electrical machinery, other than machine tools, metal products: 'Transport equipment' includes tractors and earth moving machinery; 'Electrical machinery and equipment' includes electric locomotives; 'Electronic equipment' includes office equipment, radio and TV, and communications equipment; 'Light industry' includes textiles, clothing, footwear, furniture, rubber products, glass etc.; 'Other' includes construction.
Source: UN, ESC (1976) p. 5.

and also contains a variety of inaccuracies. The numbers do nevertheless show that ICAs and JVs — the intermediate forms — have been extensively used as technology-transfer mechanisms.

The concentration of agreements in the chemicals, electrical and non-electrical machinery, transport equipment and electronics industries is of course familiar: those industries dominate international investment, technology transfer and trade patterns in industry almost universally. JVs have been somewhat more common in electrical equipment and electronics, and less important in chemicals than have LAs. The very low level of ICA activity in chemicals in part reflects the specificities of Yugoslav law relating to such agreements: 'co-operation' involves 'the reciprocal deliveries of parts and sub-assemblies that serve to finalize a product or group of products', wording which did not relate very well to the nature of chemical production. Until 1977, ICAs provided very significant benefits to participating enterprises — the domestic firms retention quota on foreign exchange earnings, under normal conditions only 7 per cent (20 per cent beginning in 1971) was in 1966 increased to 100 per cent for ICAs. The chemical industry provided much less opportunity for 'genuine' co-operation in production (rather than co-operation in circumventing foreign exchange restrictions) and so was largely excluded.

There are also some sharp differences between regional patterns of contracting. The small European countries that make up the EFTA concluded, between 1967–77, 118 LAs, 73 ICAs and 24 JVs with Yugoslav enterprises. US corporations, between 1973–8, concluded 90 LAs, just 9 ICAs (of which 5 were via US affiliates in Europe), and 21 JVs (of which 12 were with affiliates in Europe). Indeed, for the whole period, 1968 to the present, US corporations have played a significant role in the JV programme, exceeding all other countries in terms of capital contributed (as is seen in Table 7.2 below). The question obviously arises as to why US firms — and their subsidiaries — have been so reluctant to enter ICAs. There have, in fact, been few attempts by US MNEs to establish any significant 'offshore processing' within Yugoslavia; the main interest, apparently, lies in servicing the domestic market (although there are some notable exceptions, as we shall see below). The explanation is not one of tariffs and transport costs, or low Yugoslav productivity, or supplier weaknesses alone, clearly, because US subsidiaries in Europe take advantage of ICAs as infrequently as parent companies in the US. The answer, most probably, is the greater reluctance of US corporations to integrate minority-owned enterprises, with uncertain managerial control, into an international production network.

Table 7.2: Invested Capital of JV Enterprises in Yugoslavia, By Country of Origin, 1968–80 (Million Dinars)

Country of origin of foreign partner	Number of JVs	Total foreign investment	Foreign investment per JV	Total investment	Total investment per JV	Foreign equity share %
USA	30	3,368.0	112.3	10,627.4	354.2	31.7
UK	12	1,777.9	148.2	13,914.1	1159.5	12.8
Switzerland	19	1,637.1	86.2	5,749.3	302.6	28.5
West Germany	52	1,123.0	21.6	8,065.7	155.1	13.9
Italy	31	937.6	30.3	4,330.0	139.7	21.7
France	11	290.0	26.4	1,157.0	105.2	25.1
Austria	7	254.2	36.3	1,791.2	255.9	14.2
Other	37	876.7	23.7	3,620.7	99.2	23.9
Total	199	10,264.5	51.6	49,255.4	247.5	20.7

Source: *Ekonomska politika*, July 20 1981, plus own calculations.

In considering the sectoral distribution of JVs in Yugoslavia, it would clearly be desirable to have data on the shares of output and capital within each sector accounted for by JVs as well as the sectoral distribution of JV numbers and output or capital (and the foreign capital component). The latter data are available, but only at a highly aggregate level after 1974. The most recent available data are presented in Tables 7.2 and 7.3. Table 7.2 apparently covers most, if not all, JVs concluded to December 1980; it shows the level of JV participation of the countries most actively participating in JVs, as well as the share of foreign investment in total JV equity by country. Table 7.3 covers only the 164 most significant JVs, and reveals the sectoral distribution of aggregate and foreign invested capital for the two sub-periods 1968–75 and 1976–80, as well as 1968–80 as a whole.[7]

The data in Table 7.3 lead to some interesting points. *First,* while there may have been a decline in the rate of contracting, in terms of contract numbers, between the early and late 1970s, this is not an accurate reflection of trends in the significance of foreign involvement. Between 1976–80, the annual JV capital investment was around 6.43 billion dinars, of which the foreign share totalled 1.59 billion dinars. These figures are obviously quite small; but they substantially exceed the figures for 1968–75, or even 1970–5 (taking into account the very low level of activity in the initial two years). The 1968–75 figures produce annual sums of 1.79 billion dinars and 0.27 billion dinars respectively; the 1970–5 figures cannot be more than 2.1 billion and 0.3 billion respectively. Inflation may account for some of the difference, but not all of it. It must also be recognized that a few large projects such as Dow Chemicals JVs in petrochemicals, do tend to dominate the data for the later period.[8] Indeed, between 1968–75, 58.2 per cent of the foreign capital (in the 164 larger projects) was destined for the three industries perhaps most characterized by large scale − chemicals, basic metals and motor vehicles. By the late 1970s, this figure had risen to 74.8 per cent. Notably, the chemicals industry retained its relative position; but the motor vehicles industry was replaced by basic metals as *the* major destination of foreign capital (by the mid-1970s most of the major motor vehicles JVs had already been established). A *second* interesting point is that the average foreign equity share has shown a significant jump, from around 15 per cent to 25 per cent. In chemicals, it is now very close to the 49 per cent maximum.[9]

The picture of the development of JVs that one gets from this data, then, is somewhat more optimistic than that provided by the trends in

Table 7.3: Sectoral Distribution of Invested Capital in JVs

	Chemicals	Metal products	Wood, paper	Basic metals	Food processing	Transport equipment	Electrical machinery, equipment	Rubber	Other	Total
A. *Number of JVs*										
1968–75	17	10	3	5	7	9	8	4	26	89
1976–80	10	7	5	7	10	8	6	4	18	75
1968–80	27	17	8	12	17	17	14	8	44	164
B. *Total invested capital*										
Total capital (bill. dinar)										
1968–75	1.550	.398	2.358	5.791	.367	2.053	.868	.811	.235	14.387
1976–80	4.293	1.871	.736	16.427	2.210	3.807	.527	1.367	.902	32.145
1968–80	5.843	2.269	3.094	22.218	2.577	5.860	1.395	2.178	1.137	46.532
Capital per JV (mill. dinar)										
1968–75	91.1	39.8	786.0	1,158.0	52.4	228.1	108.5	202.8	9.0	161.7
1976–80	429.3	267.3	147.2	2,346.7	221.0	475.1	87.8	341.8	50.1	428.6
1968–80	216.4	133.5	386.8	1,851.5	151.6	344.7	99.6	272.3	25.8	283.7
C. *Foreign capital*										
Foreign capital (bill. dinar)										
1968–75	.516	.139	.201	.216	.112	.547	.072	.260	.115	2.196
1976–80	1.987	.356	.241	2.742	.441	1.206	.162	.337	.476	7.930
1968–80	2.503	.495	.442	2.958	.553	1.753	.234	.597	.591	10.126
Capital per JV (mill. dinar)										
1968–75	30.4	13.9	67.0	43.2	16.0	60.8	9.0	65.0	4.4	24.7
1976–80	198.7	50.9	48.2	391.7	44.1	150.8	27.0	84.3	26.4	105.7

Foreign share of sectors' total JV capital (%)										
1968–75	33.3	34.9	8.5	3.7	30.5	26.6	8.3	32.1	48.9	15.3
1976–80	46.3	19.0	32.7	16.7	20.0	31.7	30.7	24.7	52.8	24.7
Sectors share of foreign JV capital (%)										
1968–75	23.5	6.3	9.2	9.8	5.1	24.9	3.3	11.8	5.2	100.0
1976–80	25.1	4.5	3.0	34.5	5.6	15.2	2.0	4.2	6.0	100.0

Source: *Ekonomska Politika*, July 20 1981 plus own calculations. Note that only the most significant 164 JVs are included in this table.

contract numbers alone. Nevertheless, it remains very true that the JV programme has far from fulfilled the expectations of the Yugoslav authorities. There are many factors underlying this negative assessment. They have been disappointed with and concerned about the number of JV contracts concluded; with the size of the investments engaged in, and the foreign shares of JV equity; with the extent of JV earnings retention and reinvestment; with the number of agreements cancelled or permitted to lapse after the initial contracted period expired (by end 1979, 50 of a total of 206 contracts concluded between 1968–79, according to *Ekonomska Politika*, 29 September 1980); with the import-dependence of JV production, especially relative to JV export achievement; and so on.

For their part, there are also many factors underlying the modest embracement by MNEs of the opportunities offered by the JV legislation. Besides the inherent unfamiliarity and uncertainty of investing in a socialist country, the fact that the regulations have been unclear, unfavourable and unstable has clearly been a factor. Management rights within the self-management system and profit repatriation have been particularly contentious issues.[10] The unfavourable economic situation in both Yugoslavia and the OECD countries in the 1970s; the force of official pressure toward JV export expansion;[11] the unprofitability of a number of ventures (due, in some cases, to government price controls); the inherent conflicts of interest between foreign and domestic partners in the joint-venture framework[12] must all be taken into account. In the following section we *shall* see, however, that there are a sufficient number of examples of highly developed inter-corporate relations to produce a more optimistic view of both the achievements and the potential of JVs in Yugoslavia.

But we should at this point return to the pattern of joint-venture contracting. Since we have been able to identify the great majority of JV contracts through scrutiny of the business press (especially, reports in the weekly economics and business magazine *Ekonomska Politika*, Business International's *Business Eastern Europe*, and the English-language Yugoslav monthlies *Yugoslavia Export* and *Economic Review*), we are able to present a disaggregated tabulation of JV numbers by sector. These data are presented in Table 7.4.[13] In Cory and Dunning (1982), we have compared this pattern to those of US and all foreign subsidiaries in Mexico. By and large, the most striking feature of the comparison was the similarity rather than dissimilarity in patterns.[14]

In Table 7.5 below, we present a partial listing of JV agreements

Table 7.4: Apparent Sectoral Distribution of JV Contracts in Yugoslavia, to Mid-1981

Non-manufacturing

	No.		No.
Agriculture	1	Construction & project engineering	5
Mining	1	Hotel services	1
Total, non-manufacturing	8		

Manufacturing

Sector	Number of JVs	% of Man. JVs	Sector	Number of JVs	% of Man. JVs
Food processing	20	11.3	Non-ferrous metals	3	1.7
Tobacco products	1	0.6	Non-metals & construction materials	13	7.3
Plastics & synthetics	6	3.4	Metal products	2	1.1
Pharmaceuticals, soaps and cosmetics	9	5.1	Industrial machinery & parts (non-electr.)	20	11.3
Chemicals	17	9.6	Agricultural machinery	5	2.8
Footwear & apparel	3	1.7	Electrical machinery & supplies	13	7.3
Textiles	7	4.0	Transport equipment	13	7.3
Wood & furniture	6	3.4	Instruments	9	5.1
Pulp & paper	10	5.6	Miscellaneous	1	0.6
Printing & publishing	1	0.6	Unclassified	5	2.8
Rubber and plastic products	12	6.8	Total manufacturing	177	100.0
Ferrous metals	6	3.4	Total	185	

Source: OECD (1974), plus reports in *Ekonomska Politika, Business Eastern Europe, Yugoslavia Export, Economic Review*. Note that the total number is below the aggregates reported above partly because projects with multiple contracts (renewals, new partners) are counted singly; probably our coverage is incomplete to some extent as well. Altogether, we have identified 204 individual contracts (including multiples) which is probably 10–15 below the true total. Some contracts identified in the press as JVs may in fact not have been entered into; there may, of course, also be errors in the sectoral identifications. The reader should note that some obvious disparities exist between Table 7.4, and Tables 7.1 and 7.3 above.

Table 7.5: Some Significant JVs Between MNEs and Yugoslav Enterprises

Western Corporation	Country	Year	Yugoslav partner	Product
Unilever	Netherlands	1976	PK Beograd	frozen foods
General Foods	USA	1979	Agrocoop	snack foods, beverage concentrates
Rhone Poulence	France	1970	OHIS	PVC
Chemetex Fibres	USA	1973	OHIS	polyester fibre
Dow Chemical	USA	1974	OKI	polystyrene
ICI	UK	1975	Soda-So	polyurethane
Borg Warner (Europa)	USA	1980	PIK Vrbas	ABS pellets
Bayer	FRG	1971	Lek	pharmaceuticals & cosmetics
Ciba-Geigy	Switzerland	1972	Pliva	pharmaceuticals & pharm. chemicals
Hoechst	FRG	1974	PIK Servo Mihalj, Jugohemija	plasma expanders
Boots	UK	1978	Galenika	anti-rheumatic chemicals
Hoechst	FRG	1971	Iplas, Jugohemija	synthetic dispersions
Chemische Werke Huls	FRG	1971	Chromos-Katran-Kutrilin	ethoxylated chemicals
Dow Chemical	USA	1976	INA	petrochemical complex-ethylene, propylene, vinyl chloride etc.
Dunlop	UK	1971, 1978	Fadip, Jugohemija	high pressure rubber hose, flexible hydraulic brake lines
Semperit	Austria	1971,1978	Sava	radial auto tyres
Kleber Columbes	France	1973	Miloj Zakic	radial auto tyres
Semperit	Austria	1974	Borova	radial truck & auto tyres
Goodrich	USA	1978	Tigar	radial auto tyres
Dunlop	UK	1979	Balkan	tyres for heavy trucks & construction machinery
Tragergesellschaft	FRG	1972,1973, 1977	Sladkargorska, Belisce, INCEL	wrapping paper, sanitary paper, roofing cardboard; pulp, paper & cardboard; paperboard
Armco Steel, G.E., Waterbury Farrel	USA	1972	Zeljezara Jesenica	steel mill
Davy Loewy	UK	1979	MK Smederevo	cold rolling mill
Alusuisse	Switzerland	1976	Boris Kidric	aluminium products

Company	Country	Year	Yugoslav partner	Product
Gillette	US	1973	Yugoslavia Commerce	razor blades
SKF	Sweden	1969,1975, 1977	UNIS	ball bearings, roller bearings
SKF	Sweden	1971	IKL	roller bearings
Glacyer	UK	1978	Slobodan-Penezic	sliding-bearings
Westinghouse	USA	1976	Prva Petoletka	industrial pneumatic equipment
Atlas Copco	Switzerland	1977	Fagram, Univerzal	compressors
Honeywell	USA	1978	Ei-Nis, Progres	minicomputers, electronic calculators, data terminals
Elektrolux	Switzerland	1981	Universal	high pressure washing machines, heaters
Kloeckner-Humboldt-Duetz	FRG	1972	Torpedo	tractors
Messwandler-Bau	FRG	1970	Minel	inductive transformers
Fiat	Italy	1976	Zeljezara Store	tractors
Kloeckner-Humboldt-Duetz	FRG	1980	Duro-Dakovic	combine harvestors
Bell Telephone Meg	Belgium	1972	Iskra	telecommunications equipment
Teddington Bellows	UK	1974	Duro Dakovic	power generating equipment
GTE	USA	1980	Ei-Nis	digital computer controlled PABX telephone switching equipment
Fiat	Italy	1968,1969	Zavod Crvena Zastava	autos
Volkswagenwerk	FRG	1972,1977	UNIS	autos
Automobiles Citroen	France	1972	TOMOS, Iskra	autos
Renault	France	1977,1980	IMV	autos
Daimler-Benz	FRG	1970,1972	Fap-Famos	trucks, buses, engines
Kloeckner-Humboldt-Duetz	FRG	1971	TAM	trucks, buses
General Motors	USA	1977	LZT Kikinda	cast auto parts
Eaton Corporation	USA	1972	Rudi Cajavic	electronic devices for temperature regulation for household appliances
Agfa-Gevaert	Belgium	1980	Zorka	X-ray film
Baxter-Travenol	USA	1980	Zdravlje	medical dialyzers, filters, etc.

Sources: As for Table 7.4.

concluded from 1968 to the present. The selection of JVs included in Table 7.5 is not random; on the contrary, it is primarily to support our argument that many well-known MNEs have accepted minority equity positions in JVs producing products for which sophisicated, proprietary technology; superior product quality; and/or brand identification are critical factors in the corporations' international competitive position. Indeed, corporations such as Dow Chemicals and Gillette were involved until recently almost exclusively with 100 per cent-owned subsidiaries. A combination of more restrictive entry conditions in many developing countries, and the new possibilities for pre-emptive or defensive entry into Eastern Europe, produced a re-evaluation of such strategies.

We have mentioned, at a number of points in the discussion above, the fact that MNEs have been most strongly motivated by a desire to maintain or expand sales to the local Yugoslav market. In many cases, JVs represent the foreign response to pressures and policies of the Yugoslav authorities towards increased import substitution. In a relatively recent study, Lamers (1976) surveyed 15 foreign firms (respondents to a questionnaire sent to 60 firms) involved in JVs in the chemicals, auto, electrical equipment, paper, metal processing and tyre industries. Using a 4 to 1 point scale for 'measuring' the importance of various alternative motivating factors in the decision to invest in Yugoslavia, he obtained the following results:

Maintain existing local market	32
Make profitable use of patents, know-how and licences	29
Develop new local market	27
Use Yugoslavia as a base for exports to Eastern Europe	21
Obtain raw materials	5
Take advantage of low labour costs	2
Overcome tariff barriers	2
Take advantage of favourable labour relations	1
Other	2

Source: Lamers (1976) p. 206, table 57.

The possibility of capitalizing technology, often to establish an equity stake in import-replacing production, receives a high rating by foreign firms. In the 10 of 15 firms surveyed by Lamers whose capital investment included capitalized technology, it amounted to 40 per cent or more of their capital contribution in 4 cases and between 10 to 30 per cent in the other 6. Other data support the conclusion that a significant share of MNEs equity stake in JVs is capitalized technology, although sources vary very widely on the exact numbers involved.[15]

Indeed, in many of the cases for which some details of the joint-venture agreements are known to the present author, capitalization of technology has been a significant factor. A number of them are reported on below. However, there are additional cases which deserve mention. Dow Chemicals made available within a JV (with 49 per cent share-of-capital) technology for polymerization of styrene and for production of expandable polystyrene beads which would not have been available under licence. Virtually the entire Dow capital contribution was capitalized technology. In Hoechst's JV in synthetic dispersions, capitalized technology amounted to one half of its 45 per cent equity share. The JV was negotiated after a Yugoslav proposal for a LA had been rejected; for Hoechst, security for its existing market was crucial. The Dunlop JV in hydraulic rubber hose was concluded when the domestic partner, unable or unwilling to meet Dunlop's licence fee for its technology, proposed instead a JV. Dunlop agreed; its 40 per cent share of capital represents capitalized technology.

We should add a further point. In general, foreign capital shares have been considerably lower than these above-mentioned cases — around 20 per cent in the period 1968–80. A significant proportion represents capitalized technology; another proportion represents equipment contributed by the foreign partner. In some cases this equipment is reconditioned equipment from the firms' own production lines (as was the case in the Dunlop, Gillette and some recent JVs, for example). In other cases, new equipment suppliers to major projects in the pulp and paper, basic metals and other industries have agreed to supply capital equipment through an equity stake in these projects. This, presumably, gives them an edge over other foreign equipment suppliers, especially in official eyes; however, the arrangement may amount to little more than a technology-transfer contract and a long-term loan. The 'sharing of risk' that the Yugoslav authorities expect to stimulate substantial foreign assistance in management, technology development and marketing may not amount to very much.

Finally, although the Lamers' questionnaire results give rather low weight to the significance of JVs in Yugoslavia as a source of raw materials and components, there has been a significant expansion in co-production and sourcing from Yugoslavia in recent years, as we shall see below. In fact, it is now a convenient point to turn to the individual industry studies: these will generally be presented very briefly, with the hope of illustrating the most important points only.

Industry Studies

In this section, we shall very briefly review the development of technology transfer, production co-operation and international trade activity in a few selected industries. Extensive documentation for these industries has been prepared by the author and is available upon request; here we shall simply summarize the main findings. We are, we believe, able to show that in a number of these industries the *de facto* internalization of inter-firm relations has indeed been achieved via contractual agreements — that is, ICAs and JVs.

The *motor-vehicles industry*, including parts and accessories, provides the most striking example of these developments. In *passenger cars*, domestic production commenced in 1954, when Crvena Zastava (ZCZ) began assembly under a LA with Fiat. In the ensuing 2½ decades, many LAs, ICAs and JVs have been concluded; by 1980 there were JVs between Fiat and ZCZ, Renault and IMV, VW and TAS (part of UNIS), and Citroen and Tomas and Iskra, for the domestic production and assembly of autos. A JV with General Motors for the production of cast auto parts (to be exchanged for imports of assembled Opel cars), and an ICA with Peugeot for local parts production and export (also in exchange for assembled autos), had also been concluded.

These JVs have facilitated (i) the rapid introduction of new production technology and new models into domestic production; (ii) the expansion of production capacities (albeit to the rather modest levels of approximately 250,000 at ZCZ, 80,000 at TAS, and 35,000 at IMV in 1980; as previously mentioned, the CIMOS venture was dissolved in mid-1981 following successive years of losses); and (iii) a very rapid expansion of Yugoslavia's exports of auto parts to Western European and Eastern bloc markets. These exports (or more commonly 'exchanges') have largely taken place within the framework of separate ICAs negotiated between the JV partners, as well as with their licensees in the Eastern bloc. The aim has been two-fold — to increase production specialization in order to capture economies of scale; and to cover import requirements for parts, subassemblies, CKDs and assembled cars to the extent required by Yugoslav foreign trade law and policy. Many of the parts exports by Yugoslav firms are produced under LAs negotiated with the foreign partner or their affiliates and subcontractors.

ZCZ in particular, has emerged as an innovative, aggressive firm that has developed an extensive network of parts production and supply relations throughout Western and Eastern Europe. The auto (and parts) industry as a whole supplies parts to Fiat in Italy; GM, Ford and VW in Germany; and Renault and Citroen in France (as well as to VAZ in the USSR and Polmot in Poland). The parts involved are not crucial components such as engines or transaxles or standard gears − such as are now being produced in the Latin American subsidiaries of US firms. Rather, they tend to cover radiators and heaters, spark plugs, electric motors, alternators, starters, horns, batteries, lights, wipers, electrical wiring sets, filters, shock absorbers, bumper bars, seats and so on. In the case of IMV, even domestically produced caravans are exchanged for CKD imports. However Renault is also involved in a JV producing forged metal parts for its autos; and General Motors, as previously mentioned, has recently established a JV for the production of cast parts, including differential housings. In 1981, a JV was concluded to produce safety glass for VW automobiles. There are, now, a number of JVs producing radial tyres, and the Goodrich venture in particular has led to a significant recent expansion in exports. Finally, we should note that ZCZ has begun to appear as an exporter of automobiles (as well as parts), with markets emerging in LDCs and Eastern, Southern and even Western Europe. An extensive programme of 'model exchange' has been developed with the USSR and Eastern Europe; ZCZ also widely exports the modified Fiat 128 (the Zastava-101), and produces for Fiat the 127 and 128, which Fiat has stopped producing; Fiat handles the marketing in Europe. Finally, it has assembly facilities in Egypt and Colombia. Table 7.6 presents a summary of the development of industry exports.[16]

In most of the examples cited in the preceding paragraph, one would probably not conclude that 'internalization' was essential to protect valuable proprietary technology, or to maintain stringent quality standards and/or production scheduling requirements − it is unlikely that the 'make or buy' choice in sourcing would always in each case fall to the former. However, a proper assessment of this question would require a much more extensive analysis of sourcing practices, and production process characteristics, than we are able to undertake here. Nevertheless, it does appear that Yugoslav production is becoming much more closely integrated with the auto industries of Western and Eastern Europe, and it is most unlikely that this would have been achieved without the existence of the 'intermediate' contractual arrangements that we have been discussing.

Production of *commercial motor vehicles* (vans, trucks and buses) has a somewhat longer history than is the case for autos: the first assembly of trucks was actually begun in 1940, under a Czech licence.

Table 7.6: Yugoslav Exports From the Motor Vehicle and Related Industries (millions of dinars)

	1963	1966	1969	1972	1975	1978	1979
Passenger cars (including CKD for assembly)	0.4	39.4	21.3	97.5	287.4	795.9	1,104.9
Buses	4.8	31.9	3.9	56.9	362.5	521.6	864.4
Trucks (over 1 ton)	1.5	72.3	17.6	20.2	69.0	111.9	292.9
Special + other road motor vehicles	1.5	8.6	10.6	16.6	64.0	883.8	167.4
Engines and parts	3.0	33.4	48.1	129.5	216.8	124.4	187.6
Transmissions and parts	0.1	1.2	8.7	48.7	272.7	1,147.9	1,032.6
Other parts	4.1	63.3	129.2	359.4	816.1	914.2	2,225.7
Caravans	–	2.4	51.3	217.2	267.7	438.8	602.3
Rubber tyres and tubes	1.6	24.9	26.7	78.0	170.2	491.2	1,013.6
Electrical equipment	0.1	16.0	21.8	64.3	107.8	362.6	315.5
Batteries	n.a.	21.6	24.7	201.3	374.0	777.2	954.2
Total	n.a.	315.0	363.9	1,289.6	3,008.0	5,796.2	8,771,9
$ US million	n.a.	25.2	29.5	75.9	173.0	311.0	461.7

Note: The last two items in the table are exaggerations of motor vehicle related exports: electrical equipment includes ignition equipment for *all* internal combustion engines and batteries includes *all* lead batteries. Motor vehicles related products include the bulk, but not all, of these exports.
Source: *Statistics of Foreign Trade*, SFR Yugoslavia, various years, plus own calculations.

The development of this sector has, since then, paralleled that of the auto industry in a number of ways: expansion in the number of producers and domestic content of production; closer involvement between domestic and foreign firms, often beginning with LAs but evolving into ICAs and JVs; and, in some lines at least, significant export expansion. ICAs and JVs have been concluded with Daimler-Benz, Kloeckner-Humboldt-Duetz, Fiat and VW; many LAs for special vehicles and parts production have also been concluded. Local firms export axles, chassis, vans and some medium trucks to Fiat; engines to KHD and Daimler-Benz; buses to Poland; and there is extensive co-operation with the Hungarian heavy motor vehicle industry. In 1978, a JV was established in Greece for the production of Yugoslav buses; the Yugoslav firms involved supply chassis mounted with engines and transmissions.

It is worth noting that in the case of Daimler-Benz, the JV in truck and engine production was entered into reluctantly, in response to increasing pressures for import substitution in the domestic market. The German firm would have preferred to have entered into a LA, but there were strong indications from the Yugoslav authorities that a JV would be necessary in order for it to be sure of its long-term position in the local market. It thus took a minimal 7 per cent initial stake in JV. It did foresee the possibility of expansion, through export, into Eastern European markets, where it had had trouble 'breaking in'. Since its foundation, however, the JV has encountered numerous production difficulties and has not been able to meet the targets for domestic content or vehicle and parts export: delays due to Yugoslav regulations, especially concerning equipment imports, to poor development of supplying firms, and to organizational problems, have all been to blame. Meanwhile, Daimler-Benz's deliveries of parts have continued at higher than expected levels. Daimler-Benz is not concerned about export competition: it does not believe that Yugoslav production can be competitive, particularly without an established service network.

Tractors, like motor vehicles, are another field in which domestic producers have become very closely interwoven with foreign firms, through licensing, industrial co-operation and joint-venture agreements. Production of tractor and tractor engines in fact dates from the early 1950s; today there are at least 8 producers of wheel and caterpillar tractors for agriculture. The industry has developed enormously recently following official encouragement of tractor purchases by private farmers that began in the late 1960s. The largest producer, IMT, has developed its own technology and is now a significant exporter, having begun its production under Massey Ferguson (US) licence agreements in 1956. In this early stage of the industries development, in fact, all producers (except Bratstvo, which copied a Soviet model) used Western licences — IMR producing wheel tractors under Landini (Italy) licence, with Perkins (UK) licensed engines built in, and caterpillar tractors under Ansaldo Fasati (Italy) licence; Tomo Vinkovic under Pasquali (Italy); and 14 Oktobar (caterpillar) under Vender (Italy), now Allied Chalmers (Italy).

Since then Torpedo, Zeljezera Store, Gorenje, Pobeda, OLT and others have entered the industry, although up until fairly recently there was a good deal of specialization by size (that is, horse power), type (wheel, caterpillar), and region (within Yugoslavia's republics). Torpedo's production of diesel engines led to a significant joint venture with Kloeckner-Humboldt-Duetz (WG) concluded in 1972, in which the firms produce diesel engines and tractors. Zeljezera Store, a steel mill, concluded a JV with Fiat-Trattori (Italy) in 1976 and in 1977 began tractor production. In 1978, 50 per cent of the 9,000 units produced were sold within Yugoslavia; the remainder was sold by Fiat in Italy and elsewhere in Europe. OLTs production is in co-operation with Ford (US). Gorenje entered into a co-operation agreement with Stey-Daimler-Puch (Austria) for the production of small tractors in 1971; in 1979 a new agreement between SDP and Pobeda was concluded, under which Pobeda will produce small tractors for resale in Western and LDC markets; in exchange SDP will sell large tractors through Pobeda. The value of exchange will be $23 million per annum, each way, over a five-year period. SDP sees such co-operation deals as the most suitable alternative to the counter-trade pressures on tractor imports, which had increased progressively since 1973. In 1978 Bratstvo concluded an agreement for the production of heavy tractors with John Deere (US) (both wheel and caterpillar types). Under the agreement, Deere supplies engines, transmissions and hydraulic equipment, with Bratstvo making counter-deliveries of other parts. In 1980, Bratstvo entered a similar arrangement with Fiat-Trattori, for the production of caterpillar tractors. In 1977, IMT entered a licensing agreement with Volvo (Sweden) under which IMT produces heavy tractors, and supplies small tractors at compensating payment in lieu of royalties. Again, this is not at all a complete listing; but it does, as previously indicated, suggest significant integration of Yugoslav tractor production into European industry.

The trade data indeed reflects this. Wheel tractor exports increased from 10.0 million dinar 1963, 85.6 million 1966 (when there existed excess capacity in the domestic industry), 15.3 million in 1969, 32.0 million in 1972, 165.9 million 1975, and 503.7 million in 1978. Until after 1975, exports were almost exclusively to LDCs; since that time significant exports to Italy, Greece and Poland have been recorded. Unfortunately, data on parts are not reported separately from other agricultural equipment, so it is not possible to analyse the impact on parts exchanges of the co-operation arrangements. One significant recent development has been the JV agreement between IMT and Kongskilde (Denmark) to establish an assembly operation in Denmark for IMT tractors.

The *household appliance or 'white goods'* industry shows an extremely interesting pattern of contractual relations. It is an industry which has seen considerable development of co-operation with foreign firms, through LAs and ICAs, in the production of final products — and joint ventures in the production of some of the more sophisticated components, particularly temperature regulation and control devices (which are generally classified as 'instruments' in most industry classification schemata). It has also enjoyed considerable export success in recent years.

The dominant firm, by far, is Gorenje, with between one-half and two-thirds of domestic production in each major appliance line. Gorenje's production is under licensing and technical assistance agreements with leading Italian and Swedish firms; it exports to Western Europe, the USA and Australia; it has its own plants in Greece, Nigeria and France. The remaining half-dozen or so major local producers have an extensive network of LAs and ICAs with German, Italian, French and Swedish firms, with the Spanish affiliate of Western Electric of the US, and with East European producers. Siemens (West Germany) takes delivery of small electric stoves produced under a LA by Sloboda; Zanussi (Italy) is supplied with electric motors, washing machine heaters and refrigerators produced within ICAs; Aspero Frigo (Italy) exchanges compressors for electric motors produced by Obod; Obod also supplies Indesit (Italy) with electric motors, pumps, valves and timers, and SEW (Germany) with electric motors; and in a recent agreement, Gasfire (Italy) will sell in Western markets dish-washing machines produced within an ICA by Iskra. The expansion of exports is illustrated clearly by the following data (note that washing machine exports have been replaced by production abroad):

Yugoslav exports

(mills. dinars)	1966	1970	1973	1976	1979
refrigerators and parts	1.4	32.3	164.5	371.4	975.0
electric cooking ranges and parts	10.8	53.4	143.3	188.6	481.0
washing machines and parts	—	34.1	173.4	170.4	0.2

The other major feature of the industry has been the JV activity in the production of temperature regulation and control devices, which are technologically sophisticated components. EGO Elektro-Geraete of Switzerland and Eaton of the USA concluded JVs in 1972; EBF of Germany following in 1973 with a JV for the production of thermostats and heating elements. Interestingly, each venture had the maximum possible foreign equity share, and (until the dissolution of the Cajavec/Eaton venture) the three shared the domestic market between them, each by and large producing on a regional basis. The dissolution of the Eaton venture followed sharp disagreements over the rate of technology flows into the venture, and the expansion of exports to Western Europe (where Eaton had existing subsidiaries), according to reports from the Yugoslav firm. The US partner put it down to financial problems and to unrealistic expectations and inexperience on both sides. The outcome does confirm that JVs are often astride a relatively fine line, given the basic conflicts of interest that in many cases exist between the partners. Eaton was mainly interested in production for the Yugoslav market, and in penetration into Eastern Europe, when it undertook the venture.

The next group of products we shall cover – *telecommunication equipment, data-processing equipment* and *office machinery* – is by and large located at the 'high-technology' end of the manufacturing spectrum. We shall treat them together (although there are important distinctions between these industries) because approximately the same few firms dominate production in each – Iskra, Ei-Nis, RIZ, Nikola-Tesla, Rudi Cajavec and UNIS.

Production of telephone and telegraph switching equipment and exchanges began in the early 1950s with Tesla producing under LM Ericsson (Sweden) licence and Iskra under licence to the ITT subsidiary Standard (WG). From that time, product range and technological level were continuously upgraded, through a combination of in-house research and development and licensing arrrangements. In addition, new producers including RIZ with Telettra (Italy), Siemens (WG), and

Ericsson (Sweden) technology; Rudi Cajavec with Marconi (Italy) technology; and Ei-Nis with Siemens (WG) and Hasler (Switzerland) technology entered the field, producing a variety of telephone and telegraph, radio relay and microwave telecommunications equipment.

With the growth of the electronics components industry during the 1960s, Yugoslav producers (using licences from Rockwell, Philips, GE, RCA, Murata, Teledyne, Siemens, Texas Instruments, AMI, Toshiba and others) expanded production rapidly, and these components were increasingly incorporated into locally-produced communications equipment. Indeed, in the early 1970s both Tesla and Iskra entered production of semi-electronic and electronic telephone exchanges, and were not far behind the leading international firms in doing so. In 1972 Iskra concluded a JV and licensing agreement with BTM (Belgium), a Bell Telephone subsidiary, to develop production in this field. Tesla's development has been in co-operation with LM Ericsson. Most recently, in 1980 Ei-Nis concluded a JV contract with GTE (US) for the production of digital computer-controlled PABX telephone switching systems.

Iskra has begun production of minicomputers under an LA with Control Data Corporation (US) entered in 1977, and does some subcontracting production within this agreement. Ei-Nis also entered this field, producing electronic calculators and other electronic data-processing equipment under LAs concluded with the Honeywell subsidiary in West Germany, Kienzle. In 1979 Ei-Nis and Honeywell (US) entered a JV for the production of minicomputers, word processors and termimals. Iskra and Ei-Nis also produce electronic teleprinters and facsimile equipment, the former under a 1970 LA with International Scanatron Systems (US), the latter under a 1975 LA with Sagem (France). Electronic calculators are produced by a number of enterprises, including Ei-Nis and Digitron in co-operation with Rockwell (US), and UNIS in a licensing and production co-operation arrangement with Olympia Werke (WG).

In fact, through a variety of agreements UNIS has become extremely closely connected with Olympia, and is now a major producer of business and office machinery. In 1971 it began production of portable typewriters under an LA with Olympia. The agreement was basically a subcontracting arrangement with Olympia technology; UNIS contracted to deliver 200,000 of its annual 220,000 output to the West German firm. In 1974, it began producing cash registers under licence to NCR (US); the arrangement included a co-operation-exchange programme. In 1976, it began production of calculators and other electronic data-processing equipment within an ICA with Olympia; in 1978 it concluded an ICA with the same firm in the production of photocopy equipment, under which UNIS was to deliver 5,000 of its 6,000 annual production. In fact, in 1980 production was expected to be 8,000, with 6,400 exported to Olympia. In 1977 it also concluded an ICA with L.M. Ericsson (Sweden) for the construction of high frequency telecommunication transmission equipment, which took the firm further into the electronics/telecommunications field.

This is in no way a complete picture of developments on the technology-contracting/production-co-operation side; however, let us at this point turn to the trade data in Table 7.7. The Soviet Union is far and away the largest market for most products in these fields; significant exports in some cases are made also to Eastern European and Third World countries. Not surprisingly, little impact has been made on Western markets, as yet, except within standard office equipment lines under the co-operation agreements mentioned above. Clearly, Yugoslav success has been, to now, in the telecommunications field; however, there are signs of increasing success in the office machinery line, within the ICAs and JVs discussed above.

Finally, we come to two different metal products in which JV activity has been prominent. We consider first *ball, roller, needle and sliding bearings*, which are actually normally classified within the non-electrical machinery branch. These are 'high technology' products which have stringent specification and quality control standards. In Yugoslavia, domestic production is largely covered by three firms — UTL, IKL, and ILK. *Ball and roller* bearing production is dominated by the former two firms, both producing since the mid-1960s, under licence and co-operation agreements concluded with SKF of Sweden, a major international firm in the industry. (UTL entered an LA in 1965, and ICA in 1967; IKL's initial agreement was in 1964.) The agreements covered technical assistance, including quality control, and envisaged some co-operation in export to cover part of the foreign exchange requirement of production. In the subsequent years, important new agreements were concluded: in 1969 a JV contract in ball-bearing production was reached between UTL and SKF (with new agreements for capacity expansions negotiated in 1975 and 1978), and in 1971 a JV in roller-bearings was concluded between IKL and SKF. SKF has made strong efforts to rationalize local production by narrowing product lines and increasing specialization between the three firms. Its emphasis is distinctly on supplying the rapidly expanding domestic market, though it has agreed to assist in exporting, under SKF

Table 7.7: Yugoslav Exports of Telecommunications Equipment and Office and Business Machinery (millions dinars)

	1966	1969	1972	1975	1978	1979
Teleprinters						
Total	—	—	—	0.6	13.8	8.1
USSR	—	—	—	0.6	8.8	7.9
Telegraph & telephone apparatus; telegraph & telephone exchanges; parts						
Total	75.1	57.1	220.8	461.6	696.7	659.7
USSR	57.3	40.2	148.0	271.5	518.2	601.9
Radio, TV, other transmission equip. & parts						
Total	27.2	2.0	55.9	101.1	216.4	237.1
Typewriters & parts						
Total	0.5	0.6	56.3	93.1	166.0	216.7
WG	—	—	53.8	89.7	150.6	174.2
Electric calculating machines						
Total		5.9	0.2	0.6	65.5	101.6
Cash registers						
Total	—	—	—	13.8	14.4	5.6
WG	—	—	—	12.1	11.2	5.3
Electronic data-processing equipment	—	—	—	—	2.5	2.2
Office machinery parts	0.4	—	0.4	6.2	4.1	5.6

Source: *Foreign Trade Statistics*, SFRJ.

trade-names, whatever is needed to cover foreign exchange obligations incurred by the joint ventures. In the field of *sliding bearings* and similar elements, ILK had for some time produced under licence of Trione, an Italian firm; in 1976 it entered a new licensing agreement with Clyco, a Western German firm, in order to undertake a major capacity expansion. In 1978 a British firm, Galcyer, signed ICA and JV agreements with a group of local producers, including Slobodan Penezic and Privi Partizan, two domestic machinery producers.

Finally, we come to our last example, *razor blades*. In 1961, polymer-coated stainless steel blades made their appearance on international markets. The single domestic blade producer in Yugoslavia produced carbon steel blades only, and following the trade liberalization accompanying the mid-1960s reforms it encountered great difficulty in maintaining its market share. In 1968 it concluded a licensing agreement with Perma Sharp to acquire the new technology, but its financial difficulties continued. In 1973 Gillette, the major blade importer (with 80 per cent of imports in the early 1970s) came under pressure from local sources to offer technical assistance to the domestic firm; but Gillette resisted any licensing arrangement. Some months later, however, it agreed to a joint venture − with 20 per cent equity participation − once it became clear that its existing market would be threatened by another refusal to co-operate. The joint venture agreement was registered in 1973. In fact Gillette, traditionally interested only in wholly-owned subsidiaries, had been forced in other countries as well to establish minority joint ventures in order to preserve markets threatened by pressures to import substitution. In Iran, for example, a 49 per cent equity venture was established at about the same time.

In the Yugoslav venture, Gillette's initial contribution was to introduce the Gillette polymer coating technology in place of that of Perma Sharp, and to add reconditioned Gillette packaging machinery to the production line. In the field, however, product technology was evolving rapidly − 'platinum plus' blades were commercialized in 1969, and twin blades a few years later. It took until 1977 before 'platinum plus' blades were introduced into the JV's production programme; and as of 1977, no plans existed for local production of twin blades. The joint venture faced no internal competition; and Gillette's exports of the new products maintained a dominant position in Yugoslav imports. Gillette entered the venture for two reasons: to protect an existing market, and if possible, to establish a base for penetration into Eastern European and some LDC markets, countries with which Yugoslavia had close relations. With respect to the first, it does appear that Gillette's local production has given it a dominant position within the domestic market: after some intense import competition in the first years of the venture, imports have been limited under the domestic import control regimes, and by expansion of domestic production, and most of the imported product is of Gillette manufacture. With respect to the second, it seems clear from the data below that the venture has met with only limited export success: a small but regular market exists in the USSR (under MEM, not Gillette trade-name), and some exports to Western Europe have been undertaken under special arrangement. Other exports are largely to Eastern Europe and the Middle East. The razor-blades case does, however, remind us that the presence of a well-known MNE within a JV arrangement need not always represent the integration of the affiliate into the corporate 'matrix'. Gillette appears to have shown substantial caution in product-technology transfers *and* trade where the Yugoslav venture is involved.

Yugoslav Trade (mills. dinars)

	1966	1969	1972	1973	1974	1975	1976	1977	1978	1979
Exports										
Total	–	2.2	4.7	7.8	16.8	18.4	18.7	10.7	14.8	14.4
W. Europe	–	–	–	1.1	10.9	–	11.4	–	4.3	–
USSR	–	–	3.4	–	–	11.2	7.0	7.4	7.4	9.0
Imports										
Total	36.8	34.3	21.2	52.6	44.8	18.6	8.4	43.7	16.1	2.3

Conclusion

It is not an easy task to 'pull together' the type of analysis that has been undertaken in this chapter. However in the conclusion we shall attempt to summarize what appear to be the most important findings.

The basic premise of the chapter is that 'market imperfections' and 'market failures' are important phenomena in international economics, affecting technology transfer, international production specialization, and trade in finalized manufactured goods. The MNE, in turn, is seen as an institution which exploits these market imperfections, substituting 'internal organization' for flawed (horizontal and vertical) external markets – as Dunning (1974), Helleiner (1975) and others have pointed out. In a sense, the Yugoslavs have accepted the implications of this model, and have increasingly sought to integrate domestic enterprises into the technology transfer/production specialization/trade activities of MNEs. Yet this 'integration' is in no way intended to be 'complete'; it has been restricted to intermediary forms, such as ICAs and JVs. Nevertheless, the Yugoslavs have held high expectations concerning the technology transfer, co-production and export possibilities of these types of arrangements.

The chapter has considered, within this framework two key aspects of Yugoslavia's participation in the international transfer of technology and in international trade in manufactured goods. On one side, we have discussed production co-operation and joint-venture activity from the foreign firms' perspective – in particular, the extent to which such arrangements appear as a form of quasi-internalization when the wholly-owned or majority-owned subsidiary is rendered infeasible by host country legislation. On the other hand, we have also been concerned with outcomes explicitly in terms of Yugoslav objectives and expectations.

With respect to the first, a few key points should be made. *First*, Western European enterprises *have* been widely involved in significant *production co-operation arrangements* with Yugoslav enterprises, both within ICAs and JVs. For US corporations, the situation has been different, with the General Motors and Goodrich joint ventures recent, and perhaps quite significant, exceptions (with respect to possible future trends). Nevertheless, in most instances these arrangements appear to be motivated primarily by concerns over market positions within Yugoslavia (which, of course, one would expect). Equipment suppliers for example, sometimes agree to equity participation in order to obtain an advantage over competitors in machinery supply. And firms often accept joint ventures and co-production in order to preserve or expand threatened markets; the export activities frequently simply reflect the increasing local pressures in this direction, and are often limited to the necessary 'minimum' level. Nevertheless, there are notable examples of an important subcontracting or sourcing role for some Yugoslav firms. The UNIS programme with Olivetti; the Zastava production of Fiat autos and, recently, vans; the production of small SDP tractors by Pobeda; are all examples of arrangements which have enabled the European firm to phase out its own production of items that have become superseded in its production programme. The Ciba-Geigy JV in the production of pharmaceuticals, raw materials is one case of an almost exclusively export-oriented venture. Yet reports suggest that this raw material supply is at highly favourable prices to the Swiss concern, and that the same is true of other export-oriented arrangements. Of course, it may well be true in the auto industry as well, where subcontracting and co-production have become most extensively developed. Yet such price discounts are common practice, and can probably be justified in terms of the valuable 'learning' which initial penetration into these types of markets involves. Of course, the stronger Yugoslav pressures on exports become, the more outcomes can become inefficient; and also, the more will foreign firms adjust through pricing practices — or withdrawal from the activities altogether.

Secondly, the number of cases of leading MNEs entering JVs to exploit sophisticated, advanced, valuable proprietary technology is sufficiently numerous that it appears that all but a small minority will eventually accept such restrictions on equity — provided, of course, the stakes, in terms of local market size, are high enough. This, we suggest, does not mean the sacrifice of effective control: rather, it implies that JV arrangements can incorporate the essential elements of internalized relationships between the parties.

With respect to outcomes, there do appear to be grounds for considerable optimism, at least in the medium to long term. In the recent past, a combination of an overvalued dinar, sluggish European markets, strong domestic inflation, and increasing pressure on foreign firms, has created problems of significant magnitude for industrial co-operation and JV arrangements. Foreign firms have been discouraged by the counter-trade pressures, and also by new regulations which, in line with other 'third world' technology transfer laws, prohibit the registration of contracts which contain restrictions on exports to third markets (unless this foreign firm has its own or has licensed facilities, in that market). Yet the cases of highly successful enterprise development — originating generally with licensed technology, and growing into increasingly closer and more complex ties with foreign firms — are now far from trivial, in terms of both number and impact.

Notes

This is a revised version of a paper prepared for a session on Empirical Analysis of the MNE at the Eastern Economics Association Convention, Montreal, March 1980. The initial research was undertaken for my doctoral dissertation 'The Transfer of Technology to Developing Countries and the Role of the Foreign Corporation: A Comparison of Yugoslavia and Mexico' (unpublished, Berkeley, 1979). I am grateful for the assistance of my supervisor, Benjamin Ward, and to the Institute of International Studies, Berkeley, for financial support.

1. Growth of per capital real GNP was 4.71% per annum during the period 1950–75 and 5.61% per annum during 1960–77, in each case lying just within the

top decile of all market economies, according to data provided in Morawetz (1977), Table A1, and World Bank (1979), Table 1. The only countries to out perform Yugoslavia in either period were the East and Southeast Asian group, including Japan, Taiwan, Korea, Hong Kong and Singapore; some of the other Southern European countries, including Greece, Spain and Portugal; and some Middle Eastern countries. Yugoslavia's exports of manufactured goods in 1976 ranked fifth amongst the low and middle income country groups in World Bank (1979), Table 12.

Total Manufactured Exports ($ US mill.)

	1963	1976
Hong Kong	617	7,822
Taiwan	129	6,922
Korea	39	6,770
Spain	227	6,025
Yugoslavia	468	3,395
Singapore	352	3,020

It should be pointed out that the rate of expansion of exports of Yugoslav *manufactured* goods slowed considerably during the 1970s, and Yugoslavia's rapidly expanding trade deficit has been the cause of great concern in recent years, leading to a major devaluation in mid-1980. The rate of growth of *total* Yugoslav *merchandise* exports in real terms has fallen from 9.8% p.a. in 1961–5, to 5.8% p.a. in 1966–70, 4.9% in 1971–5, and 4.5% in 1976–80. In 1961–5, the export-import ratio on *merchandise account* was 0.74; in 1976–80 it was 0.57. Yugoslavia's share of total world merchandise exports actually fell from 0.55% in 1966–70 to 0.44% in 1980 (*Ekonomska Politika*, 2 Feb. 1981).

2. The following table shows the changing structure of Yugoslavia's exports of manufactured goods (SITC 5–8 less 68) to developed market economies; it is taken from Cory (1979), Ch. 7, where details of the data anlysis are provided. It is noteworthy that regular structural shifts in Yugoslavia's exports occurred with respect to 'technology-intensity', but not with respect to simple factor-intensity. This suggests that technology and skills *are* more important for the countries dynamic comparative advantage.

Percentage Composition of Yugoslav Exports to Developed Market Economies, By Industry Characteristic

	Industry capital-intensity				Industry research-intensity			
	High capital inten- sive	Medium capital inten- sive	Medium labour inten- sive	High labour inten- sive	Highest	High	Medium	Low
1962	9.15	19.20	23.46	41.19	0.46	3.11	18.85	77.57
1965	14.42	13.37	26.94	47.28	2.30	6.01	17.88	73.81
1970	11.44	10.58	26.49	51.55	0.84	7.51	29.23	62.43
1975	8.91	17.99	26.24	46.84	2.40	10.73	32.45	54.43

3. Analyses of joint ventures in Yugoslavia include Sukijasovic (1973), Pavecevic (1973), Illic (1976), Dragomanovic (1978), Chittle (1975), OECD (1974), Lamers (1976), Holt (1973), McMillan and St Charles (1973), Sukijasovic (1982), among others.

4. In Yugoslavia, legislation has in the past been quite specific on what can be

designated 'co-operation' in order for participants to obtain benefits under the relevant legislation. Compensating payments and subcontracting have not always fitted comfortably within the narrow confines of relevant laws.

5. It is very difficult to present precise aggregate or annual figures because of (i) the lack of official data; (ii) the number of cancelled and short-lived agreements; (iii) the amount of double-counting (since the addition of new partners to an existing venture, or extension or expansion of an existing venture, generally requires renegotiation and reregistration procedures); and (iv) inconsistencies in published data. *Ekonomska Politika*, for instance, reported 'official data' showing 206 contracts between 1968–79 in the edition of 29 September 1980; a research group's total of 195 contracts between 1968–79 was published in the 6 October 1980 edition. The edition of 21 September 1981 reported that 8 contracts had been concluded in 1980, and presented a total of 199 for 1968–80!

6. It is suggested that 456 contracts were concluded between 1967 and mid-1976, for example. Yet registrations were, as previously indicated, running at about 40–45 p.a. in the mid-1960s, and 125–30 p.a. in the mid-1970s when registration procedures were reintroduced. The reported figure must clearly represent an extremely low estimate, especially in view of the rapid increase in licensing that undoubtedly followed the 'opening-up' of the economy with the 1965 reforms.

7. The data almost certainly reflect capital investment commitments of JVs concluded and contracted in each year, rather than the actual disbursement of funds. The ensuing comparisons between the 1968–75 and 1976–80 periods would, of course, make little sense if the latter *was* the base. Note also that the 35 JVs included in Table 7.2 but excluded from Table 7.3 represent a total invested capital of 2.723 billion dinars, and foreign invested capital of just 0.141 billion dinars. These figures represent roughtly \$5 million and \$0.2 million respectively per JV, so the excluded ventures clearly do not represent major foreign participation.

8. 14 JVs accounted for nearly 50% of the total JV capital of the 156 JVs surviving at the end of 1979.

9. The 52.8% figure for 'other' reflects the existence of some small discrepancies in the reported data.

10. In a recent paper, Scriven (1979) indicates that a freeze on new registrations was imposed in September 1975 and remained in effect for more than a year. This apparently followed a serious political rift between different factions of the government over policy towards large joint ventures involving US multinational corporations, such as Dow Chemicals and General Motors, and domestic enterprises. In June 1976 a new decree on foreign investment was introduced, which had a number of unfavourable elements for foreign firms. It has since been replaced by a new law, introduced in April 1978, which still contains clauses deemed unfavourable by foreign business. The issue of managerial authority has always been one of concern to the foreign partners of JVs. In interviews conducted by Holt (1973) and also by the present author, a lack of effective power to make and enforce decisions was cited as a source of irritation and concern on a number of occasions – although it appears to be the case that existence of workers' councils *per se* is not an important factor in this case.

11. The Yugoslav authorities pressure JVs to export for convertible currencies in at least the amounts necessary for the continuation of business operations and repatriation of capital and profit – although in line with informal guidelines a remarkable number announce plans for exporting roughly 30% of output. Of course, many never achieve this figure! In many cases the motivation of foreign firms has been to establish production in Yugoslavia for the domestic market,

frequently because of the insecurity of pre-existing arrangements for exporting to Yugoslavia. Not surprisingly, there is a great deal of dissatisfaction amongst western firms over the official policy. For many, their interest in JVs is inversely related to the extent of official pressure on the export side. The failure of the Yugoslav authorities to distinguish clearly between import-substituting (foreign-exchange saving) and export-promoting activities is one of the peculiarities of the system — a peculiarity which has been intensified under the new foreign trade system, under which foreign trade and exchange issues are increasingly being regionalized, at the republican and provincial level. One solution to the dilemma currently favoured by the authorities lies in encouraging greater foreign sourcing activity from JV enterprises.

12. For theoretical analyses see Brada (1977) and Robinson (1978). The break-up of the Rudi Cajavec-Eaton JV, discussed below, is a striking example.

13. The complete lising of JVs upon which Table 7.4 is based will be made available upon request to the author.

14. A relatively low JV incidence in Yugoslavia in the drugs, soaps and cosmetics industry, and a high incidence in the rubber products and pulp and paper products industries, did stand out in the comparison. The situation in the drug industry has been complicated by a 1976 decree requiring drug licensors to cede ownership rights over trade marks to the Yugoslav licensee: this may have affected JVs in the industry as well. An alternative possible explanation is that the Yugoslav authorities have rejected numerous proposals for ventures in 'supermarket' drugs already produced by domestic enterprises; one condition written into the joint venture legislation is that ventures introduce new and modern technology into the industry, technology not readily available locally. In the pulp and paper industry, there have been a number of paper and paper-board ventures designed to exploit Yugoslavia's forestry resources; most of the rubber ventures are associated with the motor vehicles industry.

15. In early 1976, for example, *Business Eastern Europe* reported that in the 140 JVs concluded up until that time, the capital contribution of the non-Yugoslav partners was valued at $200 million, of which 2/3 was capitalized technology. However, later data published in *Ekonomska Politika* (29 September 1980) give a very different picture: of the 8.25 billion (approximately $400 million) foreign capital invested in the 156 JVs still active through end 1979, just 21.2% is reported as representing capitalized property rights on technology. These two sets of numbers are clearly inconsistent.

16. Average dinar dollar exchange rates for the period covered are as follows (dinars to the $US):

1963	3.00	1971	15.17	1975	17.39
1966	12.50	1972	17.00	1976	18.19
1969	12.50	1973	16.19	1978	18.64
1970	12.50	1974	15.91	1979	19.00

For the purposes of comparison with data presented through the remainder of this paper, Yugoslavia's exports of manufacture is provided.

Exports, million dinar

Industry groups	SITC class	1963	1966	1969	1972	1973	1974	1975	1976	1977	1978
Chemicals	5	77	870	1,143	2,340	2,998	6,522	6,450	6,449	6,046	8,566
Manufactures classified by material	6	508	3,529	5,396	10,257	13,835	21,161	20,068	24,398	21,978	22,967
Transport & machinery	7	462	3,743	3,755	9,292	11,975	15,010	19,405	24,879	30,615	32,836
Misc. manufactures	8	218	1,790	2,531	5,773	6,521	7,804	9,699	13,006	13,342	14,582
Total		1,265	9,932	12,825	27,752	35,329	50,497	55,622	68,732	71,981	78,951
Total $US mill.		422	795	1,026	1,632	2,182	3,174	3,199	3,779	3,933	4,155

8 MACROECONOMIC THEORIES OF FOREIGN DIRECT INVESTMENT: AN ASSESSMENT

H. Peter Gray

Introduction

This chapter assesses the contribution provided to an understanding of the process of foreign direct investment (FDI) by theories which attribute a primary, if not an exclusive role to national as distinct from firm- or industry-level determinants. Harry G. Johnson (1972) identified as one of the major requirements of a satisfactory theory of FDI, the ability to identify the complementarity of the micro-orientation of industrial organization theory and the macro-orientation of international trade theory.[1] In terms of Dunning's eclectic theory of FDI (1979), Johnson posits ownership advantages and internalization incentives as micro-oriented and location-specific variables as macro-oriented.

This chapter reviews three macroeconomic theories: the capitalization-rate hypothesis of R.Z. Aliber (1970, 1971), the comparative-advantage theory of K. Kojima (1973, 1977) and the level-of-development approach of J.H. Dunning (1981a). These are reviewed in sequence. The fourth section addresses Johnson's assertion that the location-specific (national) variables are exclusively, or even primarily, national in scope.

The 'Capitalization Rate' Hypothesis

This hypothesis avers that:[2]

> . . . the pattern of direct foreign investment reflects that source-country firms capitalize the same stream of expected earnings at a higher rate than host-country firms. This difference in capitalization rates results because the market (the world-wide family of investors) attached different capitalization rates to income streams dominated in different currencies. Source-country firms are likely to be those in countries where the capitalization rates are high; host-country firms are those in countries where capitalization rates are low.

Relying as it does on differences in the attributes of national currencies, the capitalization-rate hypothesis is the essence of a macroeconomic theory. The difference in capitalization rates for equities and, therefore, in firms' cost of capital, derives from a premium on the rate of discount implicitly charged by investors on equities denominated in the currency which is considered to be relatively vulnerable. A weak currency with some anticipated likelihood of depreciation in the foreign-exchange market will generally incur a higher schedule of interest rates: the 'currency premium' derives from the uncertainty about exchange risk *in addition* to any perceived likelihood of depreciation. Firms located in nations with strong currencies will have equities that enjoy higher capitalization rates: the currency premium applies to rates of interest and discount in countries with weak currencies.[3]

Assuming a firm to have an ownership advantage in the form of a cost-reducing patent and that the international market for such a patent is efficient, the existence of a difference in capitalization rates will affect the price that a firm in a country with a weak currency can offer for a patent to the point that the owner of the patent, with its higher rate of capitalization, finds the patent yields a higher return when exploited through a foreign subsidiary. This gain more than offsets the inherent additional costs that derive from doing business in a foreign country. Thus, outflows of FDI will tend, *ceteris paribus*, to take place from countries with strong currencies to countries in which indigenous firms have relatively low rates of capitalization. A second assumption of the capitalization-rate hypothesis is that the equity market will capitalize the flow of earnings from the foreign subsidiary at the rate of capitalization applied to source-country revenues and not at that applied to earnings denominated in the currency of the host country.

This failure to recognize that the subsidiary's earnings are denominated in a currency which demands a currency premium does not sit well with the idea of even reasonably efficient capital markets. Such treatment of a subsidiary's earnings can be better explained by Rugman's (1979) theory of higher capitalization rates accruing to multinational corporations (MNCs) by virtue of the smaller variability of their earnings streams which, in turn, derives from the international diversification of MNCs' assets in countries with negatively correlated fluctuations in demand. But the Rugman thesis is micro-oriented in that the difference in capitalization rates accrues to a firm because of the firm's own characteristics and not from the currency of denomination of the market in which its equity is traded. Yet another (micro-oriented) cause of differences in capitalization rates is that

MNCs are large corporations with tremendous financial strength and have higher capitalization ratios than smaller firms in potential host countries (Hood and Young, 1979, p. 52).

Any decision to make an investment, new or takeover, is based on a comparison of cost with the net present value of the expected net cash flows (allowance having been made for political risk in the case of FDI). Aliber's thesis can be conceived of as identifying national (currency) characteristics as imparting a competitive edge to all firms in the country with the stronger currency. The lower rate of discount in that country affects the denominator of the net present value computation. But if a corporation in a strong-currency country can obtain financial capital more cheaply, the competitive edge may equally well be identified in the larger net flow of cash (i.e. in the numerator of the net present value computation).

The imposition of mandatory controls over FDI in the United States in 1968 would, according to the capitalization-rate hypothesis, impose a currency premium on (weaken) the US dollar and inhibit the outflow of FDI from the United States. As Table 8.1 shows, US multinationals increased their rate of investment in the European Economic Community after the imposition of controls over FDI, with the exception of 1968 when the MNCs were unfamiliar with the regulations. US multinationals increased their flows of investment in their subsidiaries and the source of most of the additional flow of funds was foreign, host-country markets with their higher rates of interest.

It is possible that the capitalization-rate hypothesis relies in mistaken causality. The capitalization-rate hypothesis prerequires the existence of ownership-specific advantages on the part of the investing firm: these serve to counter the inherent additional costs of doing business in a foreign country. When a nation is a major source of FDI, the cause may be traced to a surge of development of or to an unexploited accumulation of ownership-specific advantages, a nation blessed in this way is likely to have a dynamic, fast-growth economy with attendant buoyancy in equity markets and high capitalization rates. Certainly, this explanation could apply to the United States economy in the late 1950s and early 1960s. The surge of technology transfer will have weakened the relative strength of the US economy and, together with the formation of the EEC, provided a high growth impetus to the European economies.

The capitalization-rate hypothesis has little to offer in explanation of the pattern or mix of FDI by industry. Beyond the observation that the capital intensity of an industry will affect the importance of a

Table 8.1: Sources of Funds for Subsidiaries in the EEC, 1966-72

Year	Total $ mn	Undistributed profits $ mn	percent	External funds from the United States $ mn	percent	External funds from foreign sources[a] $ mn	percent
1966	1,107	46	4	494	44	567	52
1967	1,040	97	9	284	27	659	64
1968	1,023	159	16	87	9	777	75
1969	1,749	351	20	249	14	1,149	66
1970	2,016	195	10	414	21	1,407	65
1971	2,440	216	9	1,035	42	1,189	49
1972	2,550	488	19	590	23	1,472	58

Note: a. Depreciation is also a major source of funds to foreign subsidiaries. Depreciation was not controlled by the legislation and, therefore, represented a potential source of inter-subsidiary loans that would allay the restrictiveness of the controls. This did not seem to be of great quantitative significance. Of the sources listed, external funds from foreign resources are the uncontrolled sources.
Source: US Department of Commerce, *Survey of Current Business*, July 1975, p. 33.

currency premium (or difference in capitalization rates), there is no explanation of the pattern of FDI by industry except on micro-economic grounds — variations in the value of the firm's ownership-specific resource. Similarly, 'cross-hauling' (bilateral FDI) is explained by the retention of investments made when relative capitalization rates were different but also by the inadequacy of the market for the sale of patents (Aliber, 1970, p. 33). Simultaneous cross-hauling must indicate that the effect of any differences in capitalization rates can be swamped by ownership-specific advantages.

Different rates of capitalization may play larger roles in takeover bids than in new, green-fields ventures and differences in capitalization rates may explain why foreign firms with high capitalization rates rather than domestic firms take over a going entity. The competitive edge of the foreign firm lies in the fact that it can raise money in its home market through the sale of equity at better terms than can a firm whose equity is traded in the same market as the takeover candidate. This possibility does not imply that the low rate of capitalization of the takeover candidate makes it a cheap acquisition since the take-over bid is usually made at prices significantly above the price quoted immediately prior to the announcement of the intent. Even so, as Aliber (1970, p. 32) points out, the existence of certain complementarities not necessarily available to other host-country firms may prove decisive. An example of such a complementarity is the recent takeover of the Crocker National Bank (in San Francisco) by the Midland Bank Limited. Any US bank seeking to take over Crocker National would be forced to run the gauntlet of the Board of Governors of the Federal Reserve System and the Anti-Trust Division of the Department of Justice. Midland also had the important benefit from the acquisition of a substantial deposit base in an important world currency and access to the discount window of the Federal Reserve System. Both of these aspects of the takeover would be of significant importance to Midland (Gray and Gray, 1981), but of negligible benefit to US banks.

In fact, Aliber overstates his case for takeovers by arguing (1971) that the monopolistically-competitive theory of Hymer and Kindleberger cannot explain takeovers. A takeover may be preferable to a green-fields venture on several grounds unconnected with differences in capitalization rates. The most important of these is the acquisition of a marketing-distribution organization and an established share of the host-country market. In this way the high fixed costs associated with market development are reduced. The barrier-to-entry of the costs of establishing a product in a new market is the essence of the Hymer-Kindleberger approach to market imperfections.

It is worth noting here that the capitalization-rate hypothesis, despite its frequent references to interest rate differences, can only apply to equity financing in the context of international investment. A corporation whose equity is marketed in a country with a strong currency will have an advantage in the cost of equity capital. It is unlikely to have an equal (or any) advantage in debt since any corporation of the magnitude needed to effect a takeover may reasonably be expected to be able to borrow in international markets (in a strong-currency country). The advantage of having equity denominated in a strong currency is, then, a function of the marginal debt/equity ratio.

It is also possible that Aliber's causality may be reversed so that direct investment funds will flow from the weak-currency to the strong-currency country. If equity is internally financed through retained earnings, the corporation will seek investment (assets) in a country with a higher capitalization rate than is available domestically. If it can borrow in international markets at competitive terms, the corporation may establish a green-fields venture in the strong-currency country. There is no assurance that flows of retained profits will necessarily be smaller in weak-currency countries. This possibility suggests that it would be possible to determine the effects of different capitalization rates primarily through the mix of green-fields or takeover investments in the two directions — takeover investments being more likely on balance to flow from strong-currency to weak-currency countries and vice versa.

The Comparative-advantage Theory[4]

Comparative advantage depends upon *national* resource endowments and determines the pattern of international trade. It is, therefore, essentially macroeconomic in scope. In fact, the comparative-advantage theory of FDI of Professor Kiyoshi Kojima takes place in response to evolutionary changes in dynamic comparative advantage as relative factor endowments in nations change through time. This mechanism to generate FDI is contrasted with the kind generated by monopolistic or oligopolistic attributes of corporations. Much of Kojima's theorizing is devoted to a Pigovian welfare analysis of the relative social benefits of the two kinds of FDI. Macroeconomic FDI is found to be immeasurably superior.

These two mechanisms to bring about FDI are members of a group of five but the other three receive only cursory treatment. These are: natural resource orientation; internalization advantages; and market orientation induced by trade barriers. The neglect of natural resource orientation is somewhat surprising since it is also fundamentally macroeconomic and generates very large comparative advantage in certain primary products. Instead the emphasis is on the distinction between (macroeconomic) FDI undertaken to facilitate the transfer of production from high-wage to low-wage countries as comparative advantage changes (so-called labour orientation) and (microeconomic)FDI undertaken to exploit oligopolistic factor and product markets. The superiority of macroeconomic FDI derives from its trade-creating effect while microeconomic FDI is seen as trade-supplanting. The frame of reference is limited to manufacturing FDI in developing nations by corporations based in developed nations.

The narrow emphasis on rich/poor or North/South flows of investment is unfortunate as is the simple identification of macroeconomic FDI with trade creation and of microeconomic FDI with trade supplanting. Within the limits of Kojima's analysis, the welfare criterion that trade-creating FDI is superior to trade-supplanting FDI is probably valid.[5] But the approach is so narrow that it inevitably presents a much stronger case for the comparative advantage theory than can be justified.

Part and parcel of the narrow North/South emphasis is the reliance upon a deceptively simple theory of international trade which is deemed to exist almost exclusively because of differences in the relative endowments of capital and labour in the source- and host-countries (Kojima, 1973). Acceptance of the two-factor model of international trade embellished by differences in technological availability can be traced to an earlier article (Kojima, 1970) claiming to substantiate the capital/labour version of the factor-properties theory for manufactured exports of six nations. Here the labour-intensity of exports of manufactured goods was shown to relate to differences in the gross domestic product per capita of the individual nations. This test attributed differences in the relative costs of capital and labour in the exporting nations uniquely to differences in per capita GDP on the grounds that capital is internationally mobile and, therefore, has the same cost in each country. By testing the pattern of exports against the measure for the cost of labour, the article puts all inputs other than labour into a composite input.[6] In the process, the study neglects the contributions to the pattern of trade of those variables which have been used to resolve the infamous Leontief Paradox. The analysis neglects the contributions to the pattern of trade of proprietary technology, skilled labour, cultural distinctions and of the general level of non-proprietary technology embodied in the different economies.[7] In effect, the study tests the validity of a Ricardian or labour-productivity theory of international trade in which all inputs other than labour are contained in the engineering relationship specified by the production functions instead of being attributed to the availability or cost of the individual co-operating factors.

It is impossible to disentangle the theoretical implications of the two contrasting mechanisms by which FDI is generated from the welfare analysis to which the distinction is applied. The explanatory value of the comparative-advantage theory of FDI must, therefore, be considered in the context of the welfare analysis. First, the essentials of the welfare analysis are summarised and the comparative-advantage theory is then assessed from three different standpoints:

(i)   the impact of historical time on nations' abilities to effect FDI by means of the comparative-advantage mechanism;
(ii) the possible existence of multiple blocs among which FDI may take place instead of the simple North/South framework;
(iii) the potential value to developing host-countries of high-technology FDI.

The superiority of comparative-advantage FDI over microeconomic

FDI derives from the fact that the former leads to increased international trade from the developing to the developed bloc while the latter reduces the volume of trade. An exact relationship between trade volume and welfare is assumed. The argument relies upon a dynamic condition in which labour becomes progressively relatively more costly in the developed world. This follows from pro-trade biased or neutral economic growth in both blocs involving greater rates of capital formation in the developed world. In consequence, certain products change from having their location of comparative advantage in the developed world to having it in the developing world. This is the 'wild geese flying' analogy of Professor Kaname Akamatsu (1962), which entertains the concept of a ranking of goods by comparative advantage in which the lines of separation of potential exports to non-traded goods and of non-traded goods to potential imports shift as the cost of labour increases. By recognizing the changed circumstances in international trade and accommodating them by the transfer to the new location of comparative advantage a bundle of managerial skills, technology and capital through FDI, the inherent efficiency of the industry in the host country is increased just as the industry changes its role in international trade. Global welfare is promoted and the process of adjustment in both countries is facilitated as internationally mobile inputs relocate to combine with immobile factors of production. Microeconomic FDI supplants international trade by creating, in developing hosts, industries which are at the top of the ranking (i.e. those in which the source-country's comparative advantage is the greatest). These industries transfer technology which is inappropriate to the host's resource endowment and create enclaves of modernity from which negligible spread effects emanate.

(i) One of the complaints of Kojima with respect to the pattern of investment of US multinationals (MNCs) is that their FDI is predominantly attributable to microeconomic phenomena. Rather, US MNCs should invest abroad in traditional industries such as steel, textiles and shipbuilding because FDI in these industries would be trade-creating. Instead these industries languish behind tariff protection in the United States and no FDI takes place because such FDI would not 'generate any monopolistic or oligopolistic advantages or gains' (Kojima, 1977, pp. 5-6). This pattern of FDI is in sharp contrast to that of Japanese firms which transfer technology in standardized goods at the centre or dividing line of the ranking of goods by comparative advantage.

There are two problems with this distinction. First, the introduction of the potential for monopolistic gains as a factor in the determination of FDI induced by comparative advantage reduces the macroeconomic quality of the theory. Second, the distinction fails to recognize the 'newness' of international production. The growth of manufacturing MNCs in the modern concept, in which production and marketing decisions are made on a global basis, dates from the late 1950s. At this time innovations in communications and managerial techniques transformed the ability of corporations to integrate the operations of geographically-distant production and marketing subsidiaries with those of source-country units.

At the time that the US standardized industries had a technological lead and/or a comparative advantage, the time of the multinational manufacturing corporation had not arrived. Japan is the first nation to undergo the transformation from labour surplus to labour shortage in the era of multinationals. Japan is, therefore, the first nation that is likely to have been able to conduct FDI according to the theory of dynamic comparative advantage on a large scale.

It is also possible that any comparative advantage which US standardized industries enjoyed in the 1930s and 1940s derived primarily from sheer economies of scale as much as, if not more than, industry-specific proprietary technology. Advantages derived from scale economies cannot generate the gains which Kojima attributes to macroeconomic, labour-oriented FDI. Moreover, of the four industries cited (Kojima, 1973, p. 14), three (steel, shipbuilding and cotton growing) are not likely to result in successful FDI if only because the first two are defence-related and FDI in agriculture involves the alienation of agricultural land from host-country citizens and this quickly becomes an emotional issue.

(ii) If the comparative-advantage theory of FDI is to have a broader framework, it must encompass FDI within the developed bloc as well as FDI between the two blocs of North and South.

When FDI takes place between two developed countries, the cause may be the erection of a tariff barrier by the host nation which has a comparative advantage in the production of the good *in terms of the immobile factors of production*. The use of protectionism to induce FDI is well established. Any such FDI is inherently inefficient in terms of global welfare in static terms and can only be justified by resort to growth and employment considerations.

When FDI takes place because the good can be produced more

cheaply than it can be imported as a result of the transfer of proprietary know-how, skilled workers and possible, venture capital, then the act is efficient in terms of global welfare. The inducement to invest is a qualified version of comparative advantage but in the somewhat restricted sense of having some factors of production recognized as potentially internationally mobile and under the control of a corporation. The concept of the ranking of goods by comparative advantage needs to be restructured: the ranking must be computed in terms of the mobility of certain factors and must recognize the different abilities of different countries to combine the mobile factors of production with their own immobile factors. In other words, FDI involving micro-economic variables such as proprietary knowledge may be efficient in the sense that it obeys the criterion of comparative advantage and the proprietary technology is easily assimilated into the host economy. This kind of FDI supplants unproductive trade and is potentially creative of productive trade — it supplants exports from the source to the potential host and creates the possibility of exports from the host to the source country. Such FDI is the essence of the product cycle.[8] The change in comparative advantage comes about through the evolution of the product from 'new' to 'standardized' rather than through evolutionary changes in relative endowments of factors of production.

What Kojima has captured in his comparative-advantage theory of FDI is *the transfer of technology* that promotes the adjustment process to changed conditions of international competitiveness and that is most suitable for *absorption by the host country*. Such technological transfers are equally feasible among developed nations when the technology comprises proprietary know-how. This suggests that the efficiency criterion depends as strongly on the ease of assimilation of the transferred technology as upon the effects upon foreign trade.

(iii) The contention that the production of high-technology goods by MNCs in developing countries is inefficient, neglects an important constraint. Developing countries (with the exception of important oil-exporters) labour under a chronic shortage of foreign exchange. This shortage may be caused by a price-inelastic foreign demand for the country's goods after some point is reached so that there is a maximum amount of foreign exchange that the country can earn. If unconstrained import demand (at that rate of exchange or terms of trade) is price-inelastic and excessive, the developing country is forced to limit imports by some non-price mechanism. This may be through the imposition of prohibitive limits on certain kinds of goods deemed non-essential, by planning or by foreign-exchange controls. If the high-technology good would not be imported under these conditions or imported only for highly intra-marginal uses, then the amount of international trade destroyed by microeconomic FDI may be zero or negligible.

Under such circumstances, FDI may enable the country to have available a larger volume of the high-technology good. By having it produced domestically by an MNC, the foreign exchange costs of the good may be substantially reduced so that use of the good can be increased – presumably with desirable effect.

The Level of Development Approach

Dunning's level of development approach is an attempt to validate some aspects of the eclectic theory of international production and therefore explicitly countenances the existence of (microeconomic) ownership-specific advantages and internalization incentives as well as macro-economic variables. However, any study which attempts to explain the net outward investment position of different countries by virtue of per capita GNP must be considered a macroeconomic theory of FDI.

Plotting the net outward investment position (NOI) against per capita GNP produces a quite well-defined J-curve whereby countries' NOI tends to decrease from zero as per capita income increases from abject poverty (Figure 8.1). Negative NOI obtains a maximum value at about $1,500.[9] Countries with incomes ranging from $2,000 to $4,750 show a steadily declining negative NOI and constitute Dunning's third stage of development. Finally, six countries with incomes ranging from $2,600 to $5,600 have positive and sharply increasing NOI. There is an overlap in the income ranges of groups 3 and 4. Dunning is able to improve his 'fit' by separating resource-based economies from industrial nations – the former having consistently higher rates of net investment inflow (negative NOI) at given levels of income.

While the use of an income measure is macroeconomic, it is the changing balance of ownership, internalization and location-specific advantages which is recognized as being identified by the income variable. In turn, it is the balance among these genera of factors in the eclectic theory that will affect the propensity of the country to be a net outward or a net inward investor. Poor nations have no corpora-tions with ownership-specific advantages, nor do they constitute a very attractive host country for FDI. Improvements in the economy of nations in the second stage (income between $400 and $1,500) make

Figure 8.1: Illustration of Relationship between Direct Investment Flows and Income Levels (investment 1967-1975, annual average)

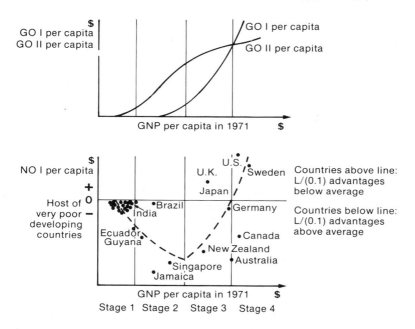

This diagram is presented for illustrative purposes only, it is not drawn to scale, nor is the line statistically estimated

the countries attractive places in which to invest but no outward investment takes place. In Stage 3, NOI starts to increase although it remains negative: some corporations have ownership-specific advantages and begin FDI while the country may seek to attack investment in those sectors in which its own firms are relatively weak but its location-specific advantages are strong. Stage 4 identifies countries with positive NOI and therefore with strong ownership advantages in its corporations but this stage does not necessarily reflect weak location-specific advantages since gross inward investment per capita increases steadily as income increases (see Table 8.2).

Dunning's paper sheds some very interesting light on the investment patterns of different nations. Even so, its weakness is one that derives inevitably from the macroeconomic or aggregative nature of the approach and from the use of net investment flows as the dependent

Table 8.2: Direct Investment Flows Per Capita 1967–75 by GNP Per Capita of Country

GNP per capita (1971)	Investment (annual average) per capita ($) Weighted average[a] 1967–75		
	Outward	Inward	Net outward
1 – over $4,000	33.0	16.3	16.7
2 – $2,500 to $4,000	20.0	15.7	4.3
3 – $1,000 to $2,500	3.2	12.9	– 9.7
4 – $500 to $1,000	0.4	8.6	– 8.2
5 – $400 to $500	0.2	7.4	– 7.2
6 – $300 to $400	0.2	3.2	– 3.0
7 – $125 to $300	0	3.1	– 3.1
8 – less than $125	0	0.5	– 0.5

a. Weighted average – obtained by summing outward/inward/net outward investment flows from the x countries in the group and dividing by the population of the x countries. This gives a country with a large population a dominating influence on the result for an income group, e.g. USA in over $4,000 group. (GNP per capita data from UN *Statistical Year Book*.)
Source: Dunning (1981a), Table 3.

variable. The level-of-development approach is predestined to ignore the very important component of intra-group FDI. Dunning's own data (1980) indicate the quantitative significance of this flow. The six countries with positive NOI (Finland, Japan, the Netherlands, Sweden, the United Kingdom and the United States) averaged (unweighted) a per capita inflow of $19.3 (when Japan is excluded the unweighted average increases to $22.8). Out of 56 countries in the sample, only 24 had per capita inward investment in excess of $9.00 and of these four had positive NOI. With the exception of Brazil, all of the countries with absolutely large inflows are rich countries. Those with inflows in excess of $500 million per anuum were: Australia, Belgium, Brazil, Canada, France, Italy, the Netherlands, the United Kingdom, the United States and West Germany. Between them these ten nations accounted for 76.4 per cent of the total inflow of investment and 88.3 of the total outflow.[10]

Dunning (1981a) does refine the analysis by identifying (macro-economic) measures which may reflect the three genera of determinants. What is interesting in these results in the present context is the importance of natural resource endowments and the ratio of national resource endowments to human capital as statistically significant explanatory variables.

Macroeconomic analyses of this kind, like Kojima's, can catch only certain types of FDI: in resources, investment induced by barriers to trade in host countries and investments due to large or evolving disparities in comparative advantage. The problem with concentrating on net investment flows is analogous to that of explaining the pattern of international trade using the simple, two-factor version of the factor-proportions theory. This theory simply does not account for the very high proportion of world trade that takes place among the fourteen industrialized nations. This proportion was better than 50 per cent by value in 1971. The extreme example was Belgium which, in 1971, conducted 86.3 per cent of its total international trade with other industrialized nations (not, of course restricted to trade in manufactures) (IMF, 1976). To account for the inordinately high volume of trade that takes place among industrial nations, trade in differentiated goods and trade in closely-related products must be explained. Trade in what is statistically the same industry takes place among countries with similar cost structures and resource endowments because of firm-specific traits either on the demand side for differentiated goods or on the supply side for closely related products (Gray, 1980). It is arguable that the intra-group pattern of FDI has similar traits and that, within the bloc of rich manufacturing countries, location-specific advantages and *disadvantages* are so small that impediments to international trade can create impressive amounts of FDI. The characteristics of trade among industrial nations are that cost structures are very similar and competitiveness in any product is likely to be much more a function of firm-specific characteristics than of differences in resource endowments.[11] Foreign direct investment among the group of developed, manufacturing nations also responds to similar, non-national determinants.

The Macroeconomic Quality of Location-specific Variables

A macroeconomic approach contributes to the theory of FDI only if the location-specific variables are national or macroeconomic in scope. Johnson's requirement for a satisfactory theory of FDI relies fundamentally on this point.[12]

Clearly, national characteristics must have some influence upon FDI. The relocation of labour-intensive production from rich, labour-short countries to poor, labour-plentiful countries under the auspices of MNCs is a clear example of FDI responding to macroeconomic forces. The development of natural resources by MNCs from rich countries is also macroeconomic. But the question is whether or not this facet of the theory of FDI is of sufficient importance to warrant an approach to the theory from the macroeconomic standpoint. To answer it in the most straightforward way requires an examination of the micro- and macroeconomic dimensions of the location-specific variables and to use the results to assess the contribution of the three models reviewed in the preceding sections.

The creation of a foreign subsidiary requires the joint use of internationally mobile factors of production controlled by the MNE with immobile, co-operationg factors in the host country. Only if the host-country factors are sufficiently cheap relative to their source-country equivalents will FDI take place in a free-trade world. The sets of factor prices in the source and host countries are determined by macroeconomic forces including national resource endowments and tastes and the patterns of international trade (given absolute price levels in each currency and a market-clearing rate of exchange). This traditional version of international trade theory can usefully be extended to include product-specific national resources which are not necessarily available in both (or all) countries. Similarly, quantitative differences in factors of production can be introduced into trade theory provided known differences in their productivity allow different factors to be reconciled into equivalencies.[13] All of these forces are macroeconomic and clearly they affect those investments which rely on wide disparities in the prices of immobile factors of production. These are likely to be found in the costs of low-skilled labour and the costs of availability of natural resources (mineral deposits for extractive industries and climate for tourism).

Given that these forces are macroeconomic, a model based on macroeconomic variables will clearly be able to explain a great deal of FDI. (Where efficient arm's-length markets exist, the investment will also need recourse to economies of vertical integration.) Any repercussions from FDI on the relative costs of inputs as a result of induced flows of trade and payments will diminish the factor-cost differences that give rise to FDI in the first instance (Gray, 1982).

There is one type of FDI which is labour-oriented (in Kojima's use of the term) and which deserves special attention if only because one acknowledged expert forsees it becoming as dominant in the last quarter of the twentieth century as the multinational corporation has become in the third quarter (Drucker, 1977). This is (international) production sharing. Production sharing takes place when a good is manufactured or processed in more than one country.[14] Because of the internalization incentives that are inherent in having vertically-integrated processes under a single operational control, production sharing almost inevitably involves the combination of domestic and foreign production facilities of an MNC. In its original version, the concept of production sharing involved the use of domestic and foreign facilities in the manufacture of a good destined for ultimate sale and use in the home country. When the home country is developed, the foreign facility is likely to be located in a developing, labour-rich nation. Complex parts are manufactured in the rich country and are shipped to the developing country for assembly and finishing. Some parts that do not require the use of highly-skilled labour may be manufactured in the foreign country or imported there from a third (developing) country for incorporation into the final product. The MNC reduces the total costs of production of the good by utilizing the relatively cheap skilled labour and sophisticated machinery in its home country and the relatively cheap low-skilled labour in the developing nation.[15] It is also possible that the production of the complex parts involves significant economies of scale that require that their production be carried out in an advanced country where the size of the market warrants the installation of technologically-advanced machinery. Contrarily, finishing and assembly operations may not enjoy significant economies of scale. Drucker gives the example of textiles being manufactured in Europe and shipped to Morocco (and even Malaysia) for transformation into apparel and other final goods.

In practice there is no need to restrict the concept of production to a two-country process in which some parts travel the same route in both directions, and in which the complex parts are manufactured in the country of ultimate use. In principle a good can be produced in as many different countries as there are separate processes in the manufacture. Each process that uses a particular input relatively intensively can be most cheaply performed in the country in which that particular input is the cheapest. This principle is the same as that underlying David Ricardo's principle of comparative cost advantage except that Ricardo confined his argument to the production of a finished good rather than to a single and partial manufacturing process. By virtue of the high quality of their internal communications, MNCs will be aware of any cost reductions that can be effected by production sharing so that they can realize a second internalization incentive denied to arm's-length production arrangements.

Production sharing can be defined as the combining of processes which take place in more than one country and which incur more than minimal transportation costs. Differences in factor costs in different nations provide cost reductions that exceed the increased costs of transportation. Production sharing may or may not involve the shipment of inputs in both directions over the same route as in Drucker's example. The limit to the economies which can be achieved by production sharing will be determined by: (1) the degree to which economies in input costs per unit of output are available in different countries in which an MNC has (or can establish) an operating subsidiary; and (2) the degree to which the cost savings are offset by additional costs of international transportation. These additional costs of transportation must include materials handling, losses through breakage and theft in transit and the costs of insurance as well as the more obvious costs of actual transportation.

Tariffs, duties levied on imported goods, can also constitute an impediment to production sharing. Taxes paid on imports from other countries counter any gains achieved by geographic integration and specialization of production. In practice, tariffs seem likely to constitute only minor impediments to production sharing. Tariffs levied on imported complex parts can be waived when the parts are included in exported commodities. The host country can institute a system of 'drawback' whereby normal tariffs are paid when inputs are imported into the host country but these funds are reimbursed to the MNC subsidiary when the parts leave the country as components of another good. If a host country is favourably disposed towards production sharing and the existence within its boundaries of an MNC subsidiary, it may be assumed to be willing to institute drawback procedures. Production sharing will also be encouraged if any duties levied on imports into the country of ultimate sale and use are based on value added abroad rather than on the CIF value of the import. Such a procedure will encourage the MNC to include in the final good, parts manufactured in the country of final sale and use. This arrangement must, therefore, encourage the two-country version of production sharing.

Production sharing is one of the kinds of FDI which can be analysed through the use of macroeconomic models. However, while macroeconomic models will be invaluable in analysing decisions to create manufacturing subsidiaries in particular host nations, the ability to distort actual costs through transfer-pricing techniques and differences in pressures of local demand (Gray, 1978), may weaken the macroeconomic dimensions of production sharing.

The macroeconomic effects of FDI are likely to be overemphasised by the factor-price (or international trade) model. International trade theory relates pre-eminently to a world in which factors of production are homogeneous within broad categories. Further, when FDI is being undertaken, what matters is not the relative price ratios of different factor groups within a country but the combination of actual money prices of immobile factors in the host country with the opportunity costs of the mobile factors (Gray, 1982). This subtlety is likely to escape macroeconomic theories of FDI. Similarly, many forms of FDI require product-specific kinds of resources (including gradations of skills and experience in labour) in host countries. The prices of these inputs are more likely to be determined by microeconomic forces operating in segmented factor markets (Canterbery, 1979). The more technologically-intensive the actual FDI undertaken, the smaller will be the explanatory power of macroeconomic theories.

Impediments to international trade, including tariffs, non-tariff barriers and transportation costs, suffer from the same schizophrenia as relative factor costs. *Levels* of impediments to international trade have no obvious effect upon the flow of FDI. Such elements are macroeconomic involving overall national commercial policies and geographic distances. But variation in the height of impediments to trade among goods for a single nation (a microeconomic variable) is likely to exceed macroeconomic differences in the average level among nations. This distinction between the level and the structure of tariffs is a well-established concept in the theory of commercial policy. It is probable also that the variance of effective protectiveness of non-tariff barriers around their mean (or average level) within a country will exceed the variance of effective protectiveness of tariffs around their mean. Transportation costs vary widely among goods because of differences in distance covered with average and given unit costs of transportation (macroeconomic). But transportation costs also vary because of differences in the unit rates charged on different goods (microeconomic). Unit costs of land transportation are inevitably greater than their maritime equivalents. Shipments of individual items sent breakbulk on cargo liners which berth in high-cost ports are far more expensive than the transportation costs of primary products carried in ship-load lots and loaded and discharged by specialist equipment in low-cost port facilities. Moreover, any goods carried by cargo liners are likely to be charged as nearly as possible what the traffic will bear since cargo liner rates are set by shipping conferences which act, as effectively as they can, as discriminating cartels. Macoeconomic models may identify important contributory factors to FDI but because models of this kind cannot realistically include variations in the level of impediments among products, they are forced to gloss over important contributing factors to individual investments.

Discriminatory behaviour by the governments of the countries involved, excluding commercial policy, can also be seen to exert a macroeconomic or macropolitical effect upon flows of FDI. Blatant prohibitions of outward or inward direct investment or antagonistic political behaviour such that fear of expropriation effectively precludes investment flows eliminate certain individual projects that might otherwise be undertaken. FDI in command economies is necessarily a macroeconomic consideration and is likely to take place only in response to a very important complementarity of mobile and immobile resources. But a great deal of government discrimination that affects FDI is likely to take place at the goods or microeconomic level as governments discriminate among producers by the nationality of their ownership. Kobrin (1981) has gone so far as to assert that 'most politically generated managerial contingencies faced by firms entail micro rather than macro risk and that, increasingly, most affect operations rather than ownership'.

When the macroeconomic analyses are expanded to include more than two countries, the factors determining the choice among a number of potential hosts is more likely to involve the microeconomic dimensions of the problem. This microeconomic bias derives from the fact that, when a firm plans a subsidiary in a particular industry, differences among national receptivity to or comparative advantage in that industry may be quite large even though all of the potential hosts have a similar macroeconomic profile (and 'psychic distances' from the source country).

The final aspect of location-specific variables is the question of the creation of a marketing and distribution (M and D) subsidiary. Most thories of FDI emphasize productive (manufacturing or extractive) subsidiaries to the neglect of M and D subsidiaries. This bias may follow from the greater dollar importance of the productive unit. An M and D subsidiary may be expected to be closely tied to the host's cultural practices and would be staffed with indigenous employees. But the probability that a corporation will create a foreign M and D subsidiary is likely to depend much more upon the microeconomic or product-specific variables than upon the 'psychic distance' between source and host countries. Whether goods be exported or manufactured locally, the means of marketing and distribution is likely to be determined primarily by the most efficient way to bring that good to market. If it can be sold through existing wholesale distribution networks, then the need for an M and D subsidiary is small. If the product requires after-sales service and warranty support, an MNC may not be willing to trust its international reputation to an organization not under its own control. It is also possible that some firms in technology-intensive industries which chose to introduce new products to foreign markets as quickly as possible will maintain their M and D subsidiary to facilitate this since they would not be willing to instruct 'outsiders' in their new technology.

This section has considered the main location-specific variables sequentially. It suggests that while location-specific variables do have inevitable and important macroeconomic dimensions, none of them is devoid of microeconomic dimensions. This means that there are limits to the insights that may be derived from the application of models based on the types of variables that typify the standard theory of international trade with its emphasis on national characteristics and homogeneous factors of production. That macroeconomic models should have less-than-full explanatory power is not surprising: investment decisions are made by firms and with reference to market conditions in a particular product. The fundamental act is microeconomic.

Conclusion

There are clear limits to the ability of macroeconomic theories to contribute to the general understanding of FDI. These theories explain FDI induced by wide disparities in the resource bases of national economies. In so doing, they justify Johnson's assertion. But these theories (and therefore Johnson's assertion) offer little in terms of an understanding of FDI among nations with relatively similar macroeconomic profiles or with the explanation of the allocation of a particular investment project to one country from among many potential hosts with similar national characteristics.

Aliber's theory adds little to the state of the art unless the argument is restricted to FDI between the bloc of rich nations, in which sophisticated capital markets exist, and poor nations. As an explanation of FDI among developed nations Aliber's theory is weakened by the growing integration of capital markets. Moreover, the suggested

chain of causality is suspect since it could argue for a flow from weak-
currency to strong-currency countries and any difference in capitalization rates could be greater among firms according to size than according to nationality.

Kojima's analysis is the victim of the simplicity of its own frame of
reference. To point out that FDI simultaneously increases comparative
advantage and plays a positive role in instituting inevitable adjustment
in national economies is a legitimate and worthwhile accomplishment.
But Kojima has found the limit of macroeconomic models of FDI and
as Arndt (1974) and Mason (1980) show, has pushed beyond that
limit.

Dunning's paper (1981b) is an empirical foray rather than an
attempt to develop a major or general theory of FDI. It provides
interesting insights into the way in which indulgence in FDI, both as
host and as source country, changes with the level of economic development. Such a model can only go so far and, as might be expected from
an economist who holds eclectic views, does not exceed its bounds.

Johnson's assertion (1972) is, then, only partially valid. Macroeconomic theories conceal as much, if not more, than they reveal.

Appendix: National Determinants of Ownership-specific Advantages

The body of the chapter, following Johnson, has identified national
role of national characteristics has been found significant in accounting
for international trade and FDI between rich and poor countries. When
the absolutely more important pattern of trade and FDI in manufactures among industrial nations is considered, national characteristics
are less important than firm- or industry-specific variables. This conclusion suggests that national characteristics play only a minor part in
the determination of the patterns of trade and FDI among industrial
nations. The selection process of relatively efficient industries in a
nation, those with ownership-specific advantages and those successfully exporting, is determined by a process in which random factors can
play a large part. Inter-firm and inter-industry variability in R and D
quality, in entrepreneurs' animal spirits, in synergistic relationships and
the ability to exploit economies of agglomeration can all affect the
identity of the efficient firms apparently without reference to national
characteristics. The role of national characteristics may not be limited
to location-specific variables. Dunning (1979, and in more detail in

1981) has suggested that country-specific (national) characteristics have an important role to play in the determination of ownership-specific advantages.

It is useful, at this juncture, to distinguish between 'physical' national characteristics (land, natural resources, labour supply and capital) and 'social' characteristics, which include the domestic social structure, the tax structure, the treatment of R and D, and government policy with respect to balance of payments. It may be argued that the physical characteristics can be identified quite closely with location-specific variables and the social characteristics with ownership-specific advantages. An interesting side issue is whether, if social national characteristics do play an identifiable role in determining comparative advantage among industries, governments can usefully employ them to promote strength in particular industries.

Clearly, Dunning is correct: national or country-specific characteristics cannot be confined to location-specific determinants. The nineteenth-century German emphasis on scientific education and chemical research and the consequent German supremacy in chemical technology is an obvious example of comparative advantage being determined by social characteristics. Equally, the British pre-eminence in the processed food industry may be attributed to the servicing of the needs of expatriates manning the outposts of a far-flung empire. The geographical pattern of FDI by successful colonial powers in the ex-colonies also shows the important role of national characteristics (in this case 'psychic proximity').

The structure of domestic society is important: tolerance of large firms will encourage ownership examples; encouragement of unified research programmes with governmental support will generate gains in proprietary knowledge. Japanese success in the computer industry has benefited from creative support from MITI (Gray, 1979b). The emphasis on health programmes in some Western European nations has aided the development of their pharmaceutical industries and space research in the United States has produced significant side benefits for a wide range of industries.

Finally, Hood and Young (1979) indicate that ownership-specific advantages can be influenced by national physical characteristics in the sense that Japanese innovation tends to emphasize space-saving and raw-material-saving developments while US innovation is biased toward labour-saving techniques.

There are two caveats that need to be added to this list. As in all determinants of international economic phenomena, it is relative emphasis which matters. If all developed nations follow the same policies, the role of social national characteristics will be unimportant. Social characteristics probably need a long time to achieve their full effect. Their effect will only be identifiable if social policies are consistent for a long period of time. It is this last feature which qualifies the idea that governments can influence the set of industries which enjoys comparative advantage. Frequent changes of government policy may create so much uncertainty that the effect of 'indicative planning' can be destroyed.

Notes

1. 'Economic theory offers two separate approaches to these questions (of the causation of FDI and the variation in FDI by industry), that of the theory of industrial organization and that of traditional trade theory. These approaches must be used as complements, since the former is microeconomic in character whereas the latter stresses the requirements of general macroeconomic equilibrium' (Johnson, 1972, p. 2.) For an analysis of the sterility of traditional trade theory in the context of FDI, see Corden (1974).

2. Aliber (1970), p. 28. The article suffers from an unfortunate ambiguity. Aliber uses 'capitalization rate' to mean the reciprocal of the rate of discount at which future expected earnings are capitalized so that a higher capitalization rate reflects a currency denomination of the equity deemed more desirable by financial markets. In other words, price/earnings ratios will be higher, on average, in countries with strong currencies. Current practice is to use 'capitalization rate' as another name for the rate of discount: see Brigham (1979, p. 797). This ambiguity may derive from a change in terminology from 'capitalization ratio' to 'capitalization rate' without any apparent change in meaning (Aliber, 1970, p. 28).

'3. The expositional ambiguity crops up again in Aliber (1970) in the discussion of the currency premium. On p. 29, Aliber identifies the currency premium as being borne by the weak currency (a premium on interest rates) and on p. 31 the premium is attached to the strong currency (the US dollar). The idea of strong and weak currencies is also developed (in the context of a portfolio of currency holdings) in Miles and Stewart (1980).

4. The comparative-advantage theory is developed in Kojima (1973, 1977). It should be noted that Kojima did not have the benefit of considering the eclectic theory of FDI. This section must benefit from two earlier comments by Arndt (1974) and Mason (1980).

5. See Arndt (1974) and Mason (1980) for some weaknesses of Kojima's argument within his North/South context.

6. A composite input has the same analytic benefits and costs as a composite good: any results obtained gloss over changes in or differences within the composite input through time or in different countries: see Gray (1980).

7. For the argument that organizations can have 'knowledge engineered into them just as does a piece of equipment' see Mason (1980). A similar concept underlines the existence of country-specific modifiers to production functions in Gray (1976), pp. 29–44.

8. For an up-to-date assessment of the product cycle hypothesis, see Vernon (1979).

9. Dunning's J-curve (1981a) is not to be confused with that portraying the behaviour of the balance on current account and the balance of payments after a devaluation.

10. Taken from Table 5 of Dunning (1980). The weighted averages were $9.97 for six countries and $12.88 when Japan was excluded from countries with positive NOI. The United States with $9.1 per capita and Japan with $1.6 per capita dominate the values for countries with positive NOI.

11. But see the discussion of country-specific factors as determinants of ownership-specific advantages in the appendix.

12. See Johnson (1972). Johnson also believed that it was necessary to incorporate impediments to international trade explicitly into trade theory.

13. Quality differences are particularly important in natural resources where pure Ricardian rents may be earned. Industry-specific skills can also earn quasi-rents for certain kinds of labour in the short run.

14. The concept was originally developed in a two-country version in Peter F. Drucker (1977). Note that production sharing is defined in an international context: strictly, it could be intra-national in a country with quite disparate regional endowments such as northern and southern Italy.

15. Drucker (1977) argues in terms of the 'availability' of production workers in the developing nation: 'availability' and price are inter-related variables but cost of labour per unit of output seems to have become dominant recently as production sharing grows in the face of reduced rates of capacity utilization in manufacturing industries in developed nations.

9 FOREIGN BANK ENTRY INTO JAPAN AND CALIFORNIA

Adrian E. Tschoegl

Introduction

This chapter investigates foreign direct investment (FDI) in banking in California and Japan.[1] The topic is of practical and theoretical interest.

Foreign banks are increasing their presence in the United States and Japan. This phenomenon has given rise to concern among domestic bankers, regulators and law-makers. It seems worthwhile to add to the discussion some information on the factors that may influence a foreign bank's entry decision.

Most current theories of FDI have been developed to explain its occurrence in manufacturing industries. With only a few exceptions (Grubel, 1977; Aliber, 1976; Gray and Gray, 1981), multinational banking has drawn little theoretical attention. Most studies of international banking such as Lees (1976), Terrell and Key (1977) and Eiteman (1978) have tended to be descriptive and qualitative.

This paper presents empirical evidence of step-wise entry based on the behaviour of foreign banks in Japan and California. The evidence here is of a time-series nature. In addition, we use a cross-sectional approach to investigate the role of time in particular, or knowledge acquisition in general, in a bank's expansion of its activities in the two markets.

We chose California and Japan for a number of reasons. Both permit foreign banks to establish operations. The markets studied are large, with substantial foreign entry, and represent opportunities primarily for corporate and retail banking activities, though they are becoming international financial centres (Hang-Sheng, 1976; Reed, 1980). They are also well documented.

The next section provides the institutional background for the two cases, followed by a discussion of some of the relevant literature and the time-series evidence. Next the cross-sectional data and models are presented. Finally there is a summary and conclusion.

The Foreign Bank Sector in California and Japan

There are four common organizational forms: representative office, agency, branch and subsidiary. Representative offices, agencies and branches are integral parts of their parents. Unlike subsidiaries, they are not separate legal persons with limited liability.

Representative offices and agencies operate almost exclusively in the wholesale and corporate markets. However, representative offices may perform only liaison, customer solicitation and information-gathering activities. Agencies may make loans and take foreign deposits. Branches may, and subsidiaries generally do, accept domestic deposits. Subsidiaries engage in retail activities as well. The forms thus represent an ordinal scale of increasing integration with the local market environment. In California prior to July 1978, foreign banks were forbidden branches in fact, though the other three options were open to them. Japanese law or practice does not seem to provide for the agency form of organization, and foreign banks are not permitted local subsidiaries.

California

History and Market Share

Foreign banks first entered California in the mid-nineteenth century. Rothschilds established a branch in San Francisco in 1849. The Hong Kong and Shanghai Banking Corporation entered in 1875 and has remained ever since. In the 1870s, the Yokohoma Specie Bank (an ancestor of the Bank of Tokyo) also opened a branch. The first Canadian bank to enter, the Canadian Imperial Bank of Commerce, did so in 1902. In the post-Second World War period, the Sumitomo Bank and the Bank of Tokyo established subsidiaries in 1953.

Even so, the pace of expansion was relatively slow until the first half of the 1970s. Table 9.1 gives the development of the number of agencies and subsidiaries from 1965 to 1980. Table 9.2 presents the banks' activity in dollar terms.

Organizational Form and Ownership

Almost all foreign subsidiaries have an associated agency. Even banks with only a minority shareholding in a subsidiary have their own agencies. The combination of organizational forms is complementary. Only Lloyds Bank, whose subisiary is very large, has dispensed with one.

All subsidiaries are locally incorporated and operate under state

Table 9.1: Foreign Banks in California: Subsidiaries, Agencies and Representative Offices, 1965–80

	1965	1970	1975	1980
Subsidiaries	6	7	15	17
Branch offices				
per subsidiary	3.67	7.00	16.07	28.59
Agencies	9	14	44	85
Representative offices	NA	17	22	22

Source: Superintendent of Banks, State of California, *Annual Report*.

Table 9.2: Foreign Bank Activity in California (US$ million, and market share by %)

	June 1965	June 1970	June 1975	June 1980
Subsidiaries				
Assets	504.0	1,071.9	4,489.4	18,055
Market share	1.31	2.0	4.55	7.3
Loans	263.5	610.5	2,830.6	14,855
Market share	1.16	1.97	5.20	
Deposits	434.6	908.1	3,804.5	25,456
Market share	1.27	2.07	4.70	10.3
Agencies				
Assets	329.3	1,598.0	8,289.4	12,802
Market share	0.8	2.98	8.4	
Loans	168.4	398.5	4,309.3	
Market share	0.74	1.29	4.37	
Total				
Assets	833.3	2,669.9	12,778.8	43,511
Market share	2.11	4.98	12.95	17.7
Loans	431.9	1,009.0	7,139.9	
Market share	1.9	3.26	9.57	

Source: Superintendent of Banks, State of California, *Annual Report*.

charters. They are eligible for Federal Deposit Insurance and are allowed to conduct a full range of banking activities, including maintaining a network of branch offices throughout the state. None of the foreign subsidiaries has sought a national charter because prior to 1978 the requirements were too restrictive. This may change, especially since the Depository Institutions Deregulation and Monetary Control Act (1980) has changed the cost/benefit calculus of Federal Reserve System membership.

Regulation[2]

California holds foreign subsidiaries and domestic banks seeking to establish themselves as commercial banks to the same requirements.

They must satisfy the State Superintendent of Banking that their establishment will promote the public convenience and advantage, and that business conditions and the knowledge, ability and standing of the proposed officers and directors are such that they have a reasonable chance of success.

The state requirement that a bank have Federal Deposit Insurance if it is to hold domestic deposits automatically bring subsidiaries under Federal regulation. Foreign subsidiaries also come under the provisions of the Bank Holding Company Act (BHCA) of 1956, as amended in 1970. Any foreign bank establishing or acquiring control of a US banking subsidiary must receive Federal Reserve approval to do so, since having such a subsidiary automatically makes it a Bank Holding Company.[3] Therefore, a foreign bank, like a domestic bank, may not maintain a banking subsidiary and a securities affiliate in the US, or banking subsidiaries in two or more states. The BHCA 'grandfathered' existing inter-state operation of subsidiaries by five foreign and six domestic bankholding companies.[4] Foreign banks, unlike domestic banks, were also permitted a subsidiary (banking or securities) in one state and branches and agencies in the same state or others.

Under the International Banking Act of 1978, the Federal Reserve Board has the authority to impose reserve requirements on all US branches and agencies of foreign banks that have more than US $1 billion in worldwide assets. The banks will have access to Federal Reserve agencies. Branches of foreign banks that accept deposits of less than $100,000 will be required to have federal deposit insurance although branches not engaged in domestic retail deposit activities can be exempted. However, branches of foreign banks will be allowed to accept domestic deposits in only one state. The 'home' branch will be permitted to accept a full range of deposits. Other branches will be restricted in deposit taking to those that a domestic bank's Edge Act subsidiary may accept.[5]

Reciprocity

The Superintendent may take into account in granting licences whether the foreign bank's home country permits US banks to establish branches or subsidiaries there. Examination of the regulations of such countries as Canada, Australia and Mexico indicates that there would be grounds for barring their banks. Conversations with some Department officials indicate that generally it does not even consider the issue when examining applications for entry.[6]

Operations

Foreign bank subsidiaries have branch offices throughout the state in areas generally experiencing rapid rates of population growth.[7] They tend to focus their business on larger firms, but compete in all types of banking, though their portfolios are heavily weighted towards real estate and commercial leading.[8] The subsidiaries' main source of funds is domestic deposits. The distribution by type of deposit closely approximates that of all California banks. Foreign banks, however, hold a slightly lower proportion of individual savings accounts than do their domestic counterparts.[9]

While officers of large banks by and large welcome the expansion of foreign banking activity, many representatives of smaller banks view the retail competition as unnecessary at best, and as damaging at worst.[10] Community banks are especially vulnerable to market share loss because of their relatively small geographic base. In their retail activities, the subsidiaries have used generally accepted competitive techniques such as lower-cost checking accounts and automobile loans, and widespread advertising campaigns.[11] The State Banking Department has discovered no instance in which an authorized additional facility has resulted in competition destructive to banks already in the community involved.[12] The policy of requiring that a new branch appear viable and promote the public advantage and convenience protects existing institutions in stagnant or low-growth areas. Morever, much foreign expansion is via takeover of existing banks. This obviously has no effect on the number of branch offices in a community. In 1976, of some 330 branch offices of foreign subsidaries, over 200 were acquired.

Japan

History and Market Share

The Hong Kong and Shanghai Bank entered Japan in 1866 by opening an office in Yokohama. The earliest US presence in Japan seems to have been that of the International Banking Corporation which established four branches in Japan: Yokohama (1902); Kobe (1904); Tokyo (1923); and Osaka (1925).[13] After the Second World War, the first banks from the US (including one from California – Bank of America), France, the UK, the Netherlands, the Republic of China and Hong Kong all established themselves in 1949. As in the case of California, the pace of entry was slow until the late 1960s and early 1970s.

Foreign banks' market share in terms of loans or deposits has always

Table 9.3: Foreign Banks in Japan: Number of Foreign Banks, Branches and Representative Offices, 1962–78

	1962	1966	1972	1974	1976	1978
Banks	14	15	80	106	128	144
Branches	29	32	45	66	74	84
Rep. offices	4	11	55	61	77	89

Source: *Banking System in Japan*, various issues

Table 9.4: Foreign Banks' Market Share (billion yen)

End March	Number	Assets	Deposits
1973	35	1,416 (1.5)	633 (0.9)
1974	42	1,926 (1.8)	761 (0.9)
1975	50	3,506 (2.9)	989 (1.1)
1976	50	4.212 (3.1)	1,110 (1.0)
1977	53	4.665 (3.1)	1,082 (0.9)
1978	59	4,752 (2.9)	1,032 (0.8)
1979	61	5,667 (3.1)	1,308 (0.8)
1980	64	8,434 (4.1)	1,536 (0.9)

Percentage shares of totals for all banks (which include all chartered city, regional, long-term credit and trust banks, but not credit co-operations).
Source: R. Komaki, 'Foreign banks: patience please', *The Banker*, Aug. 1981.

been very limited. In 1980 their assets represented about 4 per cent of the national total of bank assets in Japan. Their deposit business is even smaller, representing less than 1 per cent of the national total.

Table 9.3 gives the number of foreign banks, branches and representative offices. Table 9.4 reports the foreign banks' market share in Japan for 1973–80.

Organizational Form and Ownership

Foreign banks are restricted to having representative offices or branches. They may own a minority share (5 per cent) in a Japanese bank, and may establish some limited non-bank subsidiaries such as consumer finance companies.

During the period 1949–70 almost no banks from the US or other developed countries were permitted to establish *de novo* branches, and a number of US banks bought the branches of Dutch banks. This prohibition was lifted in 1971. Except for banks which established branches shortly after the war, foreign banks until very recently were confined to a single branch in Tokyo. This restriction was removed in 1978.

Regulation

Each office of a foreign bank is required to seek a licence under the Bank Law as a Japanese ordinary bank. Their authorized lines of business are therefore nominally the same as those of their domestic equivalents. For instance, they may issue negotiable certificates of deposists, but not debentures. Apparently, membership in the deposit insurance scheme is compulsory for all deposit taking institutions. The branches of foreign banks are classed as 'Class A' foreign exchange banks, authorized to engage in regular exchange business in general, conclude correspondent contracts directly, and to hold foreign funds.

However, from 1949 to 1979, the Foreign Exchange and Foreign Trade Control Law governed international transactions. In general, it prohibited all foreign trade and exchange transactions not specifically authorized by executive authority. In addition, Japan has a system of 'administrative guidance'. This is a kind of moral suasion, backed by other regulatory powers, which the authorities exert over commercial banks. The authorities operate flexibly in response to specific economic and policy circumstances, and tailor their instructions to the situation of individual institutions and groups of institutions. Administrative guidance is rarely written.[14]

Japan clearly discriminates between foreign and domestic banks, both in law and in practice. By design of the regulatory authorities, Japanese and foreign banks have overlapping, but not identical roles.

Reciprocity

The Japanese government takes the issue of reciprocity very seriously. It does not permit banks from countries that do not permit Japanese banks to open branches there to establish a branch in Japan. Absence of receiprocity in some US states has been used to deny entry of US banks from those states. Apparently, through, even if a country becomes more restrictive, existing operations are permitted to continue.

Canada changed its law to permit foreign banks to establish branches and bank subsidiaries in 1980. Immediately Japan negotiated an agreement with Canada under which the five Canadian banks with representative offices there may open a branch each in 1981. Similarly, five Japanese banks will be allowed the same number of subsidiary offices in Canada. If all goes well, another two from each country will be permitted in 1982–3.[15]

Operations

Japanese authorities permit foreign banks some special privileges. They are not required to buy at par government bonds with below market coupon rates, and until recently only they were permitted to make long-term (maturity of 1 year or more) foreign currency ('impact') loans to Japanese firms.[16]

Foreign exchange transactions are the main line of business for foreign banks. Lending operations are next in importance. Their deposit business is very small.

Much of the lending is in the form of the 'impact' loans mentioned above. These were, until recently, the exclusive preserve of foreign banks. They also led to spin-off business, particularly foreign exchange commissions on conversions of the loans into yen at issuance and back into the foreign currency at repayment.

The deposit business is small for a number of reasons. Not only was branching restricted, but many foreign banks were required to promise the regulatory authorities that they would not solicit local deposits. The lack of a deposit base meant that foreign banks that want to engage in yen lending have to bring funds from outside and engage in currency swaps under quotas established by the Bank of Japan. These quotas are administered on a bank-by-bank basis and thus give the regulatory authorities great influence over the foreign banks.

Theory

According to Hymer (1976) and Kindleberger (1969), if companies wish to compete in a foreign market against local firms they must possess some form of quasi-monopolistic advantage to overcome their disadvantages *vis-à-vis* their competitors. This proposition consists of an unstated condition, two assumptions and a consequence. The conditional statement is simply 'Given that the receiving country permits FDI, then . . .' The two assumptions are the existence of: (1) local competition, actual or potential; and (2) non-trivial differential costs between foreign and local firms. The consequence is that to compete successfully, the foreign company must possess some advantage, the returns to which it can appropriate more fully by FDI than by some market transaction.

Receptivity

Receptivity, the openness of a country to FDI, is a major factor in banking. It is an important consideration since the existence of FDI requires not only that firms desire to engage in the activity, but also that host countries permit them to do so. In general, it is clearly dangerous to assume that a country is equally open across all sectors and to all origins just because it permits some foreigners to operate in some industries. California and Japan clearly differ in their receptivity within the banking sector. They follow different policies with respect to both organizational form permitted and the role of reciprocity.

Competition

The first element in the Hymer/Kindleberger (HK) proposition is the assumption of the existence of local competition. Frequently, especially in less developed countries (LDCs), there are no local firms capable of providing effective competition in the particular product lines in which the foreign investor is interested. A perhaps more interesting case, because it is less obvious, may occur when local firms do not change their policies in order to compete fully with the foreigners. A third situation which might give rise to attenuated competition is a rapidly growing host market. If one assumes that there are transient costs to the firm associated with growth, then the optimal rate of growth for existing firms might be less than that of the market as a whole. This could create an opportunity for new firms who, while perhaps higher cost producers, would still find entry attractive.

Costs

The second element of the HK theory is the assumption that foreign firms face higher costs than do local firms. These costs derive from the fact that the foreign firms must operate at a distance and in an environment that is culturally, politically, legally and economically different from their own. This assumption seems eminently reasonable and all discussions of FDI have accepted it as fact. There is evidence in the literature that physical distance and environmental 'strangeness' are important (see: Horst, 1972b; Franko, 1975; Ozawa, 1975; and Buckley and Matthew, 1979).

Even so, and despite the widely acknowledged importance of the foreign environment to the FDI decision, there is little trace in the literature of any attempt to measure the costs' magnitudes and determinants. While the argument that foreign firms face greater costs is intuitively appealing, one cannot accept it uncritically. The extra costs will be a function of the firm's nationality, industry and corporate history. In some situations they may even approach zero.

In a recent article, Johanson and Vahlne (1977) investigated the internationalization process of the firm and suggested a model linking knowledge development with increasing foreign market commitments. Concentrating on the extension of operations in individual markets, they argued that,

> . . . additional commitments will be made in small steps unless the firm has very large resources and/or market conditions are stable and homogeneous, or the firm has much experience from other markets with similar conditions. If not, market experience will lead to a step-wise increase in the scale of operations and of the integration with the market environment . . .

This thesis is an extension of the argument of an earlier article in which Johanson and Wiedersheim (1975) suggested that as the level of experientially-based knowledge about a market increases, so will the organizational commitment in that market. What the 1977 article makes clearer is that this expansion is a matter of both degree and kind.

More recently, Davidson (1980) has presented evidence based on US firm data that also supports Johanson and Vahlne, though it does not distinguish between the two types of expansion. Davidson too finds that firms' preference for near, similar markets is a function of lack of international experience. Firms with broader international operating experience are more open to less familiar markets.

In banking, in particular, Baer and Garlow (1977) investigated the internationalization process of regional banks. They found it consisted of four phases:

I.   trade financing for local exporters and importers;
II.   loans to foreign banks and participation in loan syndications;
III. direct loans to foreign non-financial firms; and
IV.   creation of foreign subsidiaries by the bank and the syndication of loans.

So far as the foreign direct investment phase is concerned, Tschoegl (1980) presents evidence both that entry into California is influenced by parent banks' degree of international experience, and that expansion of activities within the market is a function of elapsed time in that market.

Advantages

The third element of the HK proposition is the consequence that, given the existence of competition and differential costs, the foreign firm must have offsetting economic advantages. These advantages may be of three types: those which derive from multinationality *per se*; those which derive from special situations, or the fact of foreignness; and those which are bank-specific, including national origin.

Because it spans borders, the multinational bank can arbitrage disequilibria caused by foreign exchange and credit controls, and tax systems. It does this by internalizing the flows or markets (Lessard, 1979). Its ability to do so gives it an advantage *vis-à-vis* wholly domestic competitors at home or abroad, but of course, not relative to other multinationals.

Some causes of special situations could be regulations in the receiving market, or its structure. One such factor which we could not test but which we would argue is important is the highly concentrated structure of the banking industry in California. Foreign banks might be able to operate as fringe entrants under a price umbrella maintained by a dominant oligopoly. Elsewhere we offer anecdotal evidence in support of this possibility, while showing that the necessary condition – high industry concentration – exists (Tschoegl, 1980).

Another clearly important and untested factor in individual cases for the US is the interaction of anti-trust law and the prohibition on interstate banking. Because of these laws, foreign banks are able to acquire local banks without having to bid against other US banks. Thus even if the acquisition were worth less to them than to a US bank, they would still prevail.

Recent legislation has limited the other legal advantages which were commonly advanced as explanation for the foreign banks' success in the past. We feel that these were not very important, though, and doubt that the changes will have much effect.

In the case of Japan, the special situation from which foreign banks profited was the Bank of Japan's regulations prohibiting Japanese banks from making impact loans. While restricting the foreign banks in many ways, the Japanese authorities permitted them this very profitable business, presumably as compensating inducement to stay.

Foreign banks active in dollar lending but without a commensurate dollar deposit base may fear being frozen out during a credit crunch. Since credit crunches do occur, one can, therefore, expect foreign banks to insure that they have an adequate access to inputs to support their loans to their regular customers. A number of banks have mentioned this as a major motivation for their acquisition of US subsidiaries.[17]

The third category, bank-specific advantages, includes the derived advantage of preferred access to MNCs from the home country which are investing abroad on the basis of their own advantages, scale economies and differentiated products.

Much of the recent literature on FDI has emphasized the importance of factor market imperfections, especially in the markets for information, commercial knowledge or technology (Johnson, 1970; Buckley and Casson, 1976; Magee, 1977). Since most of the literature deals with manufacturing, it has concentrated on the role of R and D or technology. Physical technology is of relatively little importance in banking.

Commercial knowledge — that is, information about firms and foreign markets — would seem to hold the most explanatory power. Over time, a bank builds up a stock of knowledge about its customers. When the customers go abroad and the bank follows, or has preceded them, it has an advantage over its local competition in servicing them. It can draw on the information it already possesses quickly and at low marginal cost and thus is better able than others to respond to customer needs, be they loans or operational requirements (Grubel, 1977). Moreover, if the foreign bank does not follow, it gives other banks an entrée. The foreign bank can also sell to host-country firms its knowledge of its home market.

Since many of the banks involved in FDI are large, one might look to general internal economies of scale as an explanatory factor. However, foreign banks in general possess no size advantage in either California or Japan.

Caves (1971) has argued that product differentiation is one source of advantage for foreign firms *vis-à-vis* their local competition. Grubel (1977) maintains that it is of special importance in explaining multinational retail banking. As he himself points out though, a competitive advantage based purely on product differentiation is rather precarious since innovative responses by local firms may easily curtail it. For it to be useful, the differentiation must be one that the domestic industry cannot easily copy. National origin itself meets this requirement. Its origin may give the foreign bank an appeal to subsets of the population

— either related ethnic minorities, or other groups who attribute some special value to the nationality. California provides examples of both situations. With the possible exception of the Korean minority, Japan does not.

Behaviour Over Time

In banking, the degree of integration with the local market can be associated with the legal form of a bank's presence. Of the four common legal statuses — representative office, agency, branch and subsidiary — foreign banks in Japan may assume the first and third. In California, as noted earlier, foreign banks may assume the first, second and fourth.

For the time series evidence, each foreign bank was cross-classified by its organizational form in year t and in year t-1 (California) or t-2 or 3 (Japan). For California, the total period considered is mid-1972 to mid-1980, which provides seven non-overlapping classification periods. Table 9.5 then presents the results from summing these six annual classifications. For Japan the time span is early 1972 to early 1979 and provides two two-year and one three-year periods. Table 9.6 gives the relevant results.

For both tables, the cells labelled with a 'C' represent continuations of a status, 'EN' entries, 'EX' exits, and 'D' changes in legal form. In the event a bank was present in more than one capacity, classification was based on the highest form attained. In both tables, the number of banks not present in each pair of years is unknown. In principle, one could estimate the numbers, but doing so would add little to the already strong picture of the tables.

One must remember that a bank's assuming a legal status is subject to the approval of regulatory authorities. These may prohibit all but incremental steps. While this is certainly a factor, non-incremental transitions indicate that there are no absolute barriers. Moreover, even though the two sets of authorities involved differ in their regulatory philosophies, California being particularly open to foreign banks and Japan relatively restrictive (Tschoegl, 1980), the patterns of bank behaviour are strikingly similar across the two markets.

As far as entrances are concerned, there are few large jumps. In Japan, only six entrants out of 71 went directly from not being present to having a branch. In two of these cases, an affiliate or a shareholder already had its own branch in Japan. For California, there is only one

Table 9.5: Foreign Banks in California

		STATUS AT TIME t, t = 6/1973–6/1980			
		Subsidiary	Agency	Representative Office	Not Present
STATUS AT TIME t−1, t−1 = 6/1972–6/1979	Subsidiary	C 113	D 1	D 0	EX 0
	Agency	D 8	C 233	D 1	EX 0
	Representative Office	D 0	D 19	C 50	EX 3
	Not Present	EN 1	EN 36	EN 23	

Table 9.6: Foreign Banks in Japan

		STATUS AT TIME t, t = 3/79, 6/76 and 4/74		
		Branch	Representative Office	Not Present
STATUS AT TIME t−2 or t−3 t−2 = 4/1974 and 3/1972 t−3 = 6/1976	Branch	C 123	D 2	EX 0
	Representative Office	D 33	C 153	EX 5
	Not Present	EN 6	EN 65	

case of direct entry as a subsidiary. This occurred when a British bank (Lloyds) acquired the eighth largest bank in the state. One can speculate that it was able to do so in part because it had extensive experience with managing subsidiaries in foreign countries. One might also note that there are no cases in which a foreign bank upgraded its representative office to a subsidiary.

The proportion of non-incremental to total transitions to a subsidiary in California or a branch in Japan are 11 and 15 per cent respectively. Only in the second case is the number of direct entries statistically significantly different from zero (at the 5 per cent level). Clearly there seems to be a large qualitative gap in local market integration between subsidiaries or banches on the one hand and agencies and/or representative offices on the other.

In California, entries as agencies are more frequent that as representative offices. There are two non-exclusive explanations for this anomaly. First, there is probably little difference between a small agency and a representative office. Neither has much contact with the public and therefore requires few facilities. Second, the choice between the two forms may depend on the size and experience of the parent and the cultural and physical distance between home and host country. This is a subject for further research.

In both markets entries greatly outnumber exits. This is not surprising since both markets were growing over the period. However, an hypothesis of incautious entry would lead one to expect a much higher number of withdrawals. Moreover, all the exits were by banks that had had only representative offices.

The two cases of reduction in status in the case of California were forced on the parents by the requirements of US law. When Hong Kong and Shanghai Bank acquired Marine Midland in New York it sold its California subsidiary though it was permitted to keep its agency. Similarly, European American Banking Corporation gave up its agencies as a condition for receiving Federal Reserve approval of its reorganization in New York State.[18]

In the case of Japan, one of the two reductions of status from branch to representative office was by a company that already had a branch under its bank subsidiary's name. The exits include one case where two separate parent banks merged and consolidated their operations, and one where the members of the Inter-Alpha consortium disbanded their joint representative office in favour of each member having its own office.

There are two numerical parallels between the two tables. These may

Table 9.7: Comparative Distribution of Transitions

	California		Japan	
	No.	%	No.	%
Changes	29	32	35	32
Entries	59	65	71	64
Exits	3	3	4	4
Total transitions	91	100	111	100

represent coincidences since there it too little evidence as yet to suggest that there are any constants across countries in some of the processes involved.

The first coincidence is not obvious. If one takes the ratio of the total number of changes to the total number of continuations, i.e. divides the sum of the 'D' cells by the sum of the 'C' cells for each table, the ratios are 0.078 and 0.127 for California and Japan respectively. However, one must remember that in the latter case the time periods involved are two or three years, not one as in the former. If the Japanese data were annual, the number of changes would remain roughly the same but the number of continuations would increase. On average approximately 6–8 per cent of the foreign banks in Japan and California change their status in each year. The second coincidence is that, as Table 9.7 indicates, the proportion of total transitions accounted for by changes, entries and exits is almost identical across the two markets.

Cross-sectional Results

This section uses a cross-sectional approach to cast further light on the determinants of FDI and the role of knowledge development. It applies two different statistical techniques, each embodying a slightly different conception of market commitment.

Data and Methodology

In the case of Japan, the sample consists of those foreign banks that had a representative office of a branch there in 1978, and which were not barred by considerations of reciprocity from opening a branch. We then generate two dependent variables: one qualitative and the other cardinal. The first is, is the foreign parent represented by a branch? This variable can take on only two values: 'yes' or 'no'. The second variable is the number of branches the parent has in Japan. In this form, the variable can take on integer values between 0 and 4.

For California, the sample consists of those foreign banks that had an agency or subsidiary in California in 1978, and which were not barred by US law from establishing a subsidiary. The first variable then measures the presence or absence of a subsidiary. The second variable is the number of branch offices per subsidiary in 1978. Banks which have only agencies receive a value of zero on the measure, which then ranges between 0 and 105.

For both countries, the first variable reflects a view of the establishment of a branch or subsidiary as a change in kind. We can treat this decision as one of a binary choice based on a consideration of various relevant factors. That is, the foreign bank reviews its situation and decides whether or not ot have a subsidiary (branch) in California (Japan). The second variable treats the number of branches and subsidiaries as representing differences in degree.

The models for the first type of dependent variable are estimated using maximum likelihood logit (Press and Wilson, 1978). Those for the second type are estimated with Ordinary Least Squares. For econometric reasons, the modulus transformation procedure (Draper and John, 1980) is first applied to the dependent variable. The modulus transform is an alternative one-parameter family to the power family.

Model

The model used in all four estimations is a simple one based on that of Tschoegl (1980). Qualitiatively speaking, the dependent variable is a function of the parent bank's experience at operating internationally, its knowledge of the country, unspecified bank-specific advantages, unspecified home country-specific advantages, and the distance between the market and the parent's headquarters. Five variables (CNTRY, TIMEC/TIMEJ, SIZE, SAME, DIST) operationalize these concepts.

CNTRY equals 0 or 1 + the natural logarithm of the number of countries in which the bank in question had a branch or subsidiary. The more countries in which the parent is operating, the more likely it is that it has learned to do so at minimum cost. The variable also includes the implications of a strategy of parent representation around the world.

TIMEC reflects how long the foreign bank has had a presence in California. It takes on a value of 1 if the bank in question entered in 1978 or 1977. It is incremented by 1 for each additional pair of years. Since we do not have reliable information for years period to 1969, the maximum value attainable is 5. The variable's analog for Japan is TIMEJ, the natural log of the number of years since the foreign bank first entered Japan after the Second World War.

SIZE is the natural log of the parent's size in terms of assets in 1978. It is a proxy for all bank-specific advantages which are assumed correlated with size.

SAME equals 0 or 1 + the natural log of the number of banks from a country (other than the bank in question itself) that has a branch or subsidiary in Japan or California, respectively. It acts as a proxy for home-country-related advantages since one can presume that any factors which impel one bank from a country to enter the host country will impel others too. The measure also incorporates the concept of oligopolistic reaction (Knickerbocker, 1973). The use of the log transform is intended to reflect a decreasing marginal motivational effect.

DIST is the natural log of the distance between Tokyo and the parent bank's headquarters rounded to the nearest 500 miles. The log form gives us costs that increase with distance, but at a decreasing rate.

Results

Table 9.8 presents the results of the estimations.

Across both countries, the two models perform similarly. While Model 2 provides more statistically significant coefficients, it does not unambiguously dominate Model 1. Thus one cannot infer that one conception or the other of the increased commitment to a market (i.e. the qualitative or the extensive) better describes the situation.

Across the models, the results are similar for both countries in the sense that the signs of all coefficients are the same. The models do not work as well in the case of Japan as they do for California. Nevertheless, they do not perform badly.

The coefficients of the variables for distance, bank-specific and country-specific advantages rarely achieve statistical significance. One must remember though that the samples consist of banks that already have a presence in the host markets. These factors, then, may have their greatest effect in determining whether or not the parent is in Japan or

Table 9.8: Cross-sectional Estimations

	Japan		California	
	Model 1 (Logit)	Model 2 (OLS)	Model 1 (Logit)	Model 2 (OLS)
Constant	−4.59	−0.25	−20.45	−1.08
	(−0.94)	(−0.53)	(−1.43)	(−5.02)
CNTRY	2.06	0.18	3.77	0.25
	(3.80)	(6.32)	(1.18)	(4.18)
TIME (C/J)	0.99	0.19	8.46	0.17
	(1.29)	(3.73)	(1.23)	(3.01)
SIZE	0.28	0.01	2.99	0.11
	(0.84)	(0.52)	(1.17)	(1.39)
SAME	0.17	0.01	1.03	0.17
	(0.68)	(0.62)	(0.44)	(1.99)
DIST	−0.51	−0.09	−11.50	−0.24
	(−0.86)	(−1.49)	(−0.93)	(−1.10)
Transformation parameter		−0.08		−0.97
R^2	0.54	0.66	0.87	0.68
F		34.78		17.97
SER		0.27		0.55
χ^2 (5 df)	68.38		58.45	
N	95	95	45	48

Note: For Model 1 R^2 is an analog based on a ratio of log likelihoods.

California, but contribute relatively little beyond that.

The one variable which produces the best results, in terms of statistical significance, is CNTRY, the proxy for experience in international operations. The greater the parent's worldwide spread, the more likely it is to be more deeply committed to the host market, whether one treats the commitment as being qualitative or quantitative. The variable for experience with the host market, TIME, also tends to work well. The longer the parent has been present in the market, the greater is its commitment.

Summary and Conclusion

This chapter presented evidence that the pattern of incremental expansion that Johansen and Vahlne found for Swedish manufacturing firms abroad holds for banks from many countries in their operations in California and Japan. Direct entry to either market in the organizational form representing the greatest commitment is rare. Generally, the pattern is one of time elapsing between entry and the bank's advancement to the next organizational form.

Cross-sectional tests highlighted the role of knowledge development in the expansion of activities. Given that the parent had a presence in the country in question, the most significant variables in explaining its expansion in the country were the proxies for its experience in international operations in general and in the country in particular. The variables which attempted to account for the costs of operating at a distance or the role of bank- or country-specific advantages were far less productive.

What emerges from this study is a slightly different view of the reasons for FDI from that given by the traditional approach. This has had a negative cast since it began with the assumption that foreign direct investors faced higher costs than their local competitors. Hence they had to have offsetting advantages. We, instead, see the decision to engage in an act of FDI are more positive: banks exploit opportunities.

They may do so despite costs which may not, however, be all that important in the context of an industry with a technology that is fairly widespread throughout the world. The opportunities that exist are of three types: (a) those that are inherent in the fact of multinationality; (b) those that derive from special situations; and (c) those that derive from bank-specific advantages. The ability to do so, however, is a function of experience, both with foreign operations in general, and in the country in particular.

Notes

I would like to thank Stephen J. Kobrin for his advice and criticism. Mr Sang-Rim Choi provided research assistance. All flaws remain my own.

1. FDI involves the ownership and control of an enterprise across national boundaries.

2. California regulations discussed here are contained in Sections 1753 *et seq.*, 1756, 1756.1, 1756.2, and 1780 of the California Financial Code. US regulations are drawn from 12 United States Code Sections 72, 1814, 1815, and 1841–1850. The International Banking Act has modified some of the US laws.

3. Auerbach (1976), p. 24. Control requires that at least one entity own, control or have the power to vote 5% or more of the voting securities of any bank. An ownership of 25% or more is *prima facie* proof of control. Between 5 and 25%, there is a refutable presumption. Philippine Bank of California, which is owned in equal parts by five Philippine banks and government agencies, does not seem to have required Federal Reserve approval for its establishment. These rules do not appear to apply to individuals. Apparently, a foreign investor may, in his own right, wholly own a US bank without coming under the BHCA.

4. *Bank Stock Quarterly*, Oct. 1978, Table IV.

5. *Congressional Quarterly*, 26 Aug, 1978, p. 2258.

6. It has, on one occasion, exerted pressure on a country to permit entry into a state-chartered bank when national banks domiciled in California were already operating there and the country had banks in the state.

7. California Superintendent of Banks, Report of Foreign Banking Matters, April 1974, p. 56.

8. SCRC 1976, p. 30.

9. Ibid.

10. Ibid., p. 31.

11. Cal. Super., 65th Annual Report, p. 59.

12. Ibid., p. 54.

13. National City Bank, which eventually become Citibank, acquired International Banking Corporation in 1915 (Phelps, 1927).

14. I would like ot thank Gunter Dufey for providing much of this information.

15. *The Banker*, March 1981, p. 25.

16. The term 'impact' comes from their favourable impact on Japan's balance of power.

17. National Westminster Bank (a major UK institution) had around US $12 billion in dollar assets abroad when it acquired National Bank of North America in 1978. It made the acquisition because it felt the need for a backstop in case the supply of dollars on international markets ever dried up (*Economist*, 20 May 1978).

Also, in private conversation, an official of Banco Nacional de Mexico stated that access to dollar deposits was a motivation for his bank's acquisition of Community Bank of San Jose in 1978. Finally, see also Uemura (1979).

18. *Federal Reserve Bulletin*, June 1977.

10 MULTINATIONAL FOOD AND FISH CORPORATIONS

David P. Rutenberg

Introduction

Many of the great multinationals are food corporations, yet surprisingly little research has been done on why multinational food corporations exist. The easy theories don't fit. First, international trade theory has little relevance to multinational food corporations because, unlike multinational manufacturers, the food corporations do little importing and exporting; they manufacture and market locally in many nations. Second, from international finance theory, one might expect to see food as a facade behind which sophisticated financial manoeuvres are orchestrated. Actually, all the multinational food corporations I have studied use quite simple financial structures, and prefer each subsidiary to finance itself. (By multinational food corporations, I do not mean the great trading houses in wheat and other standardized cereals. Financially, these are very sharp.) The third theory is that of industrial organization, and explicit rivalry based on internalized advantages. This theory gives some insight into multinational food corporations.

This chapter will review briefly the management of a brand as though it were alone in its country. Actually, multiple brands are sold in many nations, and the contribution of this chapter centres around the need for executives to articulate and analyse the boundaries of their portfolio of brands and nations. Usually the corporation has internalized some particular advantage so it can help some kinds of branded products more than others. Unilever, H.J. Heinz and Weston are multinational food corporations in the international fish business, but in each case the fish divisions appear to be an awkward appendage, more akin to a conglomerate diversification. To understand why fish are near the limit of tolerance of a multinational food company we shall examine the nature of the fishing business and discuss some design criteria for multinational fish corporations.

Food Brand Management

In biology, a niche is a habitat in which one species has dominated and from which it excludes all others. By a circular definition, a species is that which occupies a niche. In marketing, the niche is a market segment, and because brands are artificial beings, several brands can coexist in one market segment. In this coexistence, their rank by market share rarely changes (overtaking is rare), and their market shares usually follow a Pareto distribution (with the lead brand slightly larger than Pareto). The strategy of each brand manager is to position his product with an eye to customers' ideal points and simultaneously to the location of his rivals. To reposition, brand managers advertise, watch for opportunities to overtake (though few occur), and hone the image of their brand and the product itself.

Brand managers do not advertise evenly. Advertising budgets of 10–18 per cent of sales price are common for the lead brand in a segment. The lead brand usually advertises with almost twice the budget of all the other brands combined. Four reasons come to mind for this behaviour. First, the lead is positioned near the ideal point of most of the customers and wants to keep rivals away. Second, the work to create a good advertising theme constitutes a huge fixed cost which can better be afforded by the brand with the largest market share. Third, advertising increases industry sales, the benefits of which are greater to the brand with the largest market share. Fourth, many lead brands are surprisingly old, each constitutes a real investment, sustained by advertisements, and protected by the product being consistently available and of consistently high quality.

Although little overtaking actually succeeds, brand managers continuously scan for openings. If a smaller rival wants to become dominant it cannot expect to overtake by emulating the lead. A rival can succeed first by discerning and exploiting some natural segmentation in the market, and dominating that narrow niche. To protect itself, the lead brand is forced into niche-splitting approaches such as proliferating sizes, or sales teams, and developing products and qualities that are genuinely hard to emulate.

When a lead brand is being nibbled by a more narrowly focused rival the lead rarely cuts price, far preferring non-price competition. Cutting price to regain one subsegment would reduce revenue from the other subsegments. The lead brand is a discriminating monopolist over the market subsegments but cannot sustain price discrimination because the price of a lead brand is so easy to communicate. The lead has to resort to non-price competition.

Furthermore, from experience curve analysis one would expect the lead brand to have a lower unit cost than its smaller rival. So a smaller rival would be rash to attempt to overtake by cutting price. The price-cutting pathway to overtaking is sensible only if the rival brand is part of a much larger corporation, able to loan years of cash flow, manufacturing prowess and marketing sophistication.

A brand manager's third means of repositioning the product is to work on the consistency of the personality which the brand projects. It is often said that a good brand has a personality like a person, with values, norms and boundaries which should not be transgressed. Just as people are different, so are brand personalities. Rolls-Royce and Woolworths are each valuable brands, yet their personalities are different. Betty Crocker promises wholesomeness, whereas Smirnoff promises high-class seduction. Each brand personality ought to be clear-cut, distinctive and congruent with the physical product. A brand manager's behaviour varies with the position of the brand. The lead brand has a personality that seems to be winning, so should not be tampered with. The corporation can be said to be 'committed' to the brand. No such inhibitions crimp the style of less committed brand managers. In their search for a subsegment, they experiment and change. In a multinational corporation, the brand does not need a different personality in each nation, though its presentation of self should be adapted. The physical product may be blended to local tastes (Nescafé is different in each nation, as is Heinz ketchup) but the personality of the brand can remain coherent. In most multinational food corporations, even in such a polycentric corporation as Unilever, the last twenty years have seen a ruthless harmonization of global brand personalities. Unfortunately, harmonization has its limits. A brand personality appropriate to be the lead is miscast in markets where a rival is already finally entrenched as lead.

Multinational Portfolio of Brands

In a multinational corporate headquarters, it is necessary to be able to visualize the corporation's involvement in of all its brands in all national markets. The most useful diagram is a matrix of brands on one axis and nations on the other. Instead of listing the brands and nations alphabetically, they can be sequenced by their importance to the corporation. Sort the nations by their number of committed brands, and do likewise by sequencing brands by the number of nations in which they are committed (see Figure 10.1).

Factor analysis can be used if more sophisticated weighting schemes

Figure 10.1: **Nations and Committed Brands**

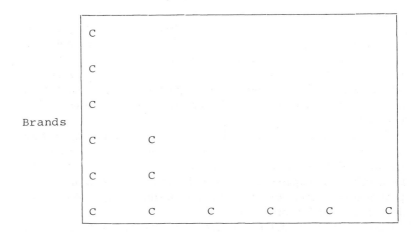

are to be considered. However, it is not the purpose of this chapter to fixate on the methodology. Our purpose is to comb out confusion, by finding ways to describe the pattern of committed cells.

First, there may be one centre of cells, or several centres. Several centres would occur if the corporation had incorporated some significant international mergers, or if several power centres coexisted as in a polycentric corporation.

Second, from the concept of experience curves, we would argue that the launch of a brand in a nation draws on the corporation's worldwide experience with the brand and simultaneously its experience with all brands in the nation.

Corporations who perceive that the brand constitutes their core skill will try to capture the advantages of the brand by spreading it worldwide. Their brand managers see each unlaunched nation as an opportunity going to waste. The opportunity constitutes both the emotional desire to spread the benefits of this brand, and also a game theoretic desire to pre-empt rivals by establishing first. However, in such brand-centred corporations, to launch a new brand is a formidable long-term investment.

On the other hand, there are corporations who perceive that their core skill lies in distribution in a nation. Some persuade retailers to reduce the shelf space available to rival brands, and justify launching a new brand on the grounds of squeezing more shelf space. However, in such a corporation, to launch in a new nation is a major investment in years of training, supervision and management.

In addition to studying the whole matrix in the current year, one can also consider a matrix of nations and brands but mark only new arrivals in the last decade. Some corporations tend to present rows of new brands, and others tend to have encouraged columns of new nations. Most do some of both, but the preponderance of their effort can be summarized as a slope if the matrix of cells is replotted on log-log paper.

Third, the brand-nation matrix of some corporations has a tight interface, whereas for others the cells are quite diffuse. From the discussion of shared experience, it is clear that an isolated brand draws on neither brand experience nor on nation experience, so is unlikely to be strong on its own. An index of diffusion (the opposite of interface clarity) could be developed.

Fourth, the fact that a lead brand in a nation constitutes a real investment has the corollary that it is expensive to establish brand leadership in a nation. This real investment does not appear on a coporation's balance sheet, so the expenses of establishing a brand appear as a loss on the corporation's income statement (strictly speaking, it is an investment with 100 per cent depreciation in the first year). The corporate executives see a trade-off between rate of expansion and *reported* profits. Conversely, a corporation with doubts about its future in a nation knows that it cannot get expropriation insurance for brand names and so will cease building its distribution network, will cut its advertising and sales force, and will raise prices as it terminates its market share. During this one- or two-year manoeuvre its reported profits will appear so abnormally high as to invite government investigation, thus fulfilling the original spectre of political risk.

Limits on a Brand

A customer perceives some benefit from paying a premium price for a branded product. From an information-processing viewpoint the customer, to be a rational economic person, ought to perform complex calculations. The customer can choose between, on the one hand, the expected time cost of making these calculations and the disutility of choosing wrongly, against, on the other hand, the price premium of a branded product. Obviously, the brand has to be instantly recognizable and has to promise the kind of product wanted for the customer to prefer it.

An effective brand personality demands that the product be of consistent quality and be always available. The investment a corporation has in its brand is at jeopardy unless assured of consistent quality and availability. In a food company either failure constitutes an emergency which draws in surprisingly senior executives.

Sardines, tuna, salmon and mackerel are fish that can be canned to consistent quality specifications, and then carried in inventory to assure availability. Although canned fish have brand names, no dominant brand names have been created to rank with Campbell soup, Heinz ketchup or Kleenex tissues. A circularity exists. Because there are many brands of canned fish, none can afford the advertising budget to differentiate itself; fish appears like the beer industry before the local brands lost to national brands. Frozen fish fillets, fish sticks, fish balls, etc., are now being sold branded. In Canada, Germany, Japan and to a lesser extent, the USA, one company is large enough to be lead. However, current brands being used are omnibus names that span many market niches. In other words, they fail to make it apparent how the customer benefits from the branding.

Limits to the Portfolio of Brands

Pursuant to normal economic thinking, a corporation should work at the margin, and add another branded product to its portfolio if the marginal revenue of so doing is expected to exceed the marginal cost. Determining the marginal revenue depends on the cross-elasticity of demand between this contemplated brand and the existing portfolio. If a food company considers adding a line of fish there probably is zero cross-elasticity of demand.

The marginal cost depends on the direct cost of producing this brand plus its effect on managerial overhead. Even a brand close to the corporation's core skill will increase the overhead as the increasing complexity of the corporation makes its executive work more difficult to co-ordinate. A style of nimble alacrity based on intimate knowledge has to give way to bureaucratic procedures into which all products must be forced to fit so that executives whose career paths were elsewhere can nevertheless evaluate the performance of each brand. Executive work is necessary only if they expect the corporation to gain from redeploying assets between products, and sharing the internalized knowledge, the core skill of the corporation, between products.

The dilemma is that there is not much economic point for having a corporation unless internalized knowledge is shared between products. If it were possible to estimate the cost of sharing between each pair of products, one could use factor analysis or other procedures to cluster like products. Given an existing cluster, one can measure the cost of adding each of several candidate products. To deal with several candidate products is an integer programming problem, the optimal solution to which is unlikely to be found by adding products one at a time.

External considerations play on the limits of the product portfolio. If one brand name covers all products then, just as the speed of a convoy is determined by the speed of the slowest ship, so the quality associated with the brand is heavily influenced by the quality of the worst item. Conversely, there is a free rider problem, in that each product manager would like to cut his quality, but be buoyed by the quality of the others.

An analytically more complicated situation occurred within the General Electric Company. Two divisions manufactured items to be medically inserted into the human body. The Medical Systems Division made pacemakers in competition with Medtronics and others. The Silicon Division made implants in competition with Dow-Corning and others. With the skyrocketing size of court settlements in US medical malpractice suits, GE executives decided that the corporation's potential liability was becoming too great. They distinguished between the cost of settlements (which could be bearable) and the adverse publicity to the GE name (which was not bearable). Too much executive work to build a coherent personality to the GE name would be imperilled. The corporation ordered its divisions to quit these products.

Fish Importers

Notwithstanding the problems of branding fish, some companies have come to *know* their market so thoroughly that they have learned to manage fish quality. To assure a more steady availability, these companies source their fish internationally. With trawlers and even processing plants in many nations, such companies appears to be multinational. Nevertheless, their focus is on their home market. We will look at a German, an American, and some Japanese companies. At first glance the German company appears especially multinational, for it is owned by Unilever, yet its core and unmovable asset is its marketing presence in Germany.

German Importers such as Unilever

In Germany 'as a result of the Schacht currency regulations in the 1930s, Unilever found itself the reluctant part owner of, *inter alia*, a fishing fleet and several cheese factories' (C. Wilson, 1968, p. 201).

In the 1950s Unilever made strategic decisions about its fishing businesses. In Britain, Unilever decided to allow its retail Mac Fisheries to diversify out of fish. In Germany, Unilever's Nordsee not only remained focused on fish, but integrated backwards, rebuilding its fish-processing plants at Bremerhaven and Cuxhaven and expanding its trawler fleet. By 1960 one third of Germany's deep-sea catch was landed by Nordsee trawlers. These trawlers were actually servicing Nordsee factory ships which froze fillets and produced fish meal at sea.

During the 1970s Nordsee's expansion continued, with a major downstream expansion. Marfels (1980, p. 174) provides details:

'Nordsee' Deutsche Hochseefischerei GmbH (Bremerhaven) is controlled by the Unilever Group which holds 19% of stock directly and another 50% via Deutsche Unilever GmbH; the remaining 31% is held by the Dresdner Bank AG. 'Nordsee' is truly a giant in the German fish industry; it is a perfect example of a vertically integrated operation encompassing all stages of production and distribution. To begin with, 'Nordsee' holds the lion's share in the German high-seas fishing fleet with 65% of the total tonnage in 1971. As of 1977, 'Nordsee' operated 36 modern ships, 15 of which had deep-freeze facilities. On the fish processing level, 'Nordsee' operates the following wholly-owned companies in Bremerhaven, Cuxhaven and Kiel: Lysell GmbH, 'Fisch ins Land' GmbH, 'Frostfilet' GmbH, Kiel-Frost GmbH & Co. KG, 'Seeadler' Fischinudstrie GmbH, Chr. Wollmeyer GmbH and 'Norfico' Feinkost GmbH; 'Nordsee' has also held 60% of the Walter von Eitzen GmbH since 1968, 40% is held by its closest competitor, Fisch-Union GmbH & Co. KG (a 1967 merger of five German firms). 'Nordsee' is also the leading wholesaler of fish via its subsidiary 'Deutsche See' Frisch- und Tiefkuhl Service GmbH (Bremerhaven) which operates a fleet of some 1,250 deep-freeze container trucks and delivers to restaurants, canteens, and food catering companies. On the retail level, 'Nordsee' operates some 300 fish specialty stores in 225 cities in Germany and

Austria. To conclude this spectrum from the sea to the consumer, 'Nordsee' also owns some 150 fish restaurants in Germany, Austria, the Netherlands, and Switzerland. The combined turnover from all of these operations exceeded DM 1 billion in 1977. This means a 100% increase from the 1971 turnover. In that year, 'Nordsee' had total sales of DM 548 million; the fish processing stage contributed DM 225 million, i.e. 50% of the total activity of 'Nordsee' . . . The Unilever-Group was able to expand share market (from 36% in 1970) by almost nine percentage points to close to 45% in 1977.

Within Unilever, Nordsee has a global product mandate to manage fish. Unilever's managerial style for all its operating units in all nations is simultaneously loose and tight. Headquarters imposes tight constraints on each subsidiary's borrowing limits, its product quality, and its use of trade marks. Within these constraints, Unilever managers have great freedom. Headquarters reallocates resources not so much by directing funds from cash cows to star products, but by reassigning their most energetic and their least energetic managers. Nordsee stays within its borrowing limits, manages its quality well, and uses its own trade mark. Furthermore, Nordsee has created the belief that fish managers are not easily exchanged with managers of other Unilever products. The consequence has been that Nordsee operates as an independent fiefdom within Unilever. Its market power was so great in Germany, Austria and Italy that Nestle's Findus conceded its rivalry with Unilever and formed a 25 per cent–75 per cent joint venture. As Nestle's managing director Pierre Liotant-Vogt (1976) reported, 'They were established before we were; they had a much larger turnover, and we were losing a lot of money while fighting hard to keep our market share.'

US Importers such as H.J. Heinz

In 1944, when their father died of a heart attack, ownership of Star-Kist Tuna of San Diego passed to Joe Bogdonovich and his six sisters. Joe, only 33 years old, ran the business in a Yugoslav way — trusting the right men, remembering all details, being tough.

Tuna fish are hunted and a good tuna captain proves his prowess as a hunter by the tuna he catches. Top captains land five times the tuna of poor captains. Captains and crews earn a percentage of the value of the catch, so good captains can recruit a good crew and reward them with the percentage of a large catch. A tuna boat costs over $2 million, so a captain needs a company to be part owner of the boat, or to provide a bank guarantee for the captain. In exchange, the company gains a little control over the captain. The company's tuna processing plant represents a large investment that is profitable only if supplied steadily with tuna. Unfortunately, tuna catch rates are erratic. When the catch rate is down, the control the company has over the captain assures that he will deliver to this company and will push his crew to keep hunting even when independent operators would tie up.

Joe Bogdonovich reinvested profits to build Star-Kist, even though this meant paying few dividends to his six sisters. Finally they decided to cash out, so Joe was forced to sell Star-Kist in 1963.

Ralston-Purina agreed to purchase Star-Kist and proceeded to draw up guidelines for its operation and systematization. I am told that they concluded that Bogdonovich himself could never be housebroken to the Ralston-Purina standards and so informed him at the formal signing of the sale. Incensed, Bogdonovich sought out H.J. Heinz and in 20 minutes sold Star-Kist to the Heinz company with the clear understanding that Joe would run it. That independence has been preserved by four means. First was the man-to-man agreement between Mr Heinz and Mr Bogdonovich. Second, the sale was actually an exchange of stock and Joe Bogdonovich became a major stockholder of the Heinz company and a board member. Third, the US operations of the Heinz company lost money through the latter 1960s and early 1970s so not only was Star-Kist holding Heinz afloat, but the Heinz executives had no time to meddle in Star-Kist affairs. Fourth, Ralston acquired the Van Kamp tuna company; however, after they had systematized its operations, it became unprofitable. The moral was noted within Heinz.

Star-Kist also gained from its affiliations with the Heinz company. Its sales quadrupled in the eighteen years since merger (8 per cent per annum), and the Star-Kist name became the lead tuna brand. If the Law of the Sea changes rules for tuna hunting, the Star-Kist market brand will nevertheless be a major asset in restructuring the tuna industry.

Japanese Importers

Five Japanese fishing companies operate internationally. Ranked by size, these are Taiyo, Nippon Suisan, Nichiro, Kyokuyo and Hoko. These companies maintain trawlers in the North Pacific, off New Zealand, off South Africa, off South America (Chile, Argentina) and in the North Atlantic.

The companies use 200-foot factory trawlers which stay in their assigned fishing ground year round. A crew occupies the trawler for 10 months, is flown to Japan for a two-month home leave, and then is flown to another trawler. On board, fish are dressed within 5 hours of being caught, and the fillets are plate frozen (a quick 3-hour process). The trawlers have on-board fish meal plants to utilize the heads and guts.

The trawlers are provisioned locally. Each trawler can hold 1,000 tons of frozen fish. Every two months the fish is transferred at sea to a carrier ship, which steams to market. Usually the carrier ships go to Japan. As profitable opportunities arise, the companies service other markets. For example, they sell some North Atlantic squid in Spain and Portugal, and some South American cod in Australia.

Packaging in Japan is chic and appropriately sized. Lead brands have advertising budgets in excess of 10 per cent of their wholesale price. Japanese consumers demand fresh fish, and are acutely aware if fish was kept too long before freezing. Many attribute this awareness to the eating of sushimi, a raw fish delicacy. A consequence is that Japanese companies face quality control problems when they purchase fish abroad. In Canada, the Japanese have had to insist on having their technicians at the processing plant whenever a Japanese order is being handled. Some aware Canadian companies welcome the technical assistance, others chafe at the intrusion. Japanese companies would have more direct control of quality if they were (part) owners of the fishing companies, but such is not encouraged by the Canadian government. Equity participation is permitted in the USA and many Alaska firms now have Japanese partners or owners. Just one of many examples is that

> in October 1973 Kyokuyo Hogei Co. Inc. (Japan's fourth largest fisheries company) acquired 99 per cent of the capital stock of Whitney-Fidalgo Seafoods Inc. for about $11 million in addition to $1.2 million worth of convertible subordinated debentures. By this transaction, Kyokuyo obtained title to seven canneries, two freezing plants, and a floating shrimp production facility . . . The Japanese company thus became the largest fish processor in Alaska, with annual revenues of $35–$45 million generated in the state. (Sullivan and Heggelund, 1979, p. 45)

Fish Trading Companies with Quick Knowledge in Many Markets and Many Oceans

In the decades of the 3-mile limit, local fishermen supplied local fish to local consumers. Simultaneously, the oceans of the world were trawled by German, Japanese, Polish and Soviet fleets, each knowing the species desired in its home market and where in the world to find them — as the three importer examples illustrated.

The worldwide move to 200-mile limits has fenced off much of the ocean that can be trawled. Many species, unwanted by their local fishermen, have in essence become trapped within someone's 200-mile limit. Although the distant markets remain, the local fishermen are unfamiliar with the particular packaging and quality that each distant market demands. Such knowledge was so deeply internalized that it was taken for granted, and has proven to be very difficult to transfer.

Joint Trawlers is a Swedish–Lebanese company which specializes in 200-mile fishing limits in the way some corporations specialize in marketing. Its Swedish heritage permits it to deal with agencies of all governments and use superbly its global communications system; its Lebanese heritage is comfortable bartering between species of fish. One of its many 1981 transactions may illustrate the company's quick knowledge of many markets and many oceans.

Joint Trawlers charterd from the Soviet government factory ships with crews, and had them anchor off Nova Scotia. During the Canadian herring season, the Canadian government permitted its fishermen to sell herring (deemed 'surplus to domestic processing and marketing capacity, or where no Canadian market exists at economically acceptable returns to fishermen') to Joint Trawlers. In Canadian idiom, these are 'over the side' sales. Joint Trawlers instructed the Soviets as to how the herring were to be packed, and was comfortable changing specifications as supply conditions changed.

In 1981 much of the Canadian herring was sent to Poland, where Joint Trawlers swapped it for Baltic herring. The herring/herring exchange rate altered through time. The Baltic herring was shipped to Nigeria, and swapped for Nigerian sardines. Again, the barter exchange rate adjusted through time. Joint Trawlers then sold the sardines in Egypt for US dollars.

The skill of Joint Trawlers is that it gains access to fish by hiring individuals able to negotiate with each government, and then sustains the ongoing communications necessary to be responsive to changing supplies, and changing market needs.

Fish Exporters

The marketing approach of understanding one's customers, and tailoring the product and its availability to the customers' needs, has been likened to the ease by which one can pull a piece of string. Nevertheless, the 200-mile limits have established property rights such that several nations are exporting fish. Some are finding it as easy as pushing a piece of string.

Much Canadian fish is exported to the USA. Only National Sea Products has invested in dominant brand names in the US market. Most East Coast Canadian fish is sold to brokers in Boston as frozen fillets and blocks.

Although the US Department of Commerce issues a daily 'blue sheet' of fish prices in the Boston market (as it issues a pink sheet for New Orleans, etc.) very little fish is now sold through the Boston market. In the 1940s several hundred ships unloaded every day at the New England Fish Exchange, and a broad-based market existed. In the 1980s there are many days in which only one small fishing boat brings its catch for auction; days occur when no ships land, and so the previous day's prices are re-reported.

Instead of going through the New England Fish Exchange, most fish transactions are negotiated privately, but at a price to be a few cents per pound premium or discount from the reported Boston price on the day the fish is delivered. So, though the Boston market is painfully thin, the total volume of transactions it affects is large. The reason for by-passing the market does not seem to be the transactions cost (low indeed) but rather the desire of a buyer to authenticate the quality he receives by dealing with known sellers (J.A. Wilson, 1980).

Trust underlies brokerage work, particularly for perishables, and many Boston fish brokers have been in the same family for three and four generations. Yet none appear to be very rich; some brokers are closing, and others explain that their children have followed other professions. The brokers' ability to respond to erratic supply and uneven quality is less prized now that fish is frozen and there are fewer and bigger buyers. (McDonald's is now a larger buyer than the US Army.)

If the fish markets were to shut down, there would no longer be an authoritative daily spot price. Contracts of sale, negotiated for several months into the future, would then have to include explicit penalty clauses for failing to deliver the stated tonnage. Fish exporters will then find it safer to own their broker, to establish a sales organization. The impetus however derives from vulnerability in the face of uncertain quantity and quality of fish.

The Problem of Uncertain Supply

One extreme myth, popular with government economists, is that fish in the water of a nation's 200-mile limit are like money in the bank. If not fished their population grows, just as money earns interest. Just as a bank needs tellers, so a nation needs fishermen.

At the opposite extreme, and popular with fishermen in the days of a 3-mile limit, is the myth that fishing is like big game hunting. The skill of one fisherman (or trawler captain) is pitted against that of the others. This myth — that nothing is predictable — has the flavour of Hemingway and appeals to the romantic in all of us.

A third myth, held by simple probabilists such as nuclear physicists, is that fish are randomly distributed throughout the ocean water. If this were so, the fish-water mixture would be so dilute that random trawling would be uneconomical. Actually each species of fish has its preferred water temperature, nutrient density, etc., and as these inputs change with the cycles of the year so the fish move in schools. In schools, fish are very highly concentrated.

From this follows a fourth myth that the abundance of fish is highly correlated with their availability (catch per unit effort). Two counter examples reveal the myth. Manhadden school near the surface so once fishermen locate a school their cost of fishing is almost a constant per fish regardless of the abundance of fish in the school (unless of course fishermen wipe out the school, in which case their cost per fish will rise on the more diluted remnants). Groundfish provide a second counter example. Some groundfish, such as sole and flounder, live at the bottom, and others, like redfish and cod, are on the ocean bottom only in the daytime. A trawler catches groundifsh by towing a net along the ocean bottom — possible only when the ocean bottom is smooth. A single boulder on a gravel bottom tears the net. Only a small percentage of the ocean floor is gravel or silt with no boulders. These are the fishable or available zones. Fish may be abundant a few miles away, but are unavailable if there are occasional boulders. A research vessel, concerned with recruitment, usually measures abundance. Availability means abundance only in the catchable areas.

Having disposed of these myths we can now proceed with statements about the stochastic nature of fish abundance.

Remarkably little statistical analysis of fish populations has yet been performed by biologists. The underlying stochastic processes are appreciably more complicated than a simple birth and death model, and when data are fitted to estimate coefficients in a variety of models there is no agreement as to tests of the better model. For example the non-recovery of the Peruvian anchoveta fishery suggests that some appropriate models should have zones of instability. This caveat of William Silvert of the Bedford Institute warns that the following studies are probably too simple.

(1) There is a life chain of smaller fish being eaten by larger fish. At the small end of the chain, pelagic fish such as capelin and herring are quite erratic in the number of young they spawn. The annual spawn of new herring varies by a factor of 10,000. This variation causes repercussions later in the chain.

(2) Only a few fish populations have been studied statistically. The number of sockeye salmon who return to spawn in the Skene River follows a log-normal distribution. The standard deviation is to high that 20 per cent of the returns are double the mean, and 20 per cent below half the mean. North Sea haddock also appear to exist following a log-normal distribution with a slightly higher standard deviation.

(3) From finance theory one would expect to find great attention given to covariance between species that taste about the same. However, biologists gather data by species, one at a time. For example, there are four races of mackerel which taste the same yet whose biological habits are quite distinct. It would be comforting to assume a zero covariance between their abundances, yet it would be very reassuring to have this hypothesis confirmed by data. I have uncovered no covariance data.

Government regulations reduce the long-run uncertainty, but increase the month-to-month and year-to-year uncertainty faced by a fishing corporation. The statistical significance of this statement is that to discuss variances and covariances of catch it is essential to give very serious thought to the time period between observations.

With 200-mile limits enacted by most nations, each government now has the problem of how to manage the species under its jurisdiction. Most have subdivided their waters, and have closed fishing in some sub-areas so as to allow particular fish species to replenish themselves. In the long run the cumulative effect should be to assure larger world fish stocks, and larger sustainable economic yields.

Getting from the (unknown) state of the late 1970s to the target (vaguely perceived) fish population is a tough problem in control theory. Even at the target maximum sustainable yield, some questions persist. For example, if the birth rate takes an erratic drop, by how much should the permitted catch be reduced? Those who believe that erratic drops will be followed by erratic rises would argue not to change the permitted catch — fishermen will catch less if they have more trouble catching. Others who believe that the underlying process is unstable (or very sluggishly stable) would feel more comfortable cutting the allowable catch immediately — though they would acknowledge that fishing companies have their own response functions, and may not have the equipment and crew to resume fishing once the allowable catch is increased.

During the transition phase that we are now in there are trade-offs to make, some of which are delicate because they appear contrary to logic. For example, the cost of fuel to steam to and from a fishing ground means that in equilibrium it is logical to fish near waters more intensively than distant waters. In steady state the fish will be less dense in near waters. During the present transition phase there are many examples of near waters being closed to fishing. Fishermen, bound for the distant open fishing grounds, see the untouchable fish on their sonar, denser than those in the distant grounds, and feel furious at the fuel they are wasting.

The Problem of Uncertain Quality

Disease affects some species in certain areas. Diseased fish can be processed for fish meal (a high-protein cattle feed whose price is set by its competition with soy-beans), or might be eaten once the diseased spots have been cut out during filleting. An interesting policy conflict may exist. It may be in the long run public policy to fish the diseased fish intensively to wipe out the disease. But it is in an individual fisherman's interest to bring home good fish. A similar long-term-short-term trade-off occurs with respect to fish size. In a fish farm small fish can be examined and young fish can be separated from mature runts. In selective breeding one eliminates the runts. A net mesh policy has the opposite effect.

Fish get damaged as they are handled. Aboard a trawler, fish are moved by fluming them along water troughs. Usually this protects them, but sometimes the fish get stuck in log-jams, and get damaged as one of the hands uses a pitch fork to try to work loose the fish. As the fish fall off the conveyor belt into the hold, some bruise. When the ship docks, the fish have to be removed. The choice of equipment involves a three-way trade-off between the time the ship will be in port, the cost of labour, and damage to the fish. In Eastern Canada fish are currently unloaded using a 10-inch diameter vacuum hose. Since that equipment became customary in the late 1970s the increment in value for premium quality fish has risen faster than the wage rate, so less damaging ways are being considered for the mid-1980s.

A branded packaged product has to be of consistent size. Fish processing plants categorize fillets by weight, and ulitize each category differently. This means that the product designers have to anticipate the distribution of size categories, and that the trawler captains have to be encouraged to fish to that distribution of fish sizes — something which was more possible before the days of tight government rules as to where and when a trawler is permitted. Fillets constitute less than 40 per cent of a fish by weight. The remaining 60 per cent is discarded at sea or processed into fish meal.

What is to be done with pieces of fish of the wrong size? Years ago they were made into chowders and bouillabaise. Nowadays they are more commonly blended into fish patties, balls, sticks. The future opportunity will be to devise products which customers find attractive, convenient and tasty, but which could be manufactured from blends of fish types — as wide a range as possible of blends which result in products of the same taste, so as to have the opportunity to adapt to whatever the boats bring in.

Fish are fresh when they are caught, and deteriorate thereafter. Holding 'fresh' fish on ice merely slows the deterioration. Whole fish can be frozen at sea but unfortunately are more difficult to process. Furthermore, a slow freezing causes large ice crystals which burst the cell walls of the fish, changing its taste and causing the flesh to feel pulpy. Fresh fish has very little smell. Fish several days old has a 'nutty' smell. Rotten fish smells fishy.

At present no scientific procedure appears to be in use to measure fish freshness. To determine freshness, the buyer smells the fish and looks the seller straight in the eye to detect lies about when it was caught. Because fish is constantly deteriorating it is not possible for disputants to bring in an outside expert to adjudicate the disagreement (as in grading lumber, for example), for by then the evidence will have changed.

The resolution of this indeterminacy has been described in general by Akerlof (1970) and in particular for New England fish by J.A. Wilson (1980). Buyers and sellers form diads of mutual trust and reputation, but have no incentive to improve quality above that which is minimally acceptable.

The problem of indeterminate quality affects not only free-market transactions, but also transfer-price transactions between profit centres of a corporation. It becomes difficult to hold managers accountable, for they cannot control quality. In North American fishing it is usual to follow a share-cropping incentive procedure and pay each crew member a pre-specified percentage of the value of the catch (from one-eighth of 1 per cent for a hand to 5 per cent for the captain). Quality is imposed as a constraint rather than an incentive, because it is not scientifically measurable.

As fish decay they create various chemical compounds, one of which is methylamine ($CH_3 NH_2$). The quantity of this chemical in a fish depends on the species of fish and its extent of the decay. One might envision a hypodermic needle used to take a fish sample for quick analysis. Inspiration for this idea comes from the buying of milk in Canada which changed from milk cans to bulk trucks in the mid-1970s. Now the truck comes to a farm, the driver draws a small sample of milk and in 2 minutes has an analysis of its bacteria count, protein, fat and water. The farmer's price depends on these qualities, and the driver will not accept (and blend into his tank) off-specification milk. Conflicts of bygone years as to whether the milk is or is not sour have faded before the impersonality of technical analysis.

A second possible device would record the temperature history of a batch of fish. It would appear to be inexpensive to combine temperature probes with digital-watch-like integrated circuits. Irreversibly temperature-sensitive wrapping papers also exist.

Fish quality control at present is so unsystematic as to be incompatible with the needs of brand management by food companies. As soon as a set of quality measures is developed that is reproduceable, unambiguous and cheap to collect, then the marketing of fish will change. As soon as quality control is mastered, multinational fish corporations will develop to manage quantity variations.

Some Design Elements of a Multinational Fish Corporation

Assuming that product quality will have been conquered, that 200-mile limits and attendant government rules continue (and become more detailed as a result of the Law of the Sea conferences), and that the value of protein continues to rise in real terms, one can predict more multinational fish companies.

The key problem of organization design is that of managing risk. Market commitments have to be made long before fish are caught. So the marketing risk and the catching risk have to be designed congruent with the financial risk that the corporation can assume. Six risk management responses exist:

First, marketing risk can be reduced by selling simultaneously in many national markets. Though some nations will preserve their market for domestic fishermen, most nations cannot afford that indulgence. In the face of supply fluctuations, it will be helpful to distinguish three categories of national markets (by the corporation's market share) and orchestrate supply to the markets in an adaptive manner.

Category (1). Medium market share and high aspirations: supply these markets with whatever fish the marketing managers request. Their task of gaining market share by establishing a brand is so elusive that they need to be spared the frustration of supply interruptions.

Category (2). High market share and weak competitors: interestingly, these markets may be able to tolerate short-term supply interruptions when competitors are hurting too. This conclusion offends marketing managers who have nurtured their market through Category 1.

Category (3). Low market share and no aspirations: supply these markets as erratically as is necessary, because good quality fish have priority for categories 1 and 2. Use different brand names, for the reputation of the product will be low due to erratic quality and supply.

The *second* multinational response is to develop multiple sources of supply, as the Japanese and Soviets have done. For each species the variance of total supply can be low if the covariances of fish availability in the various catching grounds are sufficiently low (some may even be zero). The time period for analysis of variances and covariances is probably two months, the time period in which the corporation can redeploy its physical operations.

The *third* multinational response is to develop some products that can accommodate multiple inputs, and some brands that are general enough to accommodate such blended products. The value of such blends to the corporation can only be determined by an analysis of the previous two responses.

The *fourth* response is to inventory fish. An appropriate combination of inventories has to be orchestrated between:

frozen finished product
quickly capturable fish in holding tanks of fish farms

sectors of the ocean where nobody else can fish, not throttled by government constraints as to catch rate.

These three levels of inventory have to be held in several nations of the world, as many as dictated by the cost of shipment and delays (even embargos) that nervous governments might be expected to impose.

The *fifth* response is to move trawlers and fish-processing plants between nations as the markets dictate the catch. It is not necessary to own trawlers, for in many nations foreign vessels are penalized. The crucial ingredient is to have firm relationships with fish suppliers, and yet simultaneously have some flexibility in *some* relationships so that fish delivery can adapt to forecast market requirements.

The *sixth* response is to locate the headquarters of the multinational fish company in whichever nation will give preferred access to the most useful supply of fish. An element of game theory is involved, for a company must be incorporated now in anticipation of how governments will retaliate for decades to come. The style of management of a multinational fish company, with its government awareness and ability to alter sources of supply, will probably be more similar to petroleum multinationals than to traditional multinational food corporations.

Conclusions

This chapter has explored brand management as the rationale for multinational food corporations. The challenge of brand management is to dominate a customer niche, and commit the corporation to continuing with that niche long enough that customers can learn to prefer the brand. The corporation is willing to invest in a brand only if product quality and availability is assured.

This assurance has been achieved by vertical integration to speed the movement of fish from the ocean to the customer. Examples include Unilever's Nordsee, Heinz's Star-Kist, and five large Japanese firms. The market is fixed, and the corporate task is to find fish in any of the oceans.

Joint Trawlers illustrates a geocentric view, involving arbitrage of fish between the different sources and markets. It has no brand names; and one can ponder whether negotiating and trading is yet compatible with nurturing brands.

If technical measures of fish quality can be developed (two were mentioned), then brand marketing will become viable. Once that occurs, the pressure for assured supply will drive companies to become multinational. They will know their markets, though they may have to source their fish through locally licensed ships because of government regulations in many nations.

11 INTER-INDUSTRY DETERMINANTS OF FOREIGN DIRECT INVESTMENTS: A CANADIAN PERSPECTIVE

Robert F. Owen

Introduction

Subsidiaries of foreign firms bulk increasingly large in Canadian manufacturing. Accounting for 43 per cent of sales a quarter of a century ago, foreign subsidiaries (of which 85 per cent are US controlled) comprised slightly less than 59 per cent of total sales or total assets in 1973. Yet, there remain wide variations across Canadian industries in the extent of foreign direct investment. In petroleum refining and motor vehicles, which are among the six largest Canadian industries, subsidiaries of foreign firms comprised respectively 97 and 77 per cent of total sales. However, for the other four largest industries — pulp and paper, sawmills, smelting and refining, and iron and steel — the numbers are much lower; indeed, as low as 13 and 10 per cent for the latter two.

The empirical research of this chapter offers a framework for explaining such differences in foreign direct investment levels. It seeks to identify the characteristics of 115 Canadian manufacturing industries that account for the degree of foreign investment. The analysis also considers the closely related questions of the determinants of total foreign penetration (imports plus foreign subsidiary sales as a percentage of the Canadian market) and global foreign investment participation by US multinationals. In doing so, this study affords a test of the relative significance of variables associated with the recent literature on internalization theory. The latter research, which is surveyed by Rugman (1980b), has been greatly influenced by Hymer's PhD dissertation (1976) and the subsequent writings of Kindleberger (1969) and Caves (1971, 1974). Internalization theory contends that foreign direct investment can be explained in terms of goods and factor market imperfections. Thus, multinational operations enable the firm to overcome transaction costs arising, for example, from government regulations or permit an internal market in cases of market failure — such as in the pricing of knowledge. Among the firm-specific advantages of the multinational emphasized by internalization theory are those relating to R and D, product differentiation, management, economies of scale in production, and avoidance of tariff and non-tariff barriers. Thus, this study undertakes an exhaustive test of the relative significance of both the foregoing and other variables emphasized in the foreign direct investment literature. Since the primary concern here is to examine differences between industries in foreign investment levels, economic variables and institutional aspects of the Canadian economy which could account for the overall level across industries are not specifically considered.

In contrast to earlier empirical studies on this subject which include those by Horst (1972, 1972b), Orr (1973, 1974, 1975), Caves (1974b, 1975) and Hewitt (1975) — the current analysis is a decade more recent, more disaggregate, considers several additional explanatory variables, and distinguishes between source country, foreign subsidiary and Canadian domestically-controlled firm data. In addition, a survey of these other contributions suggests that certain of this research is at least partially defective — conceptually or statistically. Briefly summarizing some of the principal empirical findings, the analysis of this chapter suggests substantial support for internalization theory. Specifically, in comparison with earlier research this study underscores the relative significance of product differentiation, in so far as it is reflected by advertising, R and D and marketing variables as an explanation of inter-industry differences in the stock of foreign direct investment. Other critical factors include plant economies of scale and the relative size of Canadian domestically-controlled firms compared with foreign subsidiary competitors and their US parent firms. Thus, large Canadian domestic firms may act as significant deterrents to both foreign investment and penetration. Moreoever, this latter finding suggests further confirmation of internalization theory, since firm size undoubtedly proxies certain of the firm-specific advantages which are not explicitly included in the analysis. However, the conclusions of this study also challenge the significance of several variables emphasized either in the internalization literature or in studies of foreign direct investment. Notably, differences in the levels of Canadian tariff and non-tariff barriers, transportation and labour costs do not appear to be significant in explaining inter-industry differences in foreign direct investment. Finally, the extension of the analysis to determinants of foreign penetration in Canada and US global foreign direct investment suggests that with a few exceptions the foregoing conclusions hold more generally.

The plan of the balance of this chapter is as follows. The next section offers a brief summary and critique of previous empirical studies relating to inter-industry determinants of foreign direct investment in

Canada. In the third section a statistical analysis of the determinants of foreign investment and penetration in Canada, as well as those of foreign participation by US multinationals, is presented. The chapter concludes with certain recommendations for further research.

Literature Survey

In this section, the focus is on previous empirical work germane to the identification of determinants of the inter-industry pattern of foreign investment. Among earlier contributions, Hewitt's PhD dissertation is the most recent, and in many respects the more comprehensive, thereby providing a useful point of departure for the present analysis.

In a provocative initial examination of the empirical relationship among control, investment, trade and commercial policy, Horst 1972b) arrived at two relatively strong conclusions. Working with cross-sectional manufacturing data at the 2-digit level, Horst found indirect evidence that US foreign investment and exports to Canada were substitutes for one another. Specifically, in terms of the notation used in this study, Horst concluded that the R and D intensity of US industries was more closely related to total US penetration of the Canadian market, ISC, than to its two components — Canadian imports from the US, IC, or foreign subsidiary sales, SC. On the basis of a second set of equations, in which the ratio of IC to ISC was considered as a dependent variable, Horst arrived at his second conclusion:

> . . . Canadian tariff policy has had a definite impact on the choice between exporting and Canadian subsidiary production — the higher the Canadian tariff the smaller the share of U.S. exports and the larger the share of Canadian subsidiary production . . . (p. 38)

Horst went on to question both the theoretical and empirical relevance of effective tariff calculations since his own analysis suggested that nominal tariff rates were just as satisfactory an explanatory variable.

Although Horst's analysis was confirmed by others (see Baumann, 1973), several of its shortcomings have also been revealed by subsequent research. When Orr (1975) disaggregated Horst's 18-industry sample to a 70-industry 3-digit level, he failed to replicate the latter's result, concluding that 'higher tariffs discourage imports but there is no evidence that U.S. controlled production in Canada is substituted for these imports' (p. 233). A further difficulty is the equation specification in Horst's paper. The ratio of IC to ISC is used as a dependent variable without including any variables which capture the interindustry variation in the size of the Canadian domestically-controlled sectors — variables relevant to the import-foreign investment decisions of US firms. Since implicitly Orr worked within this same framework, this is also a weakness of his paper. The empirical analysis in the current study attempts to capture in part the influence of this omitted variable by including a Canadian firm-size variable.

Understanding of inter-industry determinants of foreign investment was advanced by Orr's subsequent research (1973) and that of Caves (1974a). In contrast to the results reported by Horst, these authors again failed to find any significant role for nominal or effective tariffs as determinants of foreign direct investment. Moreover, both Orr and Caves stressed the importance of several factors besides R and D and tariffs in determining foreign investment patterns. They argued that foreign subsidiaries are not only able to benefit from spillover effects of the home firm's R and D efforts, but also from its advertising and sales promotion activities. In addition to these product differentiation advantages, the size of multinational enterprises facilitates the ease with which they can fully exploit economies of scale and overcome barriers to entry such as fixed capital requirements and risk.[1] Caves and Orr both cited the importance of parent firm size — a result which is well established elsewhere (see Horst, 1972b). Thus, their work suggests a much more extensive list of possible determinants of inter-industry variation in foreign investment. However, the results of these studies also indicate less of an influence for advertising and marketing variables than in the current study, while placing more emphasis on parent firm size, and in the case of Caves, multi-plant operations.

Perhaps the most thorough study in this field, to date — certainly the most taxonomic — is provided by Hewitt in his PhD dissertation. Contending that industrial organization factors are more important determinants of foreign investment than tariffs, transportation or trade factors, Hewitt focuses on oligopolistic structure and R and D intensity as the primary determinants of foreign penetration. Hewitt proposes a 'satisficing' model which emphasizes the costs of firms' acquiring information, in order to study the interrelation between R and D expenditure, seller concentration and foreign investment. However, when it comes to the empirical application of this model, Hewitt relies on regression analysis essentially similar to that of Orr and the present author.

Specifically, Hewitt first used his extensive set of independent variables to estimate separate equations to explain foreign investment, Canadian imports and total penetration. Secondly, to provide evidence for his 'satisficing' approach, Hewitt estimated a second series of equations in which industry concentration ratios were found to be positive determinants of a dependent variable involving expenditure on R and D. However, this approach is unsatisfactory. In effect, Hewitt limited his analysis of multicolenearity to the variables which co-incide with his 'satisficing' model. Moreover, the coefficients from his first set of equations undoubtedly are biased because of his misspecification of a firm-size variable in terms of the ratio of US and Candian firm sizes. Interpretation of Hewitt's variable is difficult since it does not capture the size relationship between foreign subsidiaries and Canadian domestic firms.

Statistical Analysis

In this section, the determinants of foreign investment and penetration in the Canadian market, along with those of global foreign participation by US multinationals, are examined. The discussion is divided into two subsections. In the first of these, the basic approach is outlined and the principal dependent and independent variables are introduced. In the second, the empirical results are presented and interpreted.

Notation

The letters U and C are used at the end of a variable name to distinguish respectively US and Canadian data series; whereas a D is used to desig-nate dummy variables. Unless otherwise specified the data series are for 1973. A more detailed description of the variables, along with certain of the actual data, is available in Owen (1979) and in English and Owen (1981).

AC   total assets per firm for an average of all Canadian firms
ACC   total assets per firm for Canadian-controlled firms
ADC   ratio of advertising expenditures to total sales for all firms in Canada
ADU   ratio of advertising expenditures to total sales for US firms, based on a 1965–71 average
AU   total assets per US firm, based on a 1965–71 average
CCD   consumer-convenience industry dummy variable
ETC   effective rates of tariff protection for Canadian manufacturing

in 1970

FPU   foreign investment proxy for US parent firm participation which consists of foreign dividends plus tax credits deflated by the firm's total assets, based on a 1965–71 average

HU   Herfindahl index of US industrial concentration in 1970

IC   Canadian imports as a percentage of the total Canadian market, which is defined as the sum of total imports and total sales by all firms in Canada (the latter include exports)

ISC   measure of total foreign penetration in Canada equal to the sum of imports, IC, and foreign subsidiary sales, SC

NRD   natural resource intensive dummy variable

NTD   dummy variable for non-tariff barriers in Canada

PC   measure of plant economies of scale as reflected by the number of production workers per Canadian establishment, 1967

PU   measure of plant economies of scale as reflected by the number of production workers per US establishment, 1967

RDC   ratio of R and D expenditure in total sales for all firms in Canada, 1972

RDU   proxy for R and D intensity of a US industry based on the number of scientists and engineers as a percentage of total workers, 1970

SC   foreign subsidiary sales as a percentage of the total Canadian market, which is defined as the sum of total imports and total sales by all firms in Canada (the latter include exports)

SFC   ratio of sales force expenditure to total industry shipments in Canada

Basic Approach

The necessity of estimating separate equations – based on IC, total Canadian imports as a percentage of the Canadian market; SC, foreign subsidiary sales as a share of the Canadian market; and ISC, total foreign penetration (the sum of IC and SC) – is suggested by an examination of the correlation matrix between the dependent variables used in this study.

	SC	IC	ISC	FPU
SC	1.00	−.27	.74	.51
IC		1.00	.44	−.06
ISC			1.00	.43
FPU				1.00

The negative correlation between IC and SC offers partial confirmation of Horst's hypothesis that there is substitutability between these variables. The sample of observations on which these correlations is based consists of 1973 data relating to 115 three-digit Canadian Standard Industrial Classification industries. These data are thus more disaggregated and a decade more recent than those used in the studies discussed in the previous section.

In the search for a comprehensive list of explanatory variables for these dependent variables, those which had proven significant in both the theoretical and empirical literature on foreign investment were carefully considered. With regard to SC, for example, it is apparent that industries characterized by high advertising, concentration, R and D, and large firm size are likely to be those in which foreign subsidiaries enjoy substantial advantages over domestic firms. However, the advertising variables used in earlier studies inadequately reflect other marketing activities such as sales promotion. In contrast to these variables, effective and nominal tariff rates, non-tariff barriers, and economies of scale conceivably may affect foreign investment, although no previous consensus appears to exist.

Although several of the foregoing explanatory variables appear related to the dependent variables, it is less evident whether the appropriate data for these variables should consist of source country (US) statistics, host country (Canada) series, or comparisons between the two. Earlier research has often been unsatisfactory in this respect. One of the principal difficulties is that Canadian series may be capturing both common cross-country industry similarities as well as characteristics which reflect either the vulnerability of the industry to foreign investment or the extent to which the industry is already dominated by such investment. In terms of the empirical results, in the next subsection, firm size is an important case where the data must be distinguished both by source versus host country, and within the Canadian market by foreign subsidiaries versus domestically-controlled firms.

Table 11.1 reflects the economic rationale just discussed. It summarizes prior expectations regarding the signs of simple correlation coefficients between certain of the most important variables used in this study. Note that anticipated correlations with the total penetration variable ISC, can often be determined by the expected correlation with its components, IC and SC. For example, since the effect of advertising on total imports into Canada is ambiguous, its impact on total penetration is also problematic. To simplify presentation, Table 11.1 does not include a large number of theoretically relevant variables which did not

Table 11.1: Prior Expectations for Signs of Correlation Coefficients Between Selected Variables

	Notation	Anticipated sign of correlation between variable and			
		IC	SC	ISC	FPU
Dependent variables					
1. Foreign subsidiary sales as a % of total Canadian market	SC				+
2. Canadian imports as % of total Canadian market	IC	?			
3. Total foreign penetration	ISC		?		
4. US global foreign investment participation proxy	FPU		+		
Independent variables					
5. Plant economies of scale proxies	PC, PU	+	+	?	+
6. Firm size-assets per firm (for respectively):					
a. US firms	AU	?	+	?	+
b. All Canadian firms	AC	?	?	?	?
c. Canadian domestically-controlled firms	ACC	?	?	?	?
7. Herfindahl index of industrial concentration	HU	?	+	?	+
8. Advertising to sales ratio	ADC, ADU	?	+	?	+
9. R and D intensity	RDC, RDU	+	+	+	+
10. Marketing proxy	SFC	?	+	?	+
11. Effective rate of protection in 1970	ETC	−	?	?	?
12. Non-tariff barriers	NTD	−	?	?	?
13. Natural resource intense dummy variable	NRD	?	+	?	+

prove significant in the subsequent statistical analysis.

Some final methodological considerations should be mentioned. The statistical results presented below were remarkably robust regardless of specific sample or econometric specification chosen. In order to evaluate any bias that data-processing might have introduced, care was taken to estimate the equations presented below for numerous samples from which miscellaneous industries along with any other doubtful observations were dropped. The possibility of slope changes for subsamples of the data involving consumer-convenience, non-convenience, producer or natural resources industries was also considered (see Porter, 1974; Caves, 1974a). For several variables, alternative measures besides those presented in the text were examined. For example, asset and expenditure series were used for respectively the foreign investment and R and D variables. When it came to the choice of a functional relationship to estimate, other forms such as logarithmic and log-linear ones were fitted. Since the dependent variables are constrained to values between zero and one, the appropriate estimate technique involves a logit transformation of the data. However, in practice the number of fitted values falling outside the zero-one interval was very small, indicating that departures from the ordinary least squares model were not significant.

Finally, interaction analysis, including multiplicative dummy variables, was attempted to examine possible interdependencies between explanatory variables. However, none of these alternative specifications or estimation techniques altered their basic conclusions which follow.

Empirical Results

The most important statistical findings are reported in Table 11.2. Equation 1, which primarily uses US data series for the independent variables, offers the most satisfactory explanation for the dependent variable, involving foreign direct investment in Canada. R and D, advertising, economies of scale, the natural resource dummy and marketing are all significantly positive. Moreover, the product-differentiation variables assume a much more dominant role in this equation than in the results of other researchers summarized in the previous section. The commercial policy variables, ETC and NTD, were both non-significant in explaining foreign investment levels and of the wrong sign. Note that even though cross-sectional differences in tariff levels at a point in time are not significant in explaining observed inter-industry differences in foreign investment levels, this does not preclude the possibility of a threshold effect on overall foreign investment in

Table 11.2: Principal Equations

1.ab SC = .22 + 1.78 RDU + 2.42 ADU + .00047 PU + .079 NRD + 1.45 SFC + .16 AU − .33 ACC
     (3.43)*** (3.02)*** (3.23)*** (2.97)*** (1.69)* (1.32) (2.13)** (−2.03)**
     − .0024 ETC − .060 NTD
     (−1.18) (−1.06)
     R^2 = .38 No. = 111

2.c SC = .3467 + .0792 $\overline{\text{RDU}}$ + .0628 $\overline{\text{ADU}}$ + .0609 $\overline{\text{PU}}$ + .1192 NRD + .0350 $\overline{\text{SFC}}$ + .0330 $\overline{\text{AU}}$
     (14.39)*** (4.00)*** (3.21)*** (2.98)*** (2.87)*** (1.65)* (1.66)*
     − .0415 $\overline{\text{ACC}}$
     (−2.09)**
     R^2 = .37 No. = 115

3.a SC = .20 + 2.04 RDC + 8.70 ADC + .00028 PC + .10 NRD + 2.65 SFC + .27 AC − .50 ACC
     (4.08)*** (1.66)* (3.01)*** (1.85)* (2.29)** (2.42)** (3.86)*** (−2.87)**
     R^2 = .30 No. = 115

4.ab ISC = .47 + 2.86 RDU + .60 ADU + .00049 PU + .00075 NRD + 1.89 SFC + .06 AU − .44 ACC
     (6.59)*** (4.49)*** (.73) (2.85)*** (.01) (1.59) (.75) (−2.55)***
     − .0021 ETC − .049 NTD
     (−.95) (−.80)
     R^2 = .37 No. = 111

5. FPU = −.004 + .06 RDU + .18 ADU + .003 AU − .005 ACC + .000006 PU + .01 HU
     (−4.17)*** (4.64)*** (9.66)*** (1.96)** (−1.67)* (1.79)* (1.30)
     − .005 CCD + .005 NRD + .01 SFC
     (−3.97)*** (5.18)*** (3.90)***
     R^2 = .68 No. = 115

Notes: a. The coefficients of the firm size variables, ACC, AC and AU, have been multiplied by a factor of 10^5.
b. Tariff data for distilleries, breweries, wineries and tobacco products were unavailable. Consequently, these four observations have been dropped.
c. The lines above the variable symbols indicate that the independent variables in this equation have been standardized to have zero mean and unit variance. Note that the constant term, dummy variable and dependent variable are not standardized.
Numbers in parentheses are t-statistics. The figures after 'No.' indicate the number of observations.
Dark asterisks indicate the significance of coefficients: * significant at 90% level, two tail test; ** significant at 95% level, two tail test;
*** significant at 99% level, two tail test.

Canada or a possible role historically.[2] None the less, the poor performance of ETC and NTD contrasts with the significance often attributed
to these variables by both industry spokesmen and earlier studies.

An unexpected result arises from the inclusion of the firm-size variables. Reliance on just the US firm-size variable, AU, would neglect the
statistically and economically significant impact of ACC. The beta coefficients for these two variables, which are, respectively, $+14705$ and
-17556, clearly indicate the importance of ACC. Where Canadian
domestic firms are large, there appears to be an important deterrent to
foreign investment independent of US firm size. At least one other interpretation of the negative beta coefficient for ACC — the vacuum argument — is possible. Large Canadian domestic firms can arise in sectors
where large firms have advantages, yet other motivations for foreign firms
entering the Canadian market are absent. An additional explanation for
the fall in significance of AU may be that it acts as a proxy for some of
the advantages firms enjoy in terms of product differentiation. When
there other variables are included, AU is no longer as significant.

A useful way to assess the relative contributions of each of the
explanatory variables is to consider the coefficient values in equation 2
in which these variables have been standardized to have zero mean and
unit variance. The constant term in this standardized equation suggests
that a number of significant variables have been excluded, while the
coefficient of NRD tends to confirm that foreign direct investment is
concentrated in resource-based industries. Of the other independent
variables, R and D, advertising and the economies-of-scale variable show
the strongest performance, each with roughly equal contributions.
Once again the negative contribution of ACC is greater than that of
AU.

Equation 3 differs from 1 by relying on Canadian statistics for the
same variables. An immediate conclusion is that reliance on Canadian
industry characteristics rather than US series yields for the most part
the same results. The somewhat lower coefficient for the R and D
variable in this equation may reflect the extent to which such activities
are dominated by that of US parent firms. This suggestion is both in
keeping with certain predictions of internalization theory and the
earlier studies of McFetridge and Howe (1976) and Rugman (1981b),
relating to R and D in Canada. Finally, the lessened significance of PSC
may be due to the oligopolistic structure of Canadian industry under
protection.[3]

The pattern of coefficients and t-statistics in equations 4 and 5 is
sufficiently similar to those in the preceding equations to suggest that

many of the foregoing conclusions generalize to the determinants of total foreign penetration in Canadian manufacturing industries, ISC, and global foreign investment participation by US multinationals, FPU.[4] To the author's knowledge, no previous study has attempted a comparison between the determinants of foreign direct investment in a host country and overall foreign investment participation by a source country. In the foreign penetration equation, the US firm-size and advertising variables lose significance, since they are negatively correlated with Canadian imports, IC, while the Canadian firm-size variable remains influential. In addition, RDU, ACC and PU have as good or better explanatory power in the ISC equation than in its components, while AU and ADU are not significant in the total penetration equation, having different signs in the IC and SC equations. Although there are certain conceptual difficulties in using a profit-related series to proxy US foreign investment participation, equation 5 again indicates a quite strong performance for the variables associated with internalization theory. The contributions of the R and D, advertising, marketing and consumer-convenience dummy variables are particularly noteworthy.

As important as the results presented in Table 11.2 is the inferior performance of several equations and variables not discussed thus far. A Canadian import equation is not shown separately since in general it did not fit well — suggesting that the factors determining imports should be analysed in a somewhat different framework. An analysis of Canadian imports in terms of factor endowments, comparative advantage and other trade theories would undoubtedly be more successful. There is a long list of variables which have been emphasized in the foreign investment literature, but did not prove significant in this specific study. These included nominal tariff rates, transportation costs, a relative market size variable used by Horst (1972), industries' capital-labour ratios, risk differentials among industries, the Herfindahl index of US industrial concentration, labour-cost differentials between the US and Canada, and several additional variables based either on a comparison of US and Canadian series or a breakdown of the Canadian data for foreign subsidiaries versus other Canadian firms.

A difference between the results reported in this study and earlier research is the appreciably lower R^2 s. An examination of the residuals from the regression equations suggests that this may be a more illusory problem than it appears initially. Indeed, none of the 10 largest Canadian industries fall among those industry observations with the 30 largest residuals. Indeed, the fits for motor vehicles, petroleum refining, sawmills and miscellaneous machinery are unusually good. In contrast, many of the industries where one encounters difficulty explaining foreign investment levels are those such as foundation garments, gypsum products, thread mills and wooden boxes and coffins which are among the least important Canadian industries.[5] Moreover, the data for these industries is quite likely to be imprecise since it may be largely determined by the peculiarities of only a few firms. With an appropriate choice of dummy variables, one could substantially improve the explanatory power of the equations.

Conclusions

The *curiosum* posed by foreign investment data in the introduction to this chapter has at least in part been explained. In so doing, several earlier findings have been substantiated, others clarified, and certain new determinants of foreign direct investment have been identified. In general, the analysis indicates substantial support for explanatory variables involving the firm-specific advantages emphasized by internalization theory. Indeed, product differentiation, either in the form of advertising, R and D, or marketing, plays a more central role in the current analysis than in previous studies. There are also significant plant economies of scale in industries where foreign investment and penetration are dominant. A new finding involves the relative size of Canadian domestically-controlled firms which may act as a significant deterrent to both foreign investment and penetration. Although tariff and non-tariff barriers do not appear to account for cross-sectional differences in foreign investment, certain other locational variables such as natural resources remain significant.

Rather than concluding this empirical study on an overly sanguine note with regard to our knowledge in this field, it seems appropriate to emphasize several limitations of studies such as the present one, in the hope it will encourage further research. Instead of relying on single equation techniques, a high priority is to develop complete simultaneous equation models of foreign investment behaviour such as recently undertaken by Caves *et al.* (1980). Such models avoid a major deficiency of previous studies by more clearly distinguishing exogenous from endogenous variables. Another important shortcoming of cross-sectional industry studies is the implicit equal weighting of all industry observations. Since there are serious data deficiencies even at the 3-digit level, it is imperative that more complete series be collected by both government and international organizations. Not only are industries quite heterogeneous, but firms are also becoming increasingly diversified into many essential unrelated product lines. At present, the relationship between such diversification and internationalization is little understood. (See, however, the studies by Caves, 1975 and Wolf, 1977.) Yet, to the extent that diversification studies focus on the detailed product lines of firms, and examine factors such as product differentiation, they may provide essential clues for comprehension of the foreign investment phenomenon.

Appendix A: Correlation Matrix Involving a Subset of Variables Used in Study

	Mean	Standard deviation
IC	0.2199	0.1740
SC	0.3937	0.2345
ISC	0.6134	0.2521
PU	92.6224	135.3758
ADU	0.0213	0.0274
SFC	0.0240	0.0198
RDU	0.0372	0.0365
AU	7404.0000	28891.4688
ACC	5000.4258	12865.5977
ETC	15.1095	10.3288
AC	11774.0000	32452.9102

Note: Based on 111 observations

Col. Row	IC 1	SC 2	ISC 3	PU 4	ADU 5	SFC 6	RDU 7	AU 8	ACC 9	ETC 10	AC 11
1	1.0000	-0.2662	0.4428	0.0322	-0.1834	0.0724	0.1718	-0.0977	-0.1252	-0.0908	-0.1314
2	-0.2662	1.0000	0.7464	0.1705	0.3141	0.2036	0.4305	0.2734	-0.0761	-0.1070	0.3362
3	0.4428	0.7464	1.0000	0.1808	0.1655	0.2394	0.5191	0.1869	-0.1572	-0.1553	0.2221
4	0.0322	0.1705	0.1808	1.0000	-0.1348	-0.2281	0.1021	0.1790	0.3253	-0.0473	0.4777
5	-0.1834	0.3141	0.1655	-0.1348	1.0000	0.3654	0.1288	-0.0982	-0.1368	0.0877	-0.1102
6	0.0724	0.2036	0.2394	-0.2281	0.3654	1.0000	0.1531	-0.0825	-0.2235	-0.1225	-0.1340
7	0.1718	0.4305	0.5191	0.1021	0.1298	0.1531	1.0000	0.3316	-0.0046	-0.1960	0.2983
8	-0.0977	0.2734	0.1869	0.1790	-0.0982	-0.0825	0.3316	1.0000	0.1129	0.2067	0.8908
9	-0.1252	-0.0761	-0.1572	0.3253	-0.1368	-0.2235	-0.0046	0.1129	1.0000	-0.1589	0.3556
10	-0.0808	-0.1070	-0.1553	-0.0473	0.0877	-0.1225	-0.1960	0.2067	-0.1589	1.0000	0.0810
11	-0.1314	0.3362	0.2221	0.4777	-0.1102	-0.1340	0.2983	0.8908	0.3556	0.0810	1.0000

Notes

This paper is adapted from a larger study: *The Role of Marketing in the Concentration and Multinational Control of Canadian Manufacturing Industries* (co-authored with H.E. English), Bureau of Competition Policy Research Monograph, Number 11, Consumer and Corporate Affairs, Ottawa, Canada, 1981. Generous financial support for this research was provided by the Canadian government. The research assistance of Rick Johannsen is also gratefully acknowledged. Richard E. Caves, H. Edward English, Rosalyn Frankl, Peter B. Kenne, R. Shaym Khemani, Dale Orr and Alan Rugman offered particularly detailed comments on various drafts of this paper. They are, of course, not responsible for any remaining deficiencies.

1. A detailed study for Canada of such barriers to entry is offered by Orr (1974).

2. Mark-up price differentials between industries are also relevant to the impact of tariffs. Unfortunately, a satisfactory price-cost data series was not available.

3. In a recent paper (1981b) Dunning has suggested a three-category breakdown for classifying explanatory variables of foreign direct investment — depending on whether these involve ownership, internalizing or location-specific advantages. In this context the findings of this study point to the relative importance of ownership-specific advantages such as research and development, plant economies of scale, and product differentiation. Although natural resources appear quite significant in explaining foreign direct investment in Canada other-location specific variables such as transportations costs, tariff and non-tariff barriers do not prove to be important determinants. Finally, the firm-size variables may be interpreted as proxying both certain internalizing and ownership-specific advantages of multinationals.

4. The limitations of the FPU variable, which has been used in several earlier studies including those by Wolf (1977) and Horst in the Bergsten *et al.* volume (1978), are elaborated in Owen (1979).

5. Although this suggests the presence of heteroscedasticity, formal tests for both heteroscedasticity and multicolenearity indicated that neither was very important for this particular data set. The absence of multicolenearity is also suggested by an examination of the correlation matrix in Appendix A.

12 MULTINATIONAL ENTERPRISES AND TECHNOLOGY TRANSFER

Richard E. Caves

Introduction

The transactional model of the multinational enterprise (MNE) holds that international firms arise in order to evade the failures of certain arm's-length markets, especially those for intangible assets. Premier among those assets is the knowledge that represents new products, processes, proprietary technology, and the like. Thus, theory implies and empirical evidence confirms that MNEs appear prominently in industries marked by high expenditures on research and development and rapid rates of new-product introduction and productivity advance.

Although arm's-length markets for technology are failure-prone, they do exist. Many companies that produce new knowledge are not multinational, and much technical knowledge is sold or rented between unrelated parties. Persons hostile to MNEs have often proposed that the arm's-length market for technology be expanded and the scope of MNEs' activities cut back.

Economic analysis has contributed a good deal to our understanding of the international market for technology, but the relevant theoretical and empirical material has not been pulled together and placed beside the consensus interpretation of the MNE's basic characteristics. This chapter attempts such a survey. The first two sections consider (in partial equilibrium) the MNE's role in the international production and transfer of industrial knowledge. The third summarizes theoretical contributions (general equilibrium) on the normative significance of the transfer and diffusion of technology, and also reviews empirical evidence on the dissemination of proprietary technology, revealed by theory to hold central normative importance.

The MNE as Producer of Technical Knowledge

Research on the production and distribution of industrial knowledge customarily distinguishes three phases of the process. *Invention* covers the generation of a new idea and its development to the point where the inventor can show that 'it works'. *Innovation* takes the invention to the point of being placed on the market; this phase includes building and proving out any needed production facilities as well as testing and refining the invention itself. *Diffusion* is the process by which all potential users of the innovation actually come to make efficient decisions to adopt it.[1] In relating the MNE to these stages of technological development we shall largely collapse the invention and innovation phases. The process of diffusion, however, is closely connected to the MNE's distinctive activities and requires close attention.

Foreign Investment and R and D Outlays

The affinities between R and D and the MNE are extensive. We know from many statistical studies that the extent of research and development (R and D) spending is an excellent predictor of MNE activity in an industry. Most formal R and D is undertaken by firms of at least moderate size; similarly, scale-economy considerations allot foreign investment to the larger firms. Hence, in those industries where most R and D takes place, both the R and D and the foreign investment are likely to be concentrated among the larger firms. Just as R and D promotes foreign investment, it is possible that foreign investment promotes R and D. The established MNE has in hand the knowledge needed to predict the payout to innovations in diverse national markets, not just the home market. If the MNE's information network indeed yields an advantage for this purpose, it enjoys both a higher and more certain mean expected return from investments in innovation than a similarly placed single-nation company. Therefore the causation should run both ways between MNE activity and R and D spending.[2]

Only one study has closely investigated the effects of overseas sales opportunities on R and D — Mansfield, Romeo and Wagner (1979). They find that the large US companies included in their two samples expect to draw 29 to 34 per cent of the returns from their R and D projects from overseas markets via all marketing channels — foreign subsidiaries, licensing and export of innovative goods.[3] The more research-intensive the company, the larger the share of its R and D returns comes from outside the United States. The overseas share is greater for research projects, in pursuit of basic discoveries, than for development projects, which tend to adapt innovations to a particular market's needs. The authors also asked the respondent firms how much they would cut back on R and D if they could collect no rents from overseas. The reduction would be 12 to 15 per cent if research results could not be exploited through the firms' foreign subsidiaries, 16 to 26 per cent if all overseas rents were cut off. The larger the share of the

MNEs global sales derived from its subsidiaries, the larger the cut. The more extensive is the firm's overseas activity (both exports and foreign subsidiaries), the higher is the rate of return it expects from R and D activities and the more does its R and D tend towards basic research and long-run projects.

Although one wishes more evidence were available, the study by Mansfield, Romeo and Wagner leaves little doubt that large firms carrying on research base their R and D investments on the revenues they expect to earn worldwide. This global orientation of research activities is seen in mirror image in the patents taken out in countries not themselves major research centres; most such patents are registered by foreign nationals seeking global protection from imitation of their inventions.

If foreign investment functions partly to garner rents to the parent's R and D assets, it also serves as a method of acquiring knowledge assets abroad (Alsegg, 1971, pp. 218–20). Tsurumi (1976, pp. 116–17) points out that Japanese companies expanded their foreign investment in research-intensive countries such as the United States and West Germany in order to improve their access to technology flows after companies in those nations, conscious of burgeoning Japanese competition, grew more reluctant to license. Samuelsson (1977) also finds that the acquisition of their technology assets has been an important factor explaining foreign investment through the acquisition of Swedish firms.

Overseas R and D Spending by MNEs

If MNEs take account of worldwide revenue potentials when setting their R and D budgets at home, they also increasingly decentralize R and D activities around the world. Part of the spread is due to government policies, for many goverments aim to promote R and D activity in their own soil (Behrman and Fischer, 1980, chap. 6). However, economic processes once again are at work within the firm. The MNE must determine not only how much R and D to undertake worldwide but also where to put it. This process sheds light not just on the economics of R and D activity itself, but also on the transferability of technical knowledge across national boundaries.

We expect that the MNE allocates its production facilities around the globe so as to maximize the net revenue it earns from serving any given market. If its intangible R and D output could be transferred costlessly among its various plants, the R and D lab would simply be put down in the worldwide cost-minimizing location. However, two important forces keep all R and D from settling in to some technological

Shangri-la. First, effective supervision of R and D investments seems to depend on keeping them within earshot of the parent's head office, and the centripetal pull of effective supervision is amplified by any scale economies that exist in the R and D function itself. Second, the MNE's effort to maximize the revenue from any of its markets often gains from having R and D facilities close at hand to adapt the product to local tastes or the production process to the quirks of local inputs. The former forces pull R and D toward the headquarters location, the latter disperse it among the subsidiaries.

Both statistical and survey evidence[4] on the experience of US MNEs confirms this framework. First, the agglomerative tendencies for research to remain at the corporate headquarters remain strong, and not much over 10 per cent of the US MNEs' research is carried on outside the United States. However, that percentage grew rapidly in the past two decades, so there is little doubt that MNE managers do think about the optimal location of their research labs. Another revealing fact is that overseas R and D is oriented rather more towards development and less toward basic research than R and D done in the United States.[5] The pattern confirms the expectation that research aimed at adapting economic activity to local market conditions is often undertaken in that market. However, there are exceptions: basic research is more footloose than is applied research, and some of it goes abroad to seek out particular scientific specialists.

Statistical studies find that the MNE's R and D outlays are more dispersed abroad the larger the percentage of its global sales made by subsidiaries, and the less does the firm rely on exports to serve foreign markets. Scale economies also wield a clear-cut influence: the more important are scale economies in research, the less is it decentralized overseas; however, the more a firm's overseas production is concentrated in a few subsidiaries (where R and D scale economies can be realized) the more does it decentralize its R and D.[6] With these influences controlled, MNEs also show some sensitivity to variations in the cost of R and D inputs from country to country. Decentralization was speeded in the 1960s when US R and D personnel were substantially more expensive than their counterparts abroad, and the process has apparently slowed lately as that differential disappeared (Mansfield, Teece and Wagner, 1979, Table 3).

International Transfer of Technology

We now come to the international transfer of technology and the MNE's role in the process. After describing the arm's-length market for industrial technology we turn to the transfer of technology by MNEs, which leads into the product life-cycle and overall patterns in the flow of technology and innovations among countries.

Arm's-length Markets for Technology

The market for technology entails transfers between firms of technical information (designs, descriptions, plans, etc.), including the right to use or infringe upon patents, and frequently the services of the licensor's personnel to install and debug the technology or train the licensee's personnel. Agreements may be one-shot, transferring a discrete technology, but they often join the parties in a continuous and long-lasting relation.[7] The agreement includes a royalty rate, frequently some round-number percentage of the licensee's sales revenue or factory costs, perhaps with a minimum payment. The agreement also often contains ancillary restraints: the licensee will grant back to the licensor any improvements made in the process or product; the licensee will not export to certain markets or will otherwise refrain from competing in the licensor's product markets. Licensing is more common, the less physically complex are the goods and hence the more easily can technical information be conveyed. It is discouraged in more complex products such as durable goods for which much research may involve reconfiguring the product for competitive reasons: the resulting discoveries have little value for licensing to other firms (Wilson, 1977).

The terms of licence agreements reflect competitive conditions in important ways. First, although the evidence is limited, it appears that much licensing of technology takes place across national boundaries rather than between firms in the same country. To license your technology to another firm is usually to strengthen another maker of your product; the rival in a geographically separated market can be licensed without threatening one's own product-market profits. The more international the industry and the less are markets separated by tariffs and other transaction costs, the less licensing we expect to occur. No evidence bears on this hypothesis directly, but Peck (1976, pp. 535–58) observed that the rising royalty rates on international licences in the late 1960s — just as more sellers of technology were coming on the scene — may have reflected licensors' heightened awareness that licensed technology was strengthening their potential if not actual international rivals.

Competitive considerations affect the mix of terms found in a technology license. A licensee will agree to a higher royalty rate, presumably, if he is not constrained as to the markets in which the licensed output is sold. Therefore a licensor who imposes an export restriction is foregoing licence revenue in return for protection from competition (for empirical evidence see Herskovic, 1976, pp. 40–7). Licensors of established technology tend to make that sacrifice, but not licensors of novel technology that is likely to become obsolete before the licensee's competition starts to hurt. Similarly, companies are more likely to license their peripheral technologies than those used in the firm's core business activity, and licences of core technologies are more likely to contain market restrictions on the licensee.[8]

Licensees in the technology market also behave in ways consistent with the pursuit of a reasoned corporate strategy. Licensing has its risks for them, but it pays where the alternative of doing one's own R and D is poor — for example, where the efficient scale of R and D is large relative to the efficient scale of production (Herskovic, 1976, p. 20). Licensing also pays the firm that is well fixed for using but not producing the technology. A licensee will take on licences that require a costly and specific physical investment when the technology lies close to the firm's established competence, but will avoid large investments in specialization facilities when the licensed technology involves diversifying into unfamiliar territory.[9]

The means used by licensors to extract rents through their licences are important for reasons indicated in the theory of patents. Society grants the inventor a monopoly over his discovery, that theory suggests, because otherwise the intangible knowledge that his discovery represents could be freely copied by others. The inventor would lack any profit incentive to invest in finding new discoveries. The worth of the inventor's monopoly depends not just on his securing and preserving a legal monopoly but also on exploiting it skilfully. There the market for licences comes in: use of a licensed technology yields the licensee a certain revenue, and every dollar of it the licensor extracts as royalties brings him closer to maximizing rents from his innovation. A profit-maximizing licensor, fully informed, would write license terms that leave the licensee with just a normal profit. Of course, not every licensed technology is monopolized, and competition drives down each licensor's return. Once the licensor has incurred the fixed costs of developing and proving the technology, the cost of transferring it dwindles to the variable costs of setting it up and running in the licensee's plant.[10] Any competition among licensors tends to drive their returns down to this variable cost.

We have only a little information on where in this range fall the returns actually earned by licensors. One source claims that US licensors typically shoot for a royalty rate that relieves an efficient licensee of one-third of his profits — which is not to extract the full potential rent (Baranson, 1978a, p. 64). Contractor (1980) finds that large US licensors typically face competition from other suppliers of technology,[11] but his statistical analysis only weakly confirms the negative effect of competition on the total (lifetime) returns to a licence agreement. He does find that they increase significantly with the size of the licensee's plant, which presumably is correlated with the rents that the licensee can earn from the licensed technology.[12]

Licensing versus Foreign Investment

For our purposes, however, the chief importance of the licensor's market position lies in the (potential) MNE's choice between starting a subsidiary and licensing an established firm in an arm's-length transaction in order to serve a given foreign market.

MNEs arise because of shortcomings in arm's-length markets for intangible assets, and the statistical evidence establishes the prominence of MNEs in high R and D industries.

We therefore expect the relative advantages and disadvantages of licensing and foreign investment to determine where one stops and the other starts. And the empirical evidence on their prevalence ought to confirm these advantages and disadvantages. Put a bit more formally (Davies, 1977; Buckley and Davies, 1979), an efficient local firm will see greater present value in a given project than will a foreign entrepreneur, other things being equal, because of the latter's unfamiliarity with the territory. If the foreign firm holding licensable intangible assets could negotiate licence terms to extract the local firm's entire rent, it would always license and never choose direct investment. But the choice tilts towards foreign investment when the foreigner cannot collect the full rent or when suitable local firms are not to be found (say, in a less-developed country).

Several empirical studies (especially Baranson, 1978a, and Telesio, 1979) expose the factors that govern this choice between licensing and foreign investment. They suggest, first off, that companies do contemplate foreign investment and licensing as direct alternatives, preferring foreign investment for its greater rent-extracting potential, turning to licensing only if that potential cannot be realized (Telesio, 1979, p. 37).

The following determining forces emerge:

1. Licensing is encouraged where entry barriers deter the firm from foreign investment. Barriers presumably operate when the firm decides that the market is too small, meaning that entry at minimum efficient scale is not warranted given the market's size (Telesio, 1979, pp. 19-20, 38). Telesio (pp. 21-2) also argues that market competition disposes the asset-holder towards licensing rather than entering. However, this hypothesis also must rest on barriers to entry by the foreign investor, because otherwise competition would also shrivel the rents that a potential licensee would be willing to pay.

2. Licensing is encouraged when the licensor lacks some assets needed for foreign investment. These might include a stock of accumulated knowledge and experience about foreign markets,[13] managerial skills or capital (meaning that the firm's shadow price of funds is high due to good competing uses). These considerations help to explain why the smaller the firm, the more likely does it resort to licensing rather than foreign investment (Telesio, 1979, pp. 78-80).

3. Licensing is discouraged where arm's-length licences are costly to arrange, due to haggling over complex terms, enforcing the agreement, preventing quality deterioration by the licensee when a trademarked product is involved, and preventing leakage of a technology from a licensee's hands into those of unlicensed competitors.

4. The lead time required to license an established producer is usually less than that to start a subsidiary from scratch. If so, licensing is encouraged where the rents to the intangible asset are short-lived, say, because the industry's technology is changing rapidly (Michalet and Delapierre, 1976, pp. 16-17, 24). This consideration probably explains why Telesio (1979, chaps. 5, 6) finds that the proportional reliance on licensing (relative to foreign investment) actually increases with the importance of R and D for a firm: foreign investment increases with R and D, but licensing increases even more.

5. Risk considerations affect the choice between licensing and foreign investment in diverse ways. The licensor exposes no substantial bundle of fixed assets in the foreign market and so avoids a downside risk (say, when expropriation is a possibility) that may deter foreign investment. On the other hand, the risk of leakage of a technology into the hands of competitors deters a firm from licensing its core technology. This consideration probably explains why firms diversified in product markets are more disposed to license.[14]

6. Licensing is discouraged if the opportunity cost of capital is higher in the recipient country than in the country of the potential

licensor, because the licensee then will value the expected stream of rents to the technology less than the owner of the technology (Jones, 1979, p. 264). This prediction has not been tested on national aggregates, but it is confirmed by case evidence on how the opportunity cost of funds affects companies' choices between licensing or foreign investment.

7. Licensing is encouraged by possibilities for reciprocity: if you license a technology to another enterprise, some day it may in return license one that you require. Telesio (chap. 4) finds this practice quite common in certain industries where it supplies a motive for licensing independent of those listed above. The evidence marks reciprocal licensing as one form of mutual understanding among oligopolistic rivals in certain markets, a policy not without its negative implications for competition and market performance. The process seems fairly innocent when firms thereby assist each other in filling out their product lines. It becomes less innocent when going firms cross-license each other without royalty payments but decline to license to newcomers, thereby creating a barrier to entry (Telesio, 1979, pp. 62–4).

Some additional light is shed on the trade-off between licensing and foreign investment by Davies's (1977) study of British MNEs' operations in India, where government regulations forced them to choose between licensing and joint ventures with Indian firms. The MNEs were clearly willing to hand over more extensive packages of technologies, provide more extensive auxilliary information, and take the trouble to adapt the technology to Indian conditions when an equity share was retained through a joint venture. Although joint ventures have their own limitations they apparently also avert some of the disincentives to trade in intangible assets through arm's-length agreements.

Finally, Teece (1977) provides unique data on the costs of internal and external transfers of technology. He upsets the economist's usual assumption that information once developed costs nothing to transfer. In the average project that he surveyed, the costs of transferring a production process amounted to 19 per cent of the total costs of the project receiving it, with the range (for 26 projects) running from 2 to 59 per cent. Teece found that these transfer costs vary from case to case in predictable ways: they tend to be higher the first time the technology is transferred, and higher for newer technologies. They are lower the more prevalent are similar technologies among other companies, and the more experienced in manufacturing is the recipient unit.[15]

MNEs, Technology Transfer and the Product Cycle

A well-known effort has been made by Vernon (1966) and many followers to build a model of the international diffusion of technology under the rubric of the 'product cycle'. Although primarily concerned with explaining international shifts in production and trade, this model does relate foreign investment and the transfer of technology by the MNE to the diffusion of innovations. The product cycle was recently laid to rest by its progenitor (Vernon, 1979), although with no surrender of claims for its empirical explanatory power for two to three decades following the Second World War.

The model's interest for our purposes lies in the link it forges between the diffusion of an innovation and the location decisions of MNEs, a link quite consistent with the transactional model of the MNE.[16]

The model starts with the incentive to innovate. Most innovations, we assume, are labour-saving. Process innovations substitute capital for labour, or reduce input requirements for labour more than they do for capital. Product innovations such as household durable goods often substitute capital for labour in the production of utility within the household. The payout to such innovations is therefore greatest in those countries where wages and therefore the value of human time is highest relative to the user cost of capital. Invention is an economic search process bestirred (in part) by the inventor's perception of a need to be filled and a profit to be made; given the random nature of the inventor's search, his eye most probably falls on nearby opportunities. Therefore inventions and innovations are concentrated in high-income countries. Not only invention but also early-stage production is tied closely to the high-income geographic market where the innovation has the best prospects. Methods of producing it are fluid and small scale in the early stages. Uncertainty about optimal production methods and configurations of the innovation discourages either the development of large-scale production or worldwide search for the most efficient production location. They are also deterred by low price-elasticities of demand, small market sizes, and the low levels of competition likely to prevail for a new product. Therefore production as well as consumption of the innovation initially sticks to the high-income market.

Eventually use of the new technology spreads to other countries as their rising real wages (and values of household labour time) make capital-saving more profitable and as the real price of the innovation falls. This demand is at first served by exports from high-income areas, a prediction that accords with the high R and D-intensity of the export

industries of the United States. However, as the innovation's technology and production method settle down, a search intensifies for low-
cost production locations, and this search tends to carry production
outside the highest-wage countries. Increasing price-elasticities of
demand, as users grow more familiar with the innovation, and sharper
competition in the product market pull in the same direction. Exports
from the high-income innovating countries are displaced by expanding
production in other industrial countries. Finally the shifting pattern of
production and use, as the innovation matures, may carry production
towards the less-developed countries, and the industrial countries may
lose their comparative advantage entirely. Of course, the 'mature'
innovation may get displaced by its successor before this final stage
is reached.

Most systematic empirical research on the product cycle has concentrated on patterns of production and trade rather than the activity of
the MNE (Wells, 1972). Yet the prevalence of MNEs in high-R and D
industries and the disabilities of the arm's-length market for technology
transfer both imply that the MNE functions prominently in the international dissemination of innovations. The model explains both why
the United States should have been a fertile source of innovations and a
prolific source of MNEs, and US foreign investment has been concentrated in innovative industries both early (Vernon, 1971, p. 85) and
late (Gruber, Mehta and Vernon, 1967) in the twentieth century. As an
epicycle on the product cycle, the European countries' shortages of
native raw materials bred an incentive to innovate in materials-saving
technologies, a pattern reflected in the industry composition of Europe-
based MNEs (Franko, 1976, chap. 2; also Tsurumi, 1976, pp. 174–6).

Still, not much research on the product cycle focuses specifically on
the question of how much difference the MNE's presence makes to the
speed and direction of the diffusion process. Tilton's (1971) study of
the semiconductor industry stressed the importance of newly-founded
foreign subsidiaries in transplanting US innovations to the European
countries. Older foreign subsidiaries, however, tended to behave rather
like any incumbent firm: an established company will rationally
innovate later than a new firm, if the innovation makes its facilities
obsolete but is not so good that it pays to scrap that capacity immediately. Globerman (1975) found no statistical evidence that foreign
subsidiaries in the Canadian tool and die industry adopted numerically
controlled machine tools faster than domestic firms. Stobaugh's
(1972) investigation of petrochemicals and Hufbauer's (1966) of
synthetic materials both suggest that scale economies in production

and marketing retard diffusion. The firm that introduced the innovation gains a sustained first-mover advantage and delays taking production outside the country. When diffusion does occur, scale economies point foreign investment towards large host markets.

Apparently the only statistical investigation of the speed of diffusion and its relation to MNEs is Lake (1979), who is concerned with the relation between market structures and the international diffusion of technology among MNEs. His data on the semiconductor industry in the United States and United Kingdom weakly affirm the conclusion from many single-nation studies that diffusion is faster, the more competitive is the industry in which it occurs. He also finds diffusion faster when it takes place among firms with previous experience in the process, a result consistent with Vernon's and Davidson's (1979) finding that diffusion processes are accelerating over time. Lake also claims to find that US MNEs' subsidiaries have outperformed domestic competitors in the diffusion of innovations in the United Kingdom pharmaceutical industry, but his methodology is somewhat suspect.

The most comprehensive data on the MNE's role in the diffusion of innovation have recently been assembled by Vernon and Davidson (1979). They cover the overseas spread through subsidiaries and licensees of 406 innovations introduced since 1945 by 57 US MNEs. The results do tend to confirm the hypothesis that the MNE's information network and ready apparatus for making technology transfers affect the diffusion process. The higher the MNE's initial proportion of sales made abroad (through both exports and subsidiary sales), the quicker are innovations transferred for production abroad. Transfer comes quicker when the innovation lies in the firm's principal product line and when the firm has had previous experience with transfers in this product line. Similarly, the more previous experience with transfers to a given country, the faster is the next innovation transferred to that country. The MNE with a high ratio of R and D to sales (either relative to its base industry or relative to other MNEs) transfers technology abroad more rapidly.

The Vernon-Davidson data also provide some information on the use of subsidiaries relative to licensees in the diffusion process. For a sample of 32 firms transfers to licensees were 28.5 per cent of all transfers over 1945–75, the share declining slightly from 1945–55 to 1966–75 (perhaps because the firms' networks of subsidiaries were growing more extensive). Subsidiaries were predominant in the first couple of years of the diffusion of an innovation, but then licensees started to catch up. Licensees play more of a role for 'true innovations' than for new products that imitate other firms' innovations; presumably the imitations are attuned largely to oligopolistic rivalry among firms and hence have little value for licensing (compare R.W. Wilson, 1977).

The Vernon–Davidson results and others bearing on MNEs in the product cycle do not lead us to very clear-cut formal conclusions – certainly not about the product-cycle model itself. However, they are broadly consistent with the preceding analysis of international transfers of technology and, indeed, the explanation for MNEs' activities developed in earlier chapters. They are consistent with intra-corporate transfers of technology having some advantages over the arm's-length market for licences. They are consistent with international transfers of technology being deterred by transfer costs, but firms' alacrity to incur them increasing with the gross returns expected from the transfer.

Indeed, the consistency of the evidence with rational behaviour by well-informed MNEs makes one slightly suspicious of parts of the original product-cycle formulation, which invoked myopia and uncertainty in the introductory stage of an innovation to explain why diffusion beyond the innovating country is delayed. Vernon's recent (1979) revision of his views allows that the global information network of the established MNE may sever the link between the site where the invention is first proved and the markets where the commercials innovation takes root. He also points out that the United States is reft of its predominant role as a probable site of innovation due to the convergence of wage levels and per capita incomes among the industrial countries.

General Equilibrium and Welfare Aspects

The international licensing market and the MNE's development and transfer of technology have been studied at the microeconomic level. We now consider their implications for resource allocation in the overall economy and for economic welfare.

Theoretical Contributions

Economists pursuing technology transfer into the realm of general equilibrium have had a difficult time of it. Such models are traditionally static and do not easily make room for imperfectly marketed assets like proprietary knowledge. Even if one gets around the market for intangible assets, the effects of technical change on production functions can be complex to model. The relevant contributions are complicated, and so the following summary is selective (see Pugel, 1981, for a more complete account).

Krugman (1979) presents a model that does not explicitly capture the MNE as a capital arbitrager but does develop the general-equilibrium implications of technology transfers. Krugman's starting point is the product cycle (Vernon, 1966). Suppose that new technology consists of a continuing stream of product innovations, and that these all emerge initially in one country (Home). With a random lag each new good's technology becomes known in the other country (Foreign). 'New goods' are those whose technology is still known only in Home; 'old goods' are those producible in Foreign. Labour is the only factor of production, immobile between Home and Foreign. Under these assumptions Home's labour may share the rents from the extra value that consumers everywhere place on new goods. Depending on how highly consumers value new goods relative to old ones, Home may specialize completely in new goods, in which case Home workers earn a higher wage. However, if in equilibrium Home also produces some old goods, its labour earns no premium over Foreign's. Product innovations make both Home and Foreign better off – Home by improving the terms of trade, Foreign by making more kinds of goods available for consumption so that a higher level of utility can be enjoyed. The transfer of technology, when a new good becomes an old good, also increases the world's real income (because it is now produced by cheaper Foreign labour rather than dearer Home labour). Foreign clearly gains from the technology transfer. Home, however, can either gain or lose: as consumers, Home citizens find that the relative price of the 'newly old' good has fallen, but as workers they find their wage has slightly fallen in terms of all other goods.[17]

Homogeneous, internationally mobile capital can be added to Krugman's model, with its rate of return the same in equilibrium in Home as in Foreign. Innovation tends to raise the marginal product of capital in Home and pull capital in from abroad; the transfer of technology pushes capital abroad to Foreign. Capital movements in Krugman's model are a consequence of transfers of technology, not a cause. There is also a sense in which they substitute for technology transfers in making world production as efficient as possible. That is, technology transfers shift the world's production-possibilities frontier outward because they permit producing the existing quantity of the new good at a lower resource cost. From such an equilibrium with Foreign constrained to be completely specialized in old goods, it would also be possible in some cases to attain efficiency in world production by letting enough of Foreign's capital migrate to Home to produce new goods. McCulloch and Yellen (1976) develop this proposition as well as the implications of technology transfers for labour's real income. For example, with capital immobile internationally, Home labour benefits from transfer of Home's technology advantage to Foreign if the advantage is in the capital-intensive good. Then, after the transfer, Home's capital stock must be reallocated toward the labour-intensive industry, raising the marginal product of Home's labour in terms of both new and old goods.[18]

For an effort to show the formal consequences of MNEs as transferors of technology we turn to Findlay (1978; also see Koizumi and Kopecky, 1977). In his model Foreign suffers a systematic technology gap. Being backward offers a sort of advantage: the further behind the leader you are, the more easily can you pick up the leader's innovations and narrow the gap. Findlay argues, however, that this property of 'relative backwardness' really implies not a complete catch-up but an equilibrium lag behind the frontier. He assigns the capital that Home's MNEs invest in Foreign the role of a generalized promoter of technological improvement: the more chances do Foreign's native factors have to observe Home's advanced technology used by Home's foreign subsidiaries, the faster does Foreign's technology level grow. Thus, Foreign's general rate of technical progress is higher, the larger is Foreign's stock of Home-originated MNE capital relative to domestic capital, and the lower is Foreign's technology level relative to Home's. The model contains a complex mechanism that adjusts the stocks of domestic and MNE capital in Foreign, in relation to the levels of technology in Home and Foreign. When Home's MNEs employ relatively advanced technology in Foreign, they earn high profits, which are taxed by Foreign's government. This tax revenue is channelled to finance expansion of the share of Foreign's domestic capital, cutting down the rate at which the MNE capital promotes the advance of Foreign's technology frontier. Also, Foreign's wage level is assumed to rise with the expansion of that technology frontier, and wage inflation thereupon cuts into the profits of the MNE sector and slows its investment rate. The upshot is that the relative stocks of MNE and domestic capital in Foreign possess a long-run equilbrium value that is determined jointly with the technological gap.

The assumption that MNE capital has a 'positive contagion' in spreading technological improvement has striking implications that appear in some of the model's comparative-statistics properties.

Foreign's increase in the tax rate on resident MNE capital raises the relative stock of domestic capital and lowers 'dependence' on imported capital, but it also enlarges the long-run equilibrium technology gap. So does an increase in the rate of domestic saving in Foreign. Whether the 'positive contagion' hypothesis has any empirical validity is of course a separate question: the point of Findlay's model is that, should technology transfer take this form, it has quite surprising implications for economic policy.

Other approaches to technology transfer emphasize its relation to the commodity terms of trade, as did Krugman (1979), but employ a different strategy in building the model. Berglas and Jones (1977) allow Home's superior technology to be embodied in capital goods invested abroad by one of Home's industrial sectors.[19] The capital export is likely to expand world output of the affected commodity, even though risks to Home's foreign investors inhibit the superior technology from driving Foreign's inferior technique totally from Foreign's market. Home may lose from this export of technology (and capital) if the transferred technology pertains to Home's export good, lowering its relative price and worsening Home's terms of trade. Home would than maximize its welfare by taxing the export of technology. However, if the exported technology expands the output of Home's imported good, Home would gain by subsidizing technology exports.

Kojima (1975) is similarly concerned with technology transfer in the context of sector-specific technology and capital, so that technology transfers affect a particular sector and thus the terms of trade. His analysis stems from his empirical observation that Japan's foreign investment in manufacturing has emanated from the country's import-competing sector. When it raises technology levels in the recipient countries (in Southeast Asia, say), it is their export industries that are benefiting, and so international trade tends to expand. On the other hand, he argues that foreign investment by Western countries typically proceeds from their export industries to their counterparts that are import-competing industries abroad; capital movements then tend to reduce and substitute for trade (as in the Heckscher–Ohlin model). Kojima is not so successful formally in developing either a mechanism to induce this transfer of technology or a normative framework for evaluating its effects,[20] but he does usefully suggest that sectorally-biased transfers of technology may have empirical importance.

The papers summarized so far are generally concerned with the effects of free dissemination of Home's technology to Foreign and optimal policy for Home to follow given that no proprietary owner collects rents on the exported knowledge.[21] Rodriguez (1975) concentrates on the policy alternatives available to Home's government for maximizing the contribution of the nation's proprietary technology to its own welfare. In a general-equilibrium model he shows that, under certain assumptions (notably, constant opportunity costs: the slope of a country's transformation curve does not change as factors are reallocated between sectors), Home's problem of maximizing rents from its technology is identical to the problem of maximizing monopoly rents on its trade with the rest of the world. Suppose that Home produces soft drinks and controls the secret formula for producing their flavouring. Foreign's consumers are assumed better off consuming some soft drinks than if they consume only the other goods that Foreign can produce without access to Home's exports or technology. Then Home achieves the same welfare level (also leaves Foreign in the same welfare position) whichever of the following policies Home's government adopts: (1) an optimum tariff on Home's trade with Foreign; (2) a tax on soft-drink technology licences that maximizes Home's monopoly profits; or (3) authorization of a multinational subsidiary in Foreign to monopolize the soft-drink business in Foreign's market and maximize its profits.[22] Rodriguez's model becomes somewhat more complex if his countries' transformation curves are not flat, indicating constant opportunity costs, but bowed out to reflect increasing costs; then Home needs to impose both a charge for technology licences and a tax on trade in order to maximize its real income.

The preceding theoretical papers suffer from treating Home's stock of technology as exogenous. They thus neglect the basic dilemma stemming from failures in the market for proprietary knowledge: one cannot simultaneously distribute the existing stock around the world efficiently and reward inventors so as to induce investments in new knowledge. Pugel (1980 and 1981) investigates how induced R and D investment changes the consequences of Foreign's natural bent to free-ride on imported technology or tax away any rents collected in Foreign's markets on Home's behalf. Clearly the globally optimal royalty payment for the use of technology becomes positive, and Foreign may even improve its own welfare by coughing up royalty payments so as to induce a continuing flow of cost-reducing research. Foreign's taxes on royalty payments for Home's technology now have negative externalities for Home, because in cutting R and D investments by Home's producers they render Home's own (future) unit costs of production higher than they would otherwise be. In the same vein Koizumi and Kopecky (1977) associate the production of technology with learning-by-doing in the use of the firm's capital stock. The more rents the firm can gather by transferring a cost-reducing improvement abroad, the larger capital stock it then chooses to maintain at home in order to generate such experience-based improvements. In this model transfers of technology abroad can have an adverse short-run effect on the wages of Home's labour for the usual reasons, but a positive long-run effect because of the extra capital formation induced to capture overseas rents from the technology improvements.

Empirical Evidence

The preceding models together suggest that international transfers of technology may weigh importantly in the welfare economies of foreign investment. If the MNE is a significant agent in transferring technology, the positive effect on world welfare could be large. Therefore it is important to consider empirical evidence bearing on the MNE's role as a transfer agent. However, the evidence would ideally also shed light on the adversary interest of transferor and transferee countries in capturing the associated economic rents. These rents, we have seen, raise problems for policy-makers. What they should do depends on whether private property rights attach to the knowledge. Another vital influence is the incidental effects of the transfer on the terms of trade. Most of the empirical evidence bears on two questions: to what extent does seller competition erode the rents potentially accruing to MNEs' technology? Just how superior is the technology used by MNEs, on the average, and how much of it leaks out to competing domestic factors of production?

Some evidence indicates how market competition affects the rent streams accruing from international sales of technology and how national governments seek to divert these streams. How nearly like monopolists are the commercial firms controlling Home's technology when they sell in Foreign's markets? Is rivalry among them eroding Home's total monopoly rents and transferring them to Foreign's consumers? The evidence from industry studies could not be called 'hard', but does it show a tendency for firms unsuccessful or inactive in foreign investment to license their technology abroad, thereby competing with the foreign-subsidiary sales or exports of other national companies.[23]

Indirect evidence on competition and technology licensing comes from the behaviour of governments in this area. If sellers of technology competed as Cournot price rivals, rents on technologies would tend to yield only a normal rate of return on the resources used in the transfer (not the production) of knowledge. Transferee governments could not gain from intervening in the market for technology transfers so as to force terms of trade more favourable to their citizens. However, if transferors retain appreciable monopoly power, a government might usefully intervene to override the bargains struck by its own citizen-licensees and force a cost-minimizing all-or-nothing offer on the foreign owner of the technology. The gains from government intervention should be greater where its citizens bid competitively for the licence. Peck (1976) concludes that the Japanese government has appreciably raised national welfare by intervening in its licensees' negotiations and stifling competition among them. Davies (1977) similarly claims that the Indian government managed to halve average royalty rates and cut the duration of agreements. The apparent success of these interventions does suggest that licensors otherwise command appreciable monopoly power in arm's-length transactions. And of course the discrimination in patent policy against foreign applicants, employed by many less-developed countries and some developed ones, operates to the same end (McQueen, 1975; Penrose, 1973).

Much more evidence bears on our other empirical question: to what degree do technologies and related proprietary assets transferred abroad escape from their owners' control? Given the stock of knowledge, such leakage probably increases the recipient country's welfare and world welfare, while reducing the welfare of the country that invested to produce the knowledge. But in the long run, reduced appropriability causes underinvestment in such knowledge assets, and hence potentially reduces world welfare. For the policy-maker in the country generating the technology there is another question: do its citizens who use or license technology abroad correctly value the risk to the national welfare of the knowledge thereby escaping from proprietary control? For example, Baranson (1978b) and others have voiced concern that US MNEs do indeed 'give away the store' by licensing their latest and best technologies abroad to dubious customers who are all too likely to make off with the nation's intellectual treasure.[24]

A number of studies shed light on the leakage of MNEs' intangible assets, but only Mansfield and Romeo (1980) focus closely on measuring and evaluating the leakage of specific technologies. From a sample of technology exports by US-based firms they determined the average time elapsed between a technology's introduction by one of the firms and its transfer abroad. The mean lag was six years for transfer to the firm's subsidiaries in developed countries, ten years to subsidiaries in LDCs, 13 years for transfers to joint ventures or through arm's-length licences. In most cases use of the technology abroad was not thought to speed its imitation by a foreign competitor. However, in about one-third of the cases the appearance of a competing product or process was speeded by at least two and one-half years.[25] Mansfield and Romeo also secured from domestic firms in the United Kingdom estimates of how often their innovative efforts had been speeded by technology transfers from US MNEs to their competing subsidiaries in the UK. Over half felt at least some of their products and processes had been introduced, or introduced sooner, because of the competitive effect of these transfers.

Beyond Mansfield and Romeo, a number of studies touch upon the productivity growth and level of MNEs in relation to competing domestic firms (especially in host countries). They seek to address issues that range beyond those of technology transfer, such as the question of whether MNEs are 'more efficient' than other companies. Some studies have examined productivity in foreign subsidiaries and competing domestic enterprises in Australian and Canadian markets. If the two types of firms coexist, and superior technology or productivity imported by the subsidiaries progressively spills over to their domestic rivals, the subsidiaries' superiority should appear as a differential-rent component of their value added. And if domestic firms follow more closely, the more they are exposed to the subsidiaries, the domestic firms' relative productivity should increase with the subsidiaries' share of the market. Caves (1974a) and Globerman (1976) both find reasonably strong evidence to support the hypothesis. Neither study rests upon data that permit measuring efficiency within the context of fully estimated production functions for the foreign and domestic firms, but both attempt to control for the shortcoming so far as their data permit.

The pursuit of technological (or other) advantages of MNEs through data on productivity is risky. As Hufbauer (1975, pp. 268–71) has shown, under some assumptions a MNE's productivity advantage will enlarge its market share without yielding any differential in productivity. Therefore some interest attaches to studies that have investigated company size along with productivity differentials. Parry (1974) seems to find that subsidiaries' sizes relative to their domestic competitors in Australia are greater in research-intensive industries. Caves (1980b) treats relative size and relative productivity as jointly determined, and also filters out some influences (scale economies in production; marketing assets of MNEs) that affect their revenue productivity but are unrelated to technology. At least for a few countries — and research has concentrated on the most likely cases — MNEs have appeared in statistical studies to play some role in the international transfer of technology. Case studies for these same countries provide confirming evidence (Brash, 1966, pp. 194–202) with regard to MNEs' suppliers and customers as well as competitors (also Dunning, 1958, pp. 224–5; Forsyth, 1972, pp. 145–50).

This conclusion requires gingerly treatment, however, because of the complexity of the question and the incompleteness of the statistical studies. It has not been shown, for example, that MNEs' presence reduces productivity gaps after controlling for other avenues of technology transfer. Also, other hypotheses suggested by the technology-transfer process have fared only moderately well in their statistical tests. If the MNE is a uniquely vital link in transfers of technology, then industrial productivity for countries that are mainly technology importers should be relatively higher in industries congenial to MNEs' operations. This hypothesis has been tested on Canada relative to the United States with mixed results (Caves, Porter and Spence, 1980, chap. 10; Saunders, 1980) and on the United Kingdom relative to the United States with negative results.[26] It is worth recalling that locational and policy-related variables (transportation costs and tariffs, for example) can lure foreign subsidiaries into markets where they may operate inefficiently, say, at suboptimal scales, but yet be profitable because of the dowry of intangible assets supplied by their parents (for example, Parry, 1974). These influences are adverse to the productivity of MNEs and of the industries in which they operate.

Similarly, studies of the relative productivity or profitability of MNEs and their domestic competitors demand careful interpretation. These will not be considered in detail, but their general thrust has been to find that MNEs are more profitable or display higher productivity than selected single-nation rivals.[27] The researcher imputes the result to any of the MNE's possible advantages that could raise profitability or productivity — including marketing and managerial skills,[28] product differentiation, and many factors other than technology. This whole line of inquiry leaves one fairly unsatisfied, because companies do not become multinational unless they are good at something. To find that the profits or value added or ongoing MNEs exceed the figure for single-nation rival companies is unsurprising, on the one hand, and fails to identify the exact source of the rent, on the other. Therefore the most revealing study of this type is Vendrell-Alda's (1978) exhaustive analysis of establishment-level data for Argentina. After controlling for a large number of industrial and strategic factors affecting foreign- and domestic-controlled plants in his sample, he finds no significant residual productivity differential for the foreign manager *per se*. His result suggests that any technology or productivity advantage possessed by MNEs is endogenous to the market-structure environments in which they emerge and has no pure residual component.

Conclusion

This survey has explored the behaviour of the MNE in developing and transferring technology, in relation to the arm's-length international market for technology licensing, first in microeconomic terms and in its general-equilibrium and welfare significance. MNEs tend to be found in research-intensive sectors, and there is evidence that they consciously allocate their R and D activities around the world to best advantage. R and D is pulled toward the parent's headquarters by the needs of efficient supervision and scale economies in the R and D process itself, dispersed toward the subsidiaries by the advantages of doing developmental research close to the served market (and sometimes by the goal of minimizing costs). Empirical evidence confirms that US MNEs would undertake less research in the United States if they could not expect to garner rents on it from foreign markets.

The marketing of technological knowledge is failure prone for the same general reasons as any market in knowledge assets. None the less, such a market exists in which licensor and licensee strike agreements. Empirical evidence tells something about the kinds of firms that gain from both licensor and licensee activities, and it also identifies the resource costs of technology transfers that make technical knowledge something less than the 'public good' assumed in most economic analysis. Technical knowledge may be transferred either within the MNE or between independent firms, the division depending on the MNE's assorted advantages and disadvantages. Arm's-length licensing is encouraged by risks to foreign investors and barriers to entry by subsidiaries, short economic life of the knowledge asset, simplicity of the technology, high capital costs for the potential foreign investor, and by certain types of product-market competition that favour reciprocal licensing.

The microeconomic evidence on licensing and foreign investment can be fitted into Vernon's product cycle, which employs a number of mechanisms to suggest that, as a product's technology matures, its production becomes more footloose and disseminates towards countries less active in producing new technical knowledge. The MNE seems to influence the rate of diffusion at certain stages of the cycle; by implication, the cycle runs its course more rapidly with MNEs active than if technology diffused only through arm's-length licensing and other channels.

International economists have recently provided a number of models helpful for understanding technology transfer in general equilibrium and its implications for nations' welfare. If Home, the innovating country, cannot collect rents on its technology that disseminates to Foreign, the dissemination generally makes Foreign and the world as a whole better off but leaves Home worse off. But Home may gain from the dissemination if its terms of commodity trade improve enough (say, Foreign is very efficient at making the innovation and now supplies it as a cheap import to Home). If technology disseminates through its attachment to the MNE's international movement of capital, Foreign can benefit from encouraging capital inflows. If technology transfers and capital movements are independent, however, they can be substitutes for one another: maximum world output can be attained by moving the technology to the capital or the capital to the technology. Home of course maximizes its own welfare by charging a monopoly rental for its superior technology; this rental may be an alternative to taxing exports of the innovative good, or Home may need to use both instruments to maximize its income.

Empirical evidence relevant to these theoretical welfare considerations shows that competition among suppliers of technical knowledge serves to beat down the rents they collect. It also indicates something about the leakage of proprietary knowledge from the control of MNEs: some leakage occurs, but no presumption that the MNEs themselves undervalue the risk when licensing or placing their technology abroad. There is limited aggregative evidence that the presence of MNEs is associated with the more rapid diffusion of technical knowledge, at least in industrial-country markets. Empirical research in this area must make some delicate discriminations, however, because successful MNEs at any given moment should be earning rents not accruing to their national competitors. Not all the rent-yielding assets are technological, and each of them is subject to a variety of depreciation and dissemination processes.

Notes

1. See Mansfield (1974) for a summary oriented to MNE issues of the state of our knowledge about research and development.

2. Similarly, product-market diversification has been held to favour R and D, and the statistical evidence shows a positive association with causation running both ways (e.g. Caves, Porter and Spence, 1980, chaps. 7, 8).

3. The statistical results of Severn and Laurence (1974) are consistent with the importance of global profitability to the R and D decisions of MNEs.

4. Statistical studies include Mansfield, Teece and Wagner (1979), Parry and Watson (1979), Hewitt (1980), and Hirschey and Caves (1981). Survey data and case studies are provided by Safarian (1966, chap. 6), Creamer (1976), Ronstadt (1977), Germidis (1977), and Behrman and Fischer (1980).

5. Creamer (1976, Chart 4.2) provides the following data on the functional distribution of domestic and overseas R and D by a large sample of US MNEs. In 1972 the overseas affiliates spent 69.0 per cent for development, 29.9 per cent for applied research, and 1.1 per cent for basic research. The corresponding percentages for their US parents were 59.8, 33.9 and 7.3 per cent. Parry and Watson (1979) find that in Australia 42 per cent of subsidiaries' R and D is spent modifying technology from abroad.

6. See also Hood and Young (1979). Mansfield, Teece and Wagner (1979) present direct estimates of the minimum efficient scale of overseas R and D facilities. These estimates vary a great deal, suggesting that MES depends on the exact type of work done by the lab. Quality control and 'customer engineering' have small minimum scales relative to the development of new products or components (see also Ronstadt, 1977, chap. 9). Parry and Watson (1979) report small scales for most industries, but with some exceptions.

7. Contractor (1980); Herskovic (1976, p. 24).

8. These conclusions are supported in unpublished research by Harold Crookell on the licensing policies of 22 large companies. Also see Casson (1979, pp. 20–2).

9. Unpublished research by Peter Killing documents these and other aspects of rational behaviour by licensees. Also see Herskovic (1976).

10. Plus any premium added to allow for the licensor's expected decrease in future profits due to strengthened competition from the licensee.

11. Two to five rivals in 34 per cent of the cases in Contractor's sample, five to ten in 10 per cent, eleven or more in 29 per cent; the licensor monopolizes in only 27 per cent.

12. Contractor (1980) tests a number of other hypotheses, usually getting the expected sign but not a statistically significant coefficient. In this sense he finds that the returns tend to be higher when the licensee is permitted to export (and thus presumably will pay a higher royalty rate) and when the licensor's patent has a long time to run; they are lower when the technology is old. The gross returns to the licensor increase with the direct costs he incurs implementing the agreement or adapting the technology for the licensee.

13. Telesio (1979, pp. 84–6) provides evidence from interviews. He also claims experienced firms make proportionally greater reliance on licensing (chap. 5). However, his proxy for experience is itself the extent of foreign investment, and that builds in a statistical bias towards acceptance of the hypothesis.

14. Telesio (1979, pp. 76–7) suggests that diversification may also be associated with shortages of complementary assets needed to start foreign subsidiaries for the purpose of exploiting peripheral technologies.

15. Surveys and case studies generally support Teece's findings. Tsurumi (1976, pp. 189–92) finds that the expatriate personnel needed to transfer as

technology increases with its complexity, independent of the scale of the recipient facility. And Sekiguchi (1979, pp. 65–7) notes that the effectiveness of transfers of Japanese textile technology has been impaired where recipient countries restrict the presence of foreign personnel.

16. Johnson (1968) probably does the most to bring out the analytical underpinnings of the product cycle, and his account is followed here.

17. In a somewhat similar model McCulloch and Yellen (1976) show that Home can gain if Foreign turns out to have such a comparative advantage in an innovative good that production of the 'newly-old' good shifts entirely to Foreign. Krugman's model does not allow for comparative-advantage differences among old goods. The McCulloch–Yellen paper is discussed below.

18. McCulloch and Yellen also develop the consequences of technology transfers for employment in a Brecher-type model in which the real wage is fixed in terms of the old good. Home's transfer of technology to Foreign can then either raise or lower Home's employment.

19. In an earlier paper Jones (1970) showed in the context of the Heckscher-Ohlin model how technology differences (and thus technology transfers) between countries may affect their equilibrium relative commodity prices in the absence of trade. This models allows for both differential effects between industries and differential biases in the proportional reduction of input requirements for each factor of production.

20. He suggests that technology transfers should be judged favourable to welfare if they expand trade, unfavourable if they contract it. As Berglas and Jones (1977) show, that conclusion may pertain to the welfare of the transferor country in a two-country world, but not to world welfare.

21. McCulloch and Yellen (1976) do show that free dissemination is never optimal for Home if trade is free of tariffs and Home's resources are fully employed; with unemployment due to a fixed minimum wage, the optimal royalty rate may be anything from zero to prohibitive. Berglas and Jones (1977) emphasize the relation between Home's optimal tax on technology embodied in sector-specific capital goods and Home's commodity terms of trade.

22. The license fee is assumed to take the form of a royalty per bottle of soft drinks. If instead Home holds out for a lump-sum royalty payment, it is in effect making an all-or-nothing offer that can potentially relieve Foreign's consumers of all the surplus they enjoy from soft drinks – not just the part that a simple monopolist would get. Then the technology license becomes superior to the other policies from Home's viewpoint.

23. See Tilton (1971, pp. 118–19) on AT&T's licensing policy in semiconductors, Baranson (1978a) on competition among US manufacturers of light aircraft and its consequences for licensing a Brazilian producer.

24. Baranson's (1978b) case studies yield little direct support for his normative conclusions because they fail to consider the royalties received from technology licences by the US licensors and the extent of competition from non-US technology suppliers. However, they have their own behavioural interest in documenting patterns discussed above in the second section. And they tend to concentrate on industries such as aircraft in which foreign investment is uncommon and government involvement high.

25. The acceleration was greater for process technologies. A product innovation is usually limited by 'reverse engineering': buy the innovation, take it apart, and figure out how it works. This does not depend on propinquity to the factory. Process innovations, however, can be imitated only by observing them, contacting suppliers, hiring away employees, or other methods for which distance matters.

26. Caves (1980a, pp. 153–4, 170–1); also see Dunning (1977, pp. 69–72) and Solomon and Ingham (1977). Katz (1969, chap. 7) provides positive evidence

from Argentina's experience.

27. See, for example, Dunning (1971, chap. 9); Brash (1966, chaps. 7, 10); Dunning (1977, pp. 69–72); Forsyth (1972, pp. 64–90).

28. US MNEs have apparently served as a vehicle for transferring innovations in management and organization as well as technical innovations. See the third section, above and Brash (1966, chap. 5).

BIBLIOGRAPHY

Agmon, Tamir and Kindleberger, Charles P. (eds) *Multinationals from Small Countries* (Cambridge, Mass., MIT Press, 1977)

Akamatsu, K. 'A Historical Pattern of Economic Growth in Developing Countries', *The Developing Economies* (March–August 1962)

Akerlof, G.A. 'The Market for "Lemons": Qualitative Uncertainty and the Market Mechanism', *Quarterly Journal of Economics* 84 (August 1970): 488–500

Aliber, Robert Z. 'A Theory of Direct Foreign Investment' in *The International Corporation*. Edited by Charles P. Kindleberger (Cambridge, Mass., MIT Press, 1970)

——. 'The Multinational Enterprise in a Multiple Currency World', in *The Multinational Enterprise*. Edited by John H. Dunning. (London, George Allen and Unwin, 1971)

——. 'Towards a Theory of International Banking', *Economic Review* (Federal Reserve Bank of San Francisco, Spring, 1976)

Alsegg, Robert J. *Control Relationships Between American Corporations and Their European Subsidiaries*, AMA Research Study No. 107 (New York, American Management Association, 1971)

Arndt, Helmut W. 'Professor Kojima on the Macroeconomics of Foreign Direct Investment', *Hitotsubashi Journal of Economics* 4 (June 1974)

Arrow, Kenneth J. 'Vertical Integration and Communication', *The Bell Journal of Economics* 6 (1975): 173–83

Auerbach, Kay J. 'International Banking: Where Do We Go From Here?', Federal Reserve Bank of Minneapolis, *Staff Report* 10 (1976)

Baer, Donald and Garlow, David. 'International Banking in the Sixth District', Federal Reserve Bank of Atlanta, *Economic Review* (Nov.–Dec. 1977)

Bank Stock Quarterly. 'Confinement of Domestic Banking in the United States' (October 1978)

Baranson, Jack. *Technology and the Multinational: Corporate Strategies in a Changing World Economy* (Lexington, Mass., Lexington Books, D.C. Heath, 1978a)

——. 'Technology Transfer: Effects on U.S. Competitiveness and Employment', in *US Department of Labor* (1978b)

Baumann, G.H. 'The Industrial Composition of U.S. Export and Subsidiary Sales to the Canadian Market: Note', *American Economic Review* (December 1973): 1009–12.

——. 'Merger Theory, Property Rights and the Patterns of U.S. Direct Investment in Canada', *Weltwirtschaftliches Archiv* 7 (1975)

Behrman, J.H. and Fischer, W.A. *Overseas R&D Activity of Transnational Companies* (Cambridge, Mass., Oelgeschlager, Gunn and Hain, 1980)

Berg, S. and Friedman, P. 'Joint Ventures in American Industry', *Mergers and Acquisitions* (Summer, Fall 1978; Winter 1979)

Berglas, E and Jones, R.W. 'The Export of Technology', in *Optimal Policies, Control Theory and Technology Exports*. Edited by K. Brunner and A.H.

Meltzer, Carnegie-Rochester Conference Series on Public Policy No. 7 (Amsterdam, North-Holland Publishing Co., 1977)

Bergsten, C.F., Horst, T. and Moran, T. *American Multinationals and American Interests* (Washington, Brookings Institution, 1978)

Boddewyn, Jean J. 'The Theory of Foreign Direct Divestment: A First Pass'. Paper to Eastern Regional Annual meetings of A.I.B. at New York University (April 1981)

Brada, J. 'Markets, Property Rights, and the Economics of Joint Ventures in Socialist Countries', *Journal of Comparative Economics* (1977)

——. 'East-West Technology Transfer by Means of Industrial Cooperation: A Theoretical Appraisal', in P. Marer, E. Tabaczynski (1981a)

——. 'Technology Transfer Between the United States and Communist Countries', in *Research in International Business and Finance: Technology and Economic Development*. Edited by R. Hawkins and J. Prasad. (JAI 1981b)

Brash, D.T. *American Investment in Australian Industry* (Cambridge, Mass., Harvard University Press, 1966)

Brigham, E.F. *Financial Management Theory and Practice* (Hinsdale, Ill., Dryden Press, 1979)

Buckley, Peter J. and Casson, Mark. *The Future of the Multinational Enterprise* (Basingstoke and London, Macmillan, 1976)

Buckley, Peter J. and Davies, Howard. 'The Place of Licensing in the Theory and Practice of Foreign Operations', mimeographed, University of Reading Discussion Papers in International Investment and Business Studies No. 47 (November 1979)

Buckley, Peter J. and Matthew, A. 'The Motivation for Recent First Time Direct Investment in Australia by UK Firms', *Management International Review* 19, 1 (1979)

'California State Superintendent of Banking', *Annual Reports* (1970–7)

Calvet, A. Louis. *Market and Hierarchies: Towards a Theory of International Business*, PhD Dissertation, MIT (1980)

——. 'Mergers and the Theory of Foreign Direct Investment', mimeographed (August 1981a)

——. 'A Synthesis of Foreign Direct Investment Theories and Theories of the Multinational Firm', *Journal of International Business Studies* (Spring/Summer 1981b)

Canterbery, E.R. 'A Vita Theory of Personal Income Distribution', *Southern Economic Journal* 45 (July 1979)

Casson, Mark. *Alternatives to the Multinational Enterprise* (London, Macmillan, 1979)

Caves, Richard E. 'International Corporations: The Industrial Economics of Foreign Investment', *Economica* 38 (1971): 1–27

——. 'Multinational Firms, Competition, and Productivity in Host-Country Industries', *Economica* 41 (May 1974a)

——. 'International Organization', in *Economic Analysis and the Multinational Enterprise*. Edited by John H. Dunning. (London, George Allen and Unwin, 1974b)

——. 'Causes of Direct Investment: Foreign Firms' Shares in Canadian and United Kingdom Manufacturing Industries', *Review of Economics and Statistics* 56 (August 1974c): 279–93

——. *Diversification, Foreign Investment, and Scale in North American Manufacturing Industries* (Ottawa, Information Canada, 1975)

——. 'International Trade and Industrial Organization: Introduction', *Journal of Industrial Economics* (December 1980a)

——. 'Productivity Differences among Industries', in *Britain's Economic Performance*. Edited by Richard E. Caves and L.B. Krause (Washington, Brookings Institution, 1980b)

——. 'Investment and Location Policies of Multinational Companies', *Schweiz. Z. Volkwirtsch. Statist.* 116, 3 (1980c)

Caves, Richard E., Porter, M.E. and Spence, A.M. *Competition in the Open Economy: A Model Applied to Canada* (Cambridge, Mass., Harvard University Press, 1980)

Cerovic, D. *Ugovori O Licencama* (Beograd, Institut za Spoljnu Trgovinu, 1965)

Chandler, Jr. Alfred D. *Strategy and Structure: Chapters in the History of the American Industrial Enterprise* (MIT Press, 1962)

Chandler, Jr. Alfred D. and Daems, H. (eds). *Managerial Hierarchies* (Cambridge, Mass., Harvard University Press, 1980)

Chittle, C. 'Direct Foreign Investment in Labor Managed Economy – The Yugoslav Experience', *Weltwirtschaftliches Archiv* 111 (1975)

Coase, Ronald H. 'The Nature of the Firm', *Economica* (1937): 386–405

Cobb, Miles. 'A Shot in the Arm for Edge Act Corporations', *Banking Law Journal* (March 1980)

Conference Board. *Announcements of Foreign Investment in U.S. Manufacturing Industry 1st Quarter 1977* (New York, 1977)

Contractor, Farok J. 'The "Profitability" of Technology Licensing by U.S. Multinationals: A Framework for Analysis and an Empirical Study', *Journal of International Business Studies* 11 (Fall 1980)

——. 'In Defence of Licensing: Its Increased Role in International Operations', mimeographed (March 1981)

Corden, W.M. 'The Theory of International Trade', in *Economic Analysis and the Multinational Enterprise*. Edited by J.H. Dunning (New York, Praeger Publishers, 1974)

Cory, Peter F. 'The Transfer of Technology to Developing Countries and the Role of the Foreign Corporation: A Comparison of Yugoslavia and Mexico', unpublished PhD dissertation (Berkeley, 1979)

Cory, Peter F. and Dunning, John H. 'The Eclectic Theory of International Production and MNE Involvement in Eastern Europe and Latin America', forthcoming in Marer, P. and Lombardi, J. (eds), *Multinational Corporations in Latin America and Eastern Europe* (Bloomington, Indiana, 1982)

Creamer, D.B. *Overseas Research and Development by United States Multinationals, 1966-1975* (New York, Conference Board, 1976)

Davidson, William H. 'The Location of Foreign Direct Investment Activity: Country Characteristics and Experience Curve Effects', *Journal of International Business Studies* (Fall 1980)

Davidson, William H. and McFetridge, Donald G. 'International Technology and the Theory of the Firm', mimeographed, Department of Economics, Carleton University (1980)

Davies, Howard. 'Technology Transfer through Commercial Transactions', *Journal of Industrial Economics* 26 (Fall 1977)

DeSarbo, W.S. and D.K. Hildebrand, 'A Marketer's Guide to Log-Linear Models for Qualitative Data Analysis', *Journal of Marketing* (Summer 1980)

Donham, Parker B. 'H.B. Nickerson and Sons: The Big, Big Fish in Canada's Pond', *Atlantic Insight* (October 1981)

Dragomanovic, V. 'Joint Ventures in Yugoslavia', *Yugoslav Survey* 4, 78 (1978)

Draper, N.R. and John, J.A. 'An Alternative Family in Transformations', *Applied Statistics* 29, 2 (1980)

Drucker, Peter F. 'The Rise of Production Sharing', *Wall Street Journal* (15 March 1977)

Dunning, John H. *American Investment in British Manufacturing Industry* (London, George Allen and Unwin, 1958)

——. *Studies in International Investment* (London, George Allen and Unwin, 1971)

——. 'Multinational Enterprises and the Trade Flaws of Developing Countries', *World Development*, 2, (1974): 131–8

——. 'Multinational Enterprises, Market Structure, Economic Power and Industrial Policy', *Journal of World Trade Law* (November/December 1975)

——. 'Trade, Location of Economic Activity and the MNE: A Search for an Eclectic Approach', in *The International Allocation of Economic Activity, Proceedings of a Nobel symposium held in Stockholm.* Edited by Bertil Ohlin *et al.* (London, Macmillan, 1977)

——. 'Explaining Changing Patterns of International Production: In Defence of the Eclectic Theory', *Oxford Bulletin of Economics and Statistics* 41 (November 1979): 269–96

——. 'Explaining Outward Direct Investment of Developing Countries: In Support of the Eclectic Theory of International Production', *Weltwirtschaftliches Archiv* 49 (1980)

——. 'Explaining the International Direct Investment Position of Countries: Towards a Dynamic or Developmental Approach', *Weltwirtschaftliches Archiv* 11, 1 (1981a): 30–64

——. *International Production and the Multinational Enterprise* (London, Allen and Unwin, 1981b)

Dunning, John H. and McQueen, Matthew. *Transnational Corporations in International Tourism* (New York, UNCTC, 1981), Sales No. St/CTC/18

Dunning, John H. and Norman, George. *Factors Influencing the Location of Offices of Multinational Enterprises* (London, Location of Offices Bureau and Economists Advisory Group Ltd, 1979)

——. 'The Theory of Multinational Enterprise: An Application to Multinational Office Location', mimeographed (1981)

Dunning, John H., assisted by Pearce, R.D. *U.S. Industry in Britain: An Economists Advisory Group Research Study* (Boulder, Co., Westview Press, 1977)

Economist. 'National Westminster Bank: A 4300 million Foothold in New York State', (20 May 1978)

Edwards, G.A. 'Foreign Acquisition Activity in Canada: A Long-term Perspective', *Foreign Investment Review Agency Papers* 1 (Ottawa, Information Canada, February 1977)

Eiteman, David K. 'The Spread of Foreign Banks into the United States: Far Eastern Bank Operations in California', in *International Business in the Pacific Basin.* Edited by R. Hal. Mason. (Lexington, Mass., Lexington Books, 1978)

English, H.E. and Owen, Robert F. *The Role of Marketing in the Concentration and Multinational Control of Canadian Manufacturing Industries* (Bureau of Competition Policy Research Monograph, Number 11, Consumer and Corporate Affairs, Ottawa, Canada, July 1981)

Fabinc, I., *et al.* 'Sistem Ekonomskih Odnosa sa Inostranstvom', in Konzorcij Ekonomskih Instituta za Makroprojekt, *Privredni Sistem SFRJ* (Zagreb, 1976)

Fama, Eugene F. *Foundations of Finance* (New York, 1976)

Federation of Banking Associations of Japan, *Banking System in Japan* (1966, 1969, 1972, 1974 and 1976)

Fienberg, S.E. *The Analysis of Cross-Classified Categorical Data* (Cambridge, Mass., MIT Press, 1977)

Findlay, Ronald. 'Relative Backwardness, Direct Foreign Investment, and the Transfer of Technology: A Simple Dynamic Model', *Quarterly Journal of Economics* 92 (February 1978)

Foorman, James. 'Revised Regulation K: Selected Issues Affecting Banking Edge Corporations', University of Illinois *Law Forum* (1980)

Forsyth, David J.C. *U.S. Investment in Scotland* (New York, Praeger Publishers, 1972)

——. 'Foreign-owned Firms and Labour Relations: A Regional Perspective', *British Journal of Industrial Relations* 11 (March 1973)

Fortune. 'The Ubiquitous Banker of Lothbury Street' (19 June 1978)

Frank, Lawrence G. *Joint Venture Survival in Multinational Corporations* (New York, Praeger, 1971)

——. 'International Joint Ventures in Developing Countries: Mystique and Reality', *Law and Policy in International Business* 6 (1974)

——. 'Patterns in the Multinational Spread of Continental Enterprise', *Journal of International Business Studies* (Fall 1975)

——. *The European Multinationals* (New York: Harper and Row, 1976)

——. *The European Multinationals: A Renewed Challenge to American and British Big Business* (Stamford, CT., Greylock Publications, 1976)

Freeman, C. *The Economics of Industrial Innovation* (Middlesex, Penguin, 1974)

Gabriel, Peter. *The International Transfer of Corporate Skills* (Cambridge, Mass., Harvard University Press, 1966)

Germidis, D. (ed.) *Transfer of Technology by Multinational Corporations*, Vol. I: *A Synthesis and Country Case Study* (Development Centre Studies, 1977)

Giddy, Ian and Rugman, A. 'A Model of Trade, Foreign Direct Investment, and Licensing', Columbia University Graduate School of Business Working Paper, No. 274A (1979)

Gillen, David W. and Oum, Tae H. 'A Study of the Demand for Grandfish in the U.S. Markets', Working Paper 81-11 School of Business, Queen's University (1981)

Globerman, Stephen. 'Technological Diffusion in the Canadian Tool and Die Industry', *Review of Economics and Statistics* 57 (November 1957)

——. 'Foreign Direct Investment and "Spillover" Efficiency Benefits in Canadian Manufacturing Industries', *Canadian Journal of Economics* 12 (February 1976)

Goldberg, Lawrence G. and Saunders, Anthony. 'The Determinants of Foreign Banking Activity in the United States', *Journal of Banking and Finance* 5, 1 (1981)

Gort, M. 'An Economic Disturbance Theory of Mergers', *Quarterly Journal of Economics* (November 1969)

Gray, H. Peter. *A Generalised Theory of International Trade* (London, Macmillan Press, 1976)

——. 'Gains from Diversification of Real Assets: An Extension', *Journal of Business Research* 6 (January 1978)

——. 'Intra-Industry Trade: The Effects of Different Levels of Aggregation', in *On the Economics of Intra-Industry Trade*. Edited by H. Giersch (Tubingen, J.C.B. Mohr, 1979a)

——. 'Needed a Webb-Pomerene Act for Research?' *Challenge* (November–December 1979b)

——. 'The Theory of International Trade among Industrialised Nations', *Weltwirtschaftliches Archiv* 116, 3 (1980)

——. 'Oil-Push Inflation: A Broader View', *Banca Nazionale del Lavoro Quarterly Review* (1981)

——. 'Toward a Unified Theory of International Trade, International Production and Foreign Direct Investment', *International Investment and Capital Movement*. Edited by J. Black and John H. Dunning (London, Macmillan, 1982)

Gray, Jean M. and Gray, H. Peter. 'The Multinational Bank: A Financial MNC?', *Journal of Banking and Finance* 5 (March 1981)

Grosse, Robert. 'Regional Offices in Multinational Enterprise: The Latin American Case', *Management International Review* 2 (1981a)

——. 'Banking Edge Corporations: A Multinational Enterprise Perspective', xerox, University of Michigan (1981b)

Grubel, Herbert G. 'A Theory of Multinational Banking', *Banca Nazionale del Lavoro Quarterly Review* (December 1977)

Gruber, William, Mehta, Dileep and Vernon, Raymond. 'The R&D Factor in International Trade and International Investment of U.S. Industries', *Journal of Political Economy* 75 (February 1967)

Hang-Sheng, Cheng. 'US West Coast as an International Financial Center' (Federal Reserve Bank of San Francisco) *Economic Review* (Spring 1976)

Heenan, David. 'Global Cities of Tomorrow', *Harvard Business Review* (May–June 1977)

——. 'The Regional Headquarters Decision: A Comparative Analysis', *Academy of Management Journal* (June 1979)

Heenan, David and Perlmutter, Howard. *Multinational Organization and Development* (Reading, Mass., Addison-Wesley, 1979)

Helleiner, G. 'The Role of Multinational Corporations in the Less Developed Countries Trade in Technology', *World Development* 3 (1975)

Herskovic, S. *The Import and Export of Technological Know-how Through Licensing Agreements in Israel, 1966–1974* (Jerusalem, Office of the Prime Minister, National Council for Research and Development 1976)

Hewitt, Gary. 'U.S. Penetration of Canadian Manufacturing Industries', unpublished PhD dissertation, Yale University (1975)

——. 'Research and Development Performed Abroad by U.S. Manufacturing Multinationals', *Kyklos* 33, 2 (1980)

Hirschey, R.C. and Caves, Richard E. 'Internationalization of Research and Transfer of Technology by Multinational Enterprises', *Oxford Bulletin of Economics and Statistics* 43 (May 1981)

Hirsch, Seev. 'An International Trade and Investment Theory of the Firm', *Oxford Economic Papers* 28 (July 1976): 258–70

286   *Bibliography*

Holt, J.T. 'Joint Ventures in Yugoslavia: West German and American Experience', *MSU Business Topics* (Spring 1973)

Hood, Neil and Young, Stephen. *The Economics of Multinational Enterprise* (London, Longman, 1979)

Horst, Thomas. 'The Industrial Composition of U.S. Exports and Subsidiary Sales to the Canadian Market', *American Economic Review* (March 1972a): 37–45

——. 'Firm and Industry Determinants of the Decision to Invest Abroad: An Empirical Study', *Review of Economics and Statistics* (August 1972b)

Hufbauer, Gary C. *Synthetic Materials and The Theory of International Trade* (Cambridge, Mass., Harvard University Press, 1966)

——. 'The Multinational Corporation and Direct Investment', in *International Trade and Finance: Frontiers for Research*. Edited by P.B. Kenen (New York, Cambridge University Press, 1975)

Hymer, Stephen H. *The International Operations of National Firms: A Study of Direct Foreign Investment* (Cambridge, Mass., MIT Press, 1976)

Illic, B. 'Transfer Nauka, Tehnike, i Tehnologije i Unapradenje Saradnja Sa Inostranim Partnerima', *Ekonomika Udrezenog Rada* 9 (1976)

International Monetary Fund. *Direction of Trade: Annual 1969–75* (Washington, D.C., 1976)

Isard, Walter. 'Location Theory, Agglomeration, and the Pattern of World Trade', in *The International Allocation of Economic Activity*. Edited by Bertil Ohlin (New York, Holmes & Meier, 1977)

Jacquillat, Bernard and Solnik, Bruno. 'Multinationals are Poor Tools for Diversification', *Journal of Portfolio Management* (Winter 1978)

James, Dilmus D. *Used Machinery and Economic Development* (East Lansing, Michigan State University, 1974)

Johanson, Jan and Vahlne, Jan-Eric. *The Internationalization Process of the Firm* (University of Uppsala, Department of Business Administration, December 1977)

Johanson, Jan and Wiedersheim, Paul. 'The Internationalization of the Firm – Four Swedish Cases', *Journal of Management Studies* (1975)

Johnson, Harry G. *Comparative Cost and Commercial Policy Theory for a Developing World Economy*, Wicksell Lectures (Stockholm, Almqvist & Wiksell, 1968)

——. 'The Efficiency and Welfare Implications of the International Corporation', in *The International Corporation*. Edited by Charles P. Kindleberger (Cambridge, Mass., MIT Press, 1970)

——. 'Survey of the Issues' in *Direct Foreign Investment in Asia and the Pacific*. Edited by P. Drysdale (Canberra, ANU Press, 1972)

Jones, R.W. 'The Role of Technology in the Theory of International Trade', in *The Technology Factor in International Trade*. Edited by Raymond Vernon. Universities-National Bureau Conference Series No. 22 (New York, National Bureau of Economic Research, 1970)

——. *International Trade: Essays in Theory*, Studies in International Economics, No. 4 (Amsterdam, North-Holland Publishing Co., 1979)

Katz, Jorge M. *Production Functions, Foreign Investment and Growth: A Study Based on the Argentine Manufacturing Sector, 1946-1961*, Contributions to Economic Analysis No. 58 (Amsterdam, North-Holland Publishing Co., 1969)

Kindleberger, Charles P. *American Business Abroad: Six Lectures on Direct*

Investment (New Haven, Yale University Press, 1969)

Knickerbocker, Frederick T. *Oligopolistic Reaction and Multinational Enterprise* (Boston, Division of Research Graduate School of Business Administration, Harvard University, 1973)

Kobrin, Stephen J. 'Political Assessments by International Firms: Models or Methodologies', *Journal of Policy Modelling* (1981)

Koizumi, T. and Kopcky, K.J. 'Economic Growth, Capital Movements and the International Transfer of Technical Knowledge', *Journal of International Economics* 7 (February 1977)

Kojima, Kiyoshi. 'Structure of Comparative Advantage in Industrial Countries: A Verification of the Factor Proportions Theorem', *Hitotsubashi Journal of Economics* 11 (June 1970)

——. 'A Macroeconomic Approach to Foreign Direct Investment', *Hitotsubashi Journal of Economics* 14 (June 1973)

——. 'International Trade and Foreign Investment: Substitutes or Complements', *Hitotsubashi Journal of Economics* 16 (June 1975)

——. 'Transfer of Technology to Developing Countries: Japanese Type versus American Type', *Hitotsubashi Journal of Economics* 17 (February 1977)

——. *Direct Foreign Investment* (London, Croom Helm, 1978)

Komaki, R. 'Foreign Banks: Patience Please', *The Banker* (August 1980)

Krugman, Paul. 'A Model of Innovation, Technology Transfer, and the World Distribution of Income', *Journal of Political Economy* 87 (April 1979)

Lake, A.W. 'Technology Creation and Technology Transfer by Multinational Firms', in *Research in International Business and Finance: An Annual Compilation of Research*, Vol. I: *The Economic Effects of Multinational Corporations*. Edited by R.G. Hawkins (Greenwich, Conn., JAI Press, 1979)

Lall, Sanjaya. 'The International Allocation of Research Activity by U.S. Multinationals', *Oxford Bulletin of Economics and Statistics* 41 (November 1979)

Lamers, E. *Joint Ventures Between Yugoslav and Foreign Enterprises* (Tilburg University Press, 1976)

Lecraw, David. 'Direct Investment by Firms from Less Developed Countries', *Oxford Economic Papers* 29, 4 (1977)

Lees, Francis A. *Foreign Banking and Investment in the United States* (New York, John Wiley & Sons, 1976)

Lessard, Donald R. 'Transfer Prices, Taxes, and Financial Transfers within the Multinational Firm', in *Research in International Business and Finance*, Vol. 1. Edited by Robert G. Hawkins (Greenwich, Conn., JAI Press, 1979)

Levcik, F. and Stankovsky, J. *Industrial Cooperation Between East and West* (White Plains, NY, M.E. Sharpe Inc., 1979)

Liotant-Vogt, Pierre. 'Nestlé – At Home Abroad', *Business Review* (Nov.–Dec. 1976)

Magee, Stephen P. 'Information and The Multinational Corporation: An Appropriability Theory of Direct Foreign Investment', in *The New International Economic Order*. Edited by Jagdish N. Bhagwati (Cambridge, Mass., MIT Press, 1977): 317–40

Mandelker, G. 'Risk and Return: The Case of Merging Firms', *Journal of Financial Economics* (December 1974)

Mansfield, Edwin. 'Technology and Technological Change', in *Economic Analysis and the Multinational Enterprise*. Edited by J.H. Dunning (London, George

Allen and Unwin, 1974): Chapter 6

Mansfield, Edwin and Romeo, A. 'Technology Transfer to Overseas Subsidiaries by U.S.-Based Firms', *Quarterly Journal of Economics* 94 (December 1980)

Mansfield, Edwin, Romeo, A. and Wagner, S. 'Foreign Trade and U.S. Research and Development', *Review of Economics and Statistics* 61 (February 1979)

Mansfield, Edwin, Teece, J. and Wagner, S. 'Overseas Research and Development by U.S.-Based Firms', *Economica*, 46 (May 1979): 187–96

Marer, P. 'US-Romanian Industrial Cooperation: A Composite Case Study', in *East-West Trade: Theory and Evidence*. Edited by J.C. Brada and V.S. Somanath (Indiana, International Development Institute, 1978)

Marer, P. and Tabaczynski, E. *East-West Industrial Cooperation in the 1980s: Findings of a Joint US-Polish Project* (Bloomington, Indiana University Press, 1981)

Marfels, Christian. *A Study on Evolution of Concentration in the Food Industry in the Federal Republic of Germany*, Working Paper 14 (Brussels, Commission of the European Communities, August 1980)

Mason, R.H. 'A Comment on Professor Kojima's Japanese Type Versus American Type of Technology Transfer', *Hitotsubashi Journal of Economics* 20, 2 (February 1980)

McCulloch, Rachel and Yellen, J.L. 'Technology Transfer and the National Interest', Discussion Paper No. 526 (Harvard Institute of Economic Research, Harvard University, 1976)

McFetridge, Donald G. and Howe, J.D. 'Ownership and R & D Expenditures: Some Recent Empirical Evidence', *Canadian Journal of Economics* (February 1976): 51–71

McManus, John. 'The Theory of the International Firm', in *The Multinational Firm and the Nation State*. Edited by G. Paquet (Toronto, Collier-Macmillan, 1972)

McMillan, Carl and St Charles, D. *Joint Ventures in Eastern Europe: A Three Country Comparison* (Montreal, Canadian Economic Policy Committee, 1973)

McMillan, Carl. 'East-West Industrial Cooperation', in *East-European Economics Post-Helsinki* (Joint Economic Committee, US Congress, USGPO, 1977a)

——. 'Forms and Dimensions of East-West Industrial Cooperation', in *East-West Industrial Cooperation in Business: Inter-firm Studies*. Edited by C.T. Saunders (Springer-Verlar, 1977b)

——. 'Trends in East-West Industrial Cooperation', mimeographed (Carleton University, 1980)

McQueen, D.L. 'Learning, The Multinational Corporation and the Further Development of Developed Economies', in *International Conference on International Economy and Competition Policy*. Edited by M. Ariga (Tokyo, Council of Tokyo Conference on International Economy and Competition Policy, 1975)

Meyer, Herbert E. 'This Communist Internationale Has a Capitalistic Accent', *Fortune* (February 1977)

Michalet, Charles A. and Delapierre, M. *The Multinationalization of French Firms* (Chicago, Academy of International Business, 1976)

Miles, M.A. and Stewart, M.B. 'The Effects of Risk and Return on the Currency Composition of Money Demand', *Weltwirtschaftliches Archiv* 116, 4 (1980)

Morawetz, D. *Twenty-Five Years of Economic Development: 1950–1975* (Washington, D.C., World Bank, 1977)

Moxon, Richard, W. 'Export Platform Foreign Investments in The Theory of International Production', mimeographed (1980)

Myers, Stewart C. (ed.). *Modern Development in Financial Management* (Hinsdale, Ill., Praeger Publishers, 1976)

Nambudiri, C.N.S. *et al.* 'Third World Country Firms in Third World Developing Countries: The Nigerian Experience', Presented at the Conference on Third World Multinational Corporations, East-West Center, Honolulu (September 1979)

Nelson, Ralph C. *Merger Movements in American Industry* (Princeton, Princeton University Press, 1959)

Neuberger, Egon and Duffy, William. *Comparative Economic Systems: A Decision Making Approach* (Boston, Allyn and Bacon, 1976)

Newbould, G.D., Buckley, Peter J. and Thurwell, J.C. *Going International* (New York, John Wiley, 1978)

OECD. *Foreign Investment in Yugoslavia* (Paris, 1974)

Orr, Dale. 'Foreign Control and Foreign Penetration in the Canadian Manufacturing Industries', unpublished paper (July 1973)

——. 'The Determinants of Entry: A Study of the Canadian Manufacturing Industries', *Review of Economics and Statistics* (February 1974): 58–66

——. 'The Industrial Composition of U.S. Exports and Subsidiary Sales to the Canadian Market: Comment', *American Economic Review* (March 1975) 230–4

Owen, Robert F. 'Inter-Industry Determinants of Foreign Direct Investments: A Perspective Emphasizing the Canadian Experience', *Working Papers in International Economics*, G-79-03, Princeton University (May 1979)

Ozawa, Terutomo. 'Peculiarities of Japan's Multinationalism: Facts and Theories', *Banca Nazionale del Lavoro Quarterly Review* (December, 1975)

——. 'International Investment and Industrial Structure: New Theoretical Implications from the Japanese Experience', *Oxford Economic Papers*, 31, 1 (1979)

Parry, Thomas G. 'Technology and the Size of the Multinational Corporation Subsidiary: Evidence from the Australian Manufacturing Sector', *Journal of Industrial Economics* 23 (December 1974)

Parry, Thomas G. and Watson, J.F. 'Technology Flows and Foreign Investment in the Australian Manufacturing Sector', *Australian Economic Papers* 18 (June 1979)

Pavecevic, M. 'Transfer of Foreign Technology and the Yugoslav Economy', *Yugoslav Survey* 24 (1973)

Peck, M.J. 'Technology', in *Asia's New Giant: How the Japanese Economy Works*. Edited by H. Patrick and H. Rosovsky (Washington, Brookings Institution, 1976)

Penrose, Edith. 'International Patenting and the Less-Developed Countries', *Economic Journal* 83 (September 1973)

——. *The Theory of Growth of the Firm* (Oxford, Blackwell, 1959; 2nd ed, 1980)

Phelps, Clyde W. *The Foreign Expansion of American Banks* (New York, Ronald Press Co., 1927)

Pindyck, Robert S. and Rubinfeld, Daniel L. *Econometric Models and Economic Forecasts* (New York, McGraw-Hill, 1976)

Porter, Michael E. 'Consumer Behavior, Retailer Power and Market Performance in Consumer Goods Industries', *The Review of Economics and Statistics*

(November 1974): 419–36

Press, S. James and Wilson, Sandra. 'Choosing Between Logistic Regression and Discriminant Analysis', *Journal of the American Statistical Association* 73, 364 (December 1978)

Pugel, T.A. 'Endogenous Technical Change and International Technology Transfer in a Ricardian Trade Model', International Finance Discussion Papers No. 167 (Board of Governors of the Federal Reserve System, Washington, D.C., 1980)

——. 'Technology Transfer and the Neoclassical Theory of International Trade', in *Technology Transfer and Economic Development*. Edited by R.G. Hawkins and A.J. Prasad (Greenwich, Conn., JAI Press, 1981)

Raubitschek, Ruth S. 'Product Differentiation and Brand Proliferation', unpublished Working Paper, Harvard University. Presented at the 1981 Winter Meeting of The Econometric Society

Read, R. 'Multinational Involvement in Tropical Export Crop Markets: The Case of Cocoa, Coffee and Bananas', unpublished paper (1981)

Reed, Howard C. 'Tokyo as an International Financial Center', *Journal of International Business Studies* 11, 3 (1980)

Robinson, R. *International Business Management* (New York, Holt, Reinhardt & Winston, 1978)

Robock, Stefan H. 'A Geobusiness Model and International Business Theory', mimeographed, Paper to the Academy of International Business (October 1980)

Rodriguez, Carlos A. 'Trade in Technological Knowledge and the National Advantage', *Journal of Political Economy* 83 (February 1975)

Ronstadt, Robert. *Research and Development Abroad by US Multinationals* (New York, Praeger Publishers, 1977)

Rosson, Philip J. 'Fish Marketing in Britain: Structural Change and System Performance', *European Journal of Marketing* 9, 3 (1975): 232–49

Rowan, Richard. 'There's Also Some Good News About South Korea', *Fortune* (September 1977)

Rugman, Alan M. *International Diversification and the Multinational Enterprise* (Lexington, D.C. Heath, 1979)

——. *Multinationals in Canada: Theory, Performance and Economic Impact* (Boston, Martinus Nijhoff, 1980a)

——. 'Internalization as a General Theory of Foreign Direct Investment: A Re-Appraisal of the Literature', *Weltwirtschaftliches Archiv* (June 1980b)

——. *Inside the Multinationals: The Economics of Internal Markets* (London, Croom Helm and New York, Columbia University Press, 1981a)

——. 'A Test of Internalization Theory', *Managerial and Decision Economics* (September 1981b)

Safarian, A.E. *Foreign Ownership of Canadian Industry* (Toronto, McGraw-Hill, 1966)

Samuelsson, H.F. *Utlandska direkta investeringar i Sverige* (Stockholm, Industriens Utredningsinstitut, 1977)

Saunders, R. 'The Determinants of Productivity in Candian Manufacturing Industries', *Journal of Industrial Economics* 29 (December 1980)

Schollhammer, Hans. 'The Locational Strategies of Multinational Firms', Center for International Business Studies, 1 (Los Angeles, Pepperdine University, 1974)

Scriven, J. 'Yugoslavia's New Foreign Investment Law', *Journal of World Trade Law* (1979)

Sekiguchi, S. *Japanese Direct Foreign Investment*, Atlantic Institute for International Affairs Series No. 1 (Montclair, NJ, Allenheld, Osmun & Co., 1979)

Severn, A.K. and Laurence, M.M. 'Direct Investment, Research Intensity, and Profitability', *Journal of Financial and Quantitative Analysis* 9 (March 1974)

Shapiro, Alan C. 'Capital Budgeting in the Multinational Corporation', *Financial Management* (June 1978)

Solomon, R.R. and Ingham, K.P.D. 'Discriminating Between MNC Subsidiaries and Indigenous Companies: A Comparative Analysis of the British Mechanical Engineering Industry', *Oxford Bulletin of Economics and Statistics* 39 (May 1977)

Southern California Research Council. *Foreign Investment in Southern California* Report 23 (1976)

Stobaugh, Robert B. 'The Neotechnology Account of International Trade: The Case of Petrochemicals', in Wells (1972)

Stobaugh, Robert B. *et al. U.S. Multinational Enterprises and the U.S. Economy* (Boston, Mass., Harvard Business School, 1972)

Stopford, John M. 'Changing Perspectives on Investment by British Manufacturing Multinationals', *Journal of International Business Studies* 7, 2 (Winter 1976)

Sukijasovic, M. *Joint Business Ventures Between Domestic and Foreign Firms: Developments in Law and Practice* (Belgrade, Kultura, 1973)

——. 'Yugoslavia and Multinational Enterprises', forthcoming in *Multinational Corporations in Latin America and Eastern Europe*. Edited by P. Marer and J. Lombardi (Bloomington, Indiana, 1982)

Sullivan, Jeremiah and Heggelund, Per. *Foreign Investment in the US Fishing Industry* (Lexington, Lexington Books, 1979)

Superintendent of Banks, State of California, *Annual Reports* (1972–80)

Surette, Ralph. '220-Mile Limit Brings More Offshore Problems', *Canadian Geographic* (October 1981)

Teece, David J. *The Multinational Corporation and the Resource Cost of International Technology Transfer* (Cambridge, Mass., Ballinger, 1976)

——. 'Technology Transfer by Multinational Firms: The Resource Cost of Transferring Technological Know-how', *Economic Journal* 87 (June 1977)

——. 'Internal Organization and Economic Performance: An Empirical Analysis of the Profitability of Principal Firms', *Journal of Industrial Economics* (1981)

Telesio, Piero. *Technology Licensing and Multinational Enterprise* (New York, Praeger Publishers, 1979)

Terrel, Henry S. and Key, Stephen J. 'The Growth of Foreign Banking in the United States: An Analytic Survey', *Key Issues in International Banking*, Federal Reserve Bank of Boston, Conference Series No. 18 (1977)

The Banker, 'The Top Banks in the World' (June 1970 and 1977)

The Banker's Almanac and Yearbook (London, Thomas Skinner Directories, 1977–8)

Tilton, John E. *The International Diffusion of Technology: The Case of Semi-Conductors* (Washington, Brookings Institution, 1971)

Tschoegl, Adrian E. 'Essays in Foreign Direct Investment in Banking', unpublished

PhD dissertation, Alfred P. Sloan School of Management, Massachusetts Institute of Technology (1980)

Tsurumi, Yoshihiro. *The Japanese are Coming: A Multinational Spread of Japanese Firms* (Cambridge, Mass., Ballinger Publishing Co., 1976)

Uemura, K. 'Managing the International Bank', *The Bankers Magazine* 162, 5 (September–October 1979)

United Nations, Economic and Social Council. 'A Statistical Outline of Recent Trends of Industrial Cooperation', Trade AC. 3 R. 8 (1976)

——. *Transnational Corporations in World Development: A Re-examination*, Commission on Transnational Corporations 4th session, E/C, 10/38 (New York, UN, 1978)

US Department of Labor, Bureau of International Labor Affairs, *The Impact of International Trade and Investment on Employment*. Edited by William Dewald (Washington, D.C., Government Printing Office, 1978)

US Treasury. *Report to Congress on Foreign Government Treatment of US Commercial Banking Organizations* (Washington, D.C., Government Printing Office, 1979)

Vendrell-Alda, J.L.M. *Comparing Foreign Subsidiaries and Domestic Firms: A Research Methodology Applied to Efficiency in Argentine Industry* (New York, Garland Publishers, 1978)

Vernon, Raymond. 'International Investment and International Trade in the Product Cycle', *Quarterly Journal of Economics* 80 (May 1966)

——. *Sovereignty at Bay: The Multinational Spread of US Enterprises* (New York, Basic Books, 1971)

——. *Storm Over the Multinationals* (Cambridge, Mass., Harvard University Press, 1977)

——. 'The Product Cycle Hypothesis in a New International Environment', *Oxford Bulletin of Economics and Statistics* 41 (November 1979)

——. 'Gone are the Cash Cows of Yesteryear', *Harvard Business Review* 58 (November–December 1980): 150–5

Vernon, Raymond and Davidson, William H. 'Foreign Production of Technology-Intensive Products by U.S.-Multinational Enterprises', Working Paper No. 79-5, Division of Research, Graduate School of Business Administration, Harvard University (1979)

Weber, Alfred. 'Location Theory and Trade Policy', *International Economic Papers* (1958)

Wells, Louis T. (ed.). *The Product Cycle and International Trade* (Boston, Division of Research, Graduate School of Business Administration, Harvard University, 1972)

——. 'Economic Man and Engineering Man', *Public Policy* (Summer 1973)

——. 'Foreign Investment from the Third World: The Experience of Chinese Firms from Hong Kong', *Columbia Journal of World Business* (Spring 1978)

White, Eduardo. 'The International Projection of Firms from Latin American Countries', presented at the Conference on Third World Multinational Corporations, East-West Center, Honolulu (September 1979)

Williamson, Oliver E. *Markets and Hierarchies: Analysis and Antitrust Implications: A Study in the Economics of Internal Organizations* (New York, Free Press, Macmillan, 1975)

——. 'Transaction-Cost Economics: The Governance of Contractual Relations',

The Journal of Law and Economics 22 (1979): 233-61

Wilson, Charles. *Unilever 1945-1965: Challenge and Response* (London, Cassell, 1968)

Wilson, James A. 'Adaptation to Uncertainty and Small Numbers Exchange: The New England Fresh Fish Market', *Bell Journal of Economics* (1980): 491-504

Wilson, R.W. 'The Effect of Technological Environment and Product Rivalry on R&D Effort and Licensing of Innovations', *Review of Economics and Statistics* 59 (May 1977)

Wolf, Bernard M. 'Industrial Diversification and Internationalization: Some Empirical Evidence', *Journal of Industrial Economics* 26, 2 (1977): 177-91

World Bank, *World Development Report, 1979* (1979)

Wrigley, Leonard. *Divisional Autonomy and Diversification* Doctoral Dissertation, Harvard Business School (1970)

Yoshino, Michael Y. *Japan's Multinational Enterprises* (Cambrdge, Mass., Harvard University Press, 1976)

NOTES ON CONTRIBUTORS

Alan M. Rugman is Director of the Centre for International Business Studies and Professor of Business Administration at Dalhousie University, Halifax, Nova Scotia, Canada. Currently he is also a Visiting Professor of International Business at Columbia University, New York, where he held a similar appointment in 1978–9. Professor Rugman has published 3 books, 20 articles and over 60 book reviews on international topics. His previous books include *Multinationals in Canada* (Martinus Nijhoff, 1980) and *Inside the Multinationals* (Croom Helm and Columbia University Press, 1981).

A. Louis Calvet is Assistant Professor of International Business and Finance at the University of Ottawa, Canada. He received his MBA degree from Queen's University and PhD from MIT's Sloan School of Management. Dr Calvet has lectured in Canada and South America, and worked in advisory capacities to government and private business. His research interests are diverse and have resulted in publications in the *Journal of International Business Studies, Journal of Business Finance and Accounting, Canadian Public Administration* and *Journal of Business Administration*, amongst others.

Mark C. Casson is Professor of Economics at the University of Reading. He studied at Bristol University and Cambridge University. His recent books include *Alternatives to the Multinational Enterprise* (1979), *Unemployment: A Disequilibrium Approach* (1981) and *The Entrepreneur: An Economic Theory* (1982). He is currently editing a book on *The Growth of International Business*.

Richard E. Caves is Professor of Economics at Harvard University, where he has served for many years, including a period as Department Chairman. Recognized as one of the world's leading published scholars in the joint fields of industrial organization and international economics, Professor Caves is the author or co-author of over 20 books, 50 articles and numerous book reviews in these areas. His most recent book is *Multinational Enterprise and Economic Analysis* (Cambridge University Press, 1982).

Peter F. Cory is an Assistant Professor in the Department of Economics at Boston University. He holds a Masters degree in economics from Monash University (Melbourne, Australia), and was awarded the PhD in economics by the University of California, Berkeley in 1979. He is the author of 'A Technique for Obtaining Improved Proxy Estimates of Minimum Optimal Scale', *Review of Economics and Statistics* (February 1981) and jointly with John H. Dunning, 'The Eclectic Theory of International Production and Multinational Enterprise Involvement in Eastern Europe and Latin America', forthcoming in Paul Marer and John Lombardi (eds), *Multinational Corporations in Latin America and Eastern Europe* (Indiana University Press). In 1979 he was a Visiting Assistant Professor at Queen's University in Canada.

John H. Dunning received his BSc (Econ.) from London University and his PhD from Southampton University. He has also been awarded an honorary degree from Uppsala University. He was Professor of Economics at the University of Reading from 1964 to 1975, since when he has been Professor of International Investment and Business Studies, also at the University of Reading. He has been a professorial visitor at various universities in the USA and Canada, and acted as Consultant to the British Government, OECD, UNTAD and the UN Centre on Transnational Corporations on multinational enterprises and international direct investment. He has written several books and many articles on multinational enterprises and international direct investment. His latest book *International Production and Multinational Enterprises* was published by Allen and Unwin in September 1981.

Ian H. Giddy is Associate Professor in the Graduate School of Business of Columbia University and Senior International Economist at the Claremont Economics Institute. He holds a PhD from the University of Michigan. He has acted in a consulting capacity for multinational corporations and banks and has also held appointments at the International Monetary Fund, Office of the Comptroller of the Currency and the Federal Reserve Board. The author of numerous articles and books on international financial markets, one of Professor Giddy's best-known publications (with Gunter Dufey) is *The International Money Market* (Prentice Hall, 1978).

H. Peter Gray is Professor of Economics at Douglass College, Rutgers University, New Jersey. He holds the MA degree from Cambridge

University and the PhD from the University of California. He has published widely in the field of international trade and finance and is the author of *International Trade, Investment, and Payments* (Houghton Mifflin, 1979).

Robert E. Grosse is Visiting Professor of International Business at the University of Michigan. He has degrees from Princeton University (AB) and the University of North Carolina (PhD). Professor Grosse writes generally about the theory of the multinational firms and about international business in Latin America. His recent publications include *Foreign Investment Codes and the Location of Direct Investment* (Praeger, 1980) and 'The Theory of Foreign Direct Investment', *Essays in International Business* (December 1981). He has also published several articles on the Andean Common Market, and currently is editing a book on that subject. Professor Grosse was a Fulbright Scholar in Peru during part of 1981.

Matthew McQueen received his BSc (Econ.) from the University of Wales and his MA from Sussex University. Since 1967 he has been a lecturer in Economics at the University of Reading, with special reference to development economics. He has also acted as Consultant to various bodies concerned with the developing countries, including the African, Caribbean and Pacific (ACP) Group, the European Commission, the Commonwealth Secretariat and the UN Centre on Transnational Corporations. He has written books and articles on development economics and in particular on the EEC's economic relations with the Third World, as well as a report and articles on Transnational Corporations in International Tourism.

Robert F. Owen is currently a Visiting Assistant Professor of Economics at the University of Wisconsin. He studied for his first degree at Swarthmore College, and obtained his PhD (1981) at Princeton University. His previous academic appointments include a position as Visiting Assistant Professor at Cornell University. He is co-author of *The Role of Marketing in the Concentration and Multinational Control of Manufacturing Industries* and has contributed several articles to economic journals.

David P. Rutenberg is Professor of Policy and International Business at Queen's University, Kingston, Canada. He studied at the University of Toronto and California (Berkeley) and then taught for 10 years at Carnegie-Mellon University in Pittsburgh. His *Multinational Management*, published by Little Brown in 1982, has the reader stand inside the headquarters of a multinational corporation and attempt to be rational on a global basis. He is interested in government attempts to guide the course of industrial development, permitting some to die, and supporting others. He sees the Canadian fishing industry as at a turning point; it has received too much guidance from too many governments; but will soon be expected to contribute to the national economy. This research was conducted at the Dalhousie Centre for International Business Studies.

Adrian E. Tschoegl is an Assistant Professor of International Business at the University of Michigan. He holds a PhD from the Sloan School of Management at MIT. His research interests centre on the growth, expansion and regulation of international banks. The Solomon Brothers Center for the Study of Financial Institutions has recently published his monograph *The Regulation of Foreign Banks: Policy Formation in Countries Outside the United States*.

Stephen Young is Senior Lecturer in International Business and Business Policy at the University of Strathclyde, Scotland. He holds degrees from the Universities of Liverpool and Newcastle. He started his career as an economist with the Government of Tanzania and followed this by a term as an International Economist with a British food company. His academic career has included posts at Paisley College, Scotland and a Visiting Professorship at Louisiana State University in 1979–80. Stephen Young is the author of several articles and co-author of four books, including *Chrysler UK: A Corporation in Transition* (Praeger, 1977), *The Economics of Multinational Enterprise* (Longman, 1979) and *Multinationals in Retreat: The Scottish Experience* (Edinburgh University Press, 1982).

INDEX OF NAMES

INDEX OF SUBJECTS